Economic Growth and Development Policy

Panagiotis E. Petrakis
Dionysis G. Valsamis
Kyriaki I. Kafka

Economic Growth and Development Policy

palgrave
macmillan

Panagiotis E. Petrakis
Department of Economics
National and Kapodistrian University of Athens
Athens, Greece

Dionysis G. Valsamis
Department of Economics
National and Kapodistrian University of Athens
Athens, Greece

Kyriaki I. Kafka
Department of Economics
National and Kapodistrian University of Athens
Athens, Greece

ISBN 978-3-030-43180-8 ISBN 978-3-030-43181-5 (eBook)
https://doi.org/10.1007/978-3-030-43181-5

This Palgrave Macmillan imprint is published by the registered company Springer Nature Switzerland AG.
The registered company address is: Gewerbestrasse 11, 6330 Cham, Switzerland

Acknowledgements

Our partner Dr P. Kostis contributed scientifically to this book, as did C. Zapatinas, G. Vasilis and M. Skotoris. K. Matsoukas was in charge of copy-editing. Our main collaborator, E. Gkiouli, as well as the rest of our partners, enabled us to complete our research. Support was offered by the National and Kapodistrian University of Athens.

We thank them all.

The authors.

Contents

1 The Sources and Evolution of Growth 1

2 Modern Growth Theory Arguments 37

3 Growth Prototypes and Economic Policy 71

4 Economic Policy Formation and Decision-Making 91

5 The Determinants of Economic Policy Formation 123

6 Targets, Instruments and Policy Implementation 143

7 Institutional Change and Cultural Change 153

8 Structural Changes, Structural Reforms and Economic Growth 189

9 Entrepreneurship and Economic Growth 213

10 Innovation, Creativity and Economic Growth 235

Index 265

Abbreviations

ACF	Advocacy Coalition Framework
ADM model	Arrow-Debreu-McKenzie
AT	Adjustment Target
CA	Choice Architect
CMEs	Coordinated Market Economies
DSGE	Dynamic Stochastic General Equilibrium Models
GVCs	Global Value Chains
HANK	Heterogeneous Agent New Keynesian
K + S	Keynes + Schumpeter
LMEs	Liberal Market Economies
MFP	Multi-Factor Productivity
MLG	Multi-Level Governance
MLS	Multi-Level Selection
MMEs	Mixed Market Economies
NIH	National Institutes of Health
NKPC	New Keynesian Phillips Curve
OGM	Overlapping Generation Models
RBC	Real Business Cycle
TFP	Total Factor Productivity
VoC	Varieties of Capitalism

List of Figures

Fig. 1.1 The importance of time. (Source: Authors' own creation) 16
Fig. 1.2 The level of analysis. (Source: Authors' own creation) 17
Fig. 1.3 Equilibrium or disequilibrium. (Source: Authors' own creation) 17
Fig. 1.4 Signals. (Source: Authors' own creation) 18
Fig. 1.5 Technology and entrepreneurship. (Source: Authors' own creation) 19
Fig. 1.6 Alternative visions of the future under different scenarios. (Source: Author's own creation) 30
Fig. 3.1 Characteristics of transition stages to different income levels. (Source: Authors' own creation) 83
Fig. 3.2 Stagnated idiosyncratic growth prototype. (Source: Authors' own creation) 84
Fig. 3.3 A ten-year Eurozone government debt interest rates and debt/GDP growth (quarterly data). (Source: Oxford Economics and authors' calculations) 86
Fig. 5.1 The ACF approach. (Source: Sabatier, 1988, and authors' calculations) 130
Fig. 7.1 Quality of institutions on time. (Source: Worldwide Governance Indicators-The World Bank and authors' calculations. Note: The data present an average of six variables: voice and accountability, political stability/absence of violence, government effectiveness, regulatory quality, rule of law, and control of corruption. The highest value is 100, that is, the best quality institutions) 164

Fig. 8.1 Adjustment goal, time required, speed of adjustment and social flexibility. (Source: Authors' own creation) 207
Fig. 9.1 Entrepreneurial growth process. (Source: Wright & Stigliani, 2012, and authors' creation) 220
Fig. 10.1 A macro-model of economic growth. (Source: Authors' own creation) 245

List of Tables

Table 1.1	The growth paradigm	13
Table 3.1	Optimal and idiosyncratic institutional framework	76
Table 3.2	Optimal and idiosyncratic cultural values framework	77
Table 3.3	The cultural model of middle- and high-income countries according to Hofstede	82
Table 5.1	Typology of results and processes	134
Table 7.1	The flexibility of institutions in the social context under normal conditions	161
Table 7.2	Institutions and geography diversification: Corruption Perception Index 2019	163
Table 7.3	Time flexibility of cultural behaviour in the social context (under normal conditions)	173
Table 8.1	Structural reform gaps in selected Eurozone economies	205
Table 8.2	Impact of structural reforms on GDP	206
Table 9.1	Policies for promoting entrepreneurship	227

Introduction

Implementing economic policy, more particularly, policy for economic growth and development, has been the goal of economic thought, since its inception by the ancient Greeks to the present.

Still, the field of economic policy has received comparatively less attention than theory of development. This certainly makes sense, as policy cannot exist without developing theoretical supports, although that is often the case, namely having a policy with no supporting economic theory. This happens because politicians develop policies, while economists develop theories, and communication between the two is not always the best. A prioritization of the needs of theoretical analysis is among the reasons why policy has been underdeveloped as is the great difficulty of implementing economic theory. The role played by individuals, society and its creations (institutions, culture, etc.) in economic policy is another significant factor leading to an exponential increase in problems of analysis in the field of economic policy.

The task at hand becomes even more difficult as the analysis of economic policy entails forecasting and analysing the future. Entering the variable of time in the analysis of economic policy creates uncertainty and demands complex analytic tools (i.e. mathematics for complex dynamic systems, complexities, decision multicriteria, etc.), which makes it extremely difficult to analyse economic policy, especially the policy of growth and development.

Based on these real difficulties of synthesis, economists usually examine the impact of a theoretical analysis on economic policy as a last conclusion. This approach is possibly why they fail to meet the requirements of economic reality and to formulate effective growth and development policies. These problems grew significantly after the Great Recession of 2008, as a much more complex and complicated environment has emerged that is also still largely uncharted. At all events, the best course of action would seem to be to increase the focus on issues of economic policy implementation.

The nature of this book's methodological approach is multi-disciplinary and evolutionary, as economic policy is regarded as a key object of human action which evolves over time. Thus, the writers do not hesitate to utilize analytic tools from related sciences, such as politics, individual and social psychology, administration sciences and so on. Ultimately, this is probably the only feasible way—albeit the most difficult—to study the conditions of growth and development in economic policy.

CHAPTER 1

The Sources and Evolution of Growth

1.1 Introduction

The contrasting notions of diminishing returns and productivity are at the centre of theoretical analysis of development and growth, and upon these, the whole structure of developmental thought is built.

This chapter is an introduction to the sources of growth and its development. Its purpose is to identify the sources of growth and also to provide a concise, comprehensive understanding of the evolution of the theories of development and growth.

Section 1.2 discusses the concept of diminishing returns and productivity. Section 1.3 identifies and highlights the individual sources of growth,[1] which, through their operation, reverse the effects of the principle of diminishing returns and affect productivity. Section 1.4 looks into the roots of development and growth, with particular reference to the role of the cultural background and biological genes. Section 1.5 discusses the functionality of growth sources and their two dimensions that must be considered. One is the dimension of time and refers to the time required to activate their effectiveness. It should be noted that some sources of growth have a short-term effect on the growth of the economy and some longer-term effects. A good example of this is how demand is affected by monetary policy (e.g. benchmark interest rates). Since monetary policy triggers expectations, its effects on economic activity are immediate. These may even be located at the same time as the announcement of relevant measures. On the contrary, many policies have long-term effects, such as

P. E. Petrakis et al., *Economic Growth and Development Policy*,
https://doi.org/10.1007/978-3-030-43181-5_1

those on attitudes and behaviours, which are not easy to change. The sources of growth can be related to the level of operation of the economy. That is, whether these policies are triggered and implemented under conditions of economic activity above or below the potential output. Finally, Sect. 1.6 treats the key questions that arise from developments in global economy and economic theory as it is shaped at the beginning of the twenty-first century. At the same time, the technique of scenario development is presented as a way of approaching and managing the future.

1.2 Diminishing Returns and Productivity

The original formulation of the law of diminishing returns lies in the past. In 1767, Anne Robert Jacques Turgot, considered by many to be the first to introduce the school of classical economics, argued that the output of production would gradually increase at a declining rate when specific inputs of production are constant, and others are increased proportionally (Groenewegen, 1977). A few years later, English classical economists Adam Smith and David Ricardo, studying the conditions of production in England, included the concept of diminishing returns in their analysis. Although Thomas Robert Malthus did not include in his work *Essay on the Principle of Populations* (1798) the conditions of the particular law in its theoretical delineation, its effect had already been incorporated in his reasoning and in the determination of the possibilities of agricultural production. By contrast, neoclassical economists included this law as the cornerstone of their structure, with particular emphasis on the concept of productivity.

The basic assumptions of the law of diminishing return are as follows: (a) there is no change in technology, (b) the period of application is limited, (c) all units of the different inputs are homogeneous and (d) production is measured in physical units.

The operation of the law of diminishing return can be understood either in the form of a non-continuous increase in the efficiency of the factors of production or in the form of increased production costs. In other words, the more units of production factors are used, the less additional units of product (marginal product) are produced. In an alternative view, we could argue that the average cost of production is increasing.

When this law appeared in the economic literature in the eighteenth century, the way it worked was quite evident. Particularly so when its function was applied to matters of agricultural production (limited land) or mines (specific mining potential), construction of buildings in industrial complexes and so on.

Over time, however, economies have become more complex, and the working of economy is now a complicated system; as a result, the operation of the law of diminishing returns is subject to many factors that overturn or limit its activity. Two concepts, knowledge and innovation, have contributed to the eradication of diminishing returns. Thus, the concepts of knowledge as a result of one's work and innovation were reasons for the effectiveness of the law to be suspended. At the same time, economic theory has taken care to extend its boundaries so as to include these factors in its models.

This is how endogenous growth models emerged (after the AK growth models of the 1960s up to the present), which now had the potential to alter the equilibrium points that would have arisen if there were no endogenous growth factors. Primarily through these factors, namely the accumulation of knowledge and human capital, output per factor of production continued to increase. This rate of increase in output has become the absolute measure of the efficiency of the economic system. Thus, analysis came to include the concept of productivity, that is, the quantity of goods and services that can be produced per unit of input. As productivity increases, so does the efficiency of the economic system. This is, in fact, the "Holy Grail of Economics", and as P. Krugman wrote in *The Age of Diminishing Expectations* (1994): "Productivity is not everything, but in the long run it is almost everything. A country's ability to improve its standard of living over time depends almost entirely on its ability to increase productivity".

There are five reasons leading to the application of the law of diminishing returns: (a) As long as there is an optimal combination of production factors, and one of them is kept constant, the increase in the others leads to overall marginally reduced returns. (b) If one of the factors of production is scarce, it is reasonable to assume that it will hardly be possible for it to proportionately match the change in the other inputs. (c) If there are no perfect substitutes for the factors of production, then the exhaustion of some of them leads to a restriction in their use. (d) If a combination of productive inputs is optimal in terms of output efficiency, any disturbance of constant and variable inputs will result in output below the optimal level. (e) If size is continually increasing, even in a proportionate way, across all inputs, there is a chance that signs may occur of ineffective management and, consequently, of a gradual decline in returns. The mathematical formulation of the law of diminishing returns is as follows: Given that it is dominated by a double differentiable production function $q = f(K,L)$ that expresses, for a given level of technology, the relationship between K and L, for any given value of K, we can find the value of L, that is, $L_{0\_}(K)$ so that $f_{LL}<0$ for $L>L_0>(K)$, and for any given value of L, we can find the value of K, that is $K_0(L)$ so that $f_{KK}<0$ for $K>K_0(L)$.

The evolution of productivity in all three of its forms, namely labour productivity, capital productivity and total productivity—total factor productivity (TFP)—shows the extent and rate to which the adverse effects of the law of diminishing returns are addressed. Productivity helps to create a regulatory framework for presenting productivity capacity and efficiency of economies. It therefore gives a picture of their competitiveness.

The evolution of productivity helps determine the capacity of the productive mechanism and thus to determine the position of economies in the economic cycle and predict growth or determine to what extent inflationary pressures will develop in the economy. In other words, an economy with very low or constantly declining productivity is likely to subsequently experience inflationary pressures due to the depletion of effective input combinations.

There are many ways to measure productivity, but the most common one, at the macroeconomic level, is the gross domestic product (GDP) per Working Hours. Several factors may obscure the above measurement. In terms of the gross domestic product, it is important to what extent it derives from the formal or the shadow economy, since if it derives from the shadow economy, it is nowhere recorded, and, therefore, the productivity index may not be fully representative.

When it comes to measuring labour inputs, it depends on many factors such as education, experience and so on. When calculating the contribution of labour and intermediate inputs to the output, it is possible to calculate the contribution of all other factors (technology, innovation, institutional background, etc.) to the residual growth that can take the form of a multi-factor productivity (MFP) index. One widespread type of productivity measurement in an economy is the total factor productivity, which can either be identified with the MFP or have the most general form of productivity measurement in an economy when the effects of direct inputs are not removed (capital, labour, etc.).

The devaluation of the effects of the 2008 crisis was accompanied by the decline in the change of productivity rates (total, labour and capital productivity) across virtually the entire world economy, including the developed and developing economies, which caused severe production losses (IMF, 2017).

This created the conditions for a debate to open regarding this observation (Da Costa, 2015) bringing to light a series of critical relevant questions:

1. Is the concept of productivity underestimated, given the complex level of technology that prevails today?
2. Is, on the contrary, productivity overrated given the complex working hours used?
3. Might it be too complicated to measure the impact of the operation of the service sector given its dominance in developed economies?
4. Could it be that the way technology change is evaluated and the way it is accounted for, are not sufficient or are systematically mistaken?
5. Does the widely pursued structural change policy cause productivity changes in the short and medium term?
6. If there is indeed a reduction in the rate of change in productivity—which means that, for one reason or another, the law of diminishing returns is triggered—then why does this happen?

1.3 The Development of Growth Theory

Early theories focused on understanding economic growth while attempting to identify general determinants of growth that could apply in any case under consideration. Studying how economies grow, the purpose of economic growth theories was to discover some of the laws or principles that govern this process. Modern theories tend to accept that the sources of growth change over time and differentiate between economies. This condition also implies the implementation of different economic policies that make effective use of the available economic factors, that is, by increasing productivity.

1.3.1 From the Malthusian Period to the Industrial Revolution

The foundation of classical economics (1720–1880) as the beginning of economic theory has been of paramount importance for the future development of economic science. Classical economics, with Smith (1723–1790), Ricardo (1772–1823) and Malthus (1766–1834) as their main proponents, attempted to provide a conceptual framework for the production and distribution of wealth.

In Smith's *The Wealth of Nations* (1776 [1981]), for the first time, the view is expounded that the wealth of nations derives from the role of international trade, a concept also used by Ricardo (1817) to develop his theory of comparative and absolute advantage. Ricardo (1772–1823) argued that trade is a comparative advantage for a country, which formed the central basis for arguments in favour of free trade as an essential component of development (Ricardo, 1817).

According to Smith, productivity of labour depends on the division of labour, which is a principal source of growth. Although the division of labour has been a source of conflict—as it entails the transformation of the labour force from the agricultural to the industrial sector and hence, into labour in the trade sector—Marx (1818–1883), like Smith, recognized its role in economic growth.

The period up until the industrial revolution—when the per capita income was substantially stable—is called the Malthusian Period, since it is governed by the principles of Malthus (1766–1834). The two main features of a Malthusian Period of economic growth are (a) there is no long-term tendency for an increase in real wages and (b) improvements in production capacity are offset by population growth (Crafts & Mills, 2009).

Malthus' theory (1798) on economic growth is based on a natural procedure that results from the fundamental laws of economic theory. In essence, Malthus stressed that the potential growth of the economy would result in an increase in population. In particular, the increase of employment in the low-productivity agricultural sector would reduce the per capita supply of agricultural products, thereby reducing the population due to malnutrition. To increase the supply of agricultural products, given the low productivity of labour in the agricultural sector, all people should be employed in it, thus leading the economy into the Malthusian trap. Therefore, while overall income could increase, per capita income was almost certain to remain stable.

However, Malthusian thought was unable to include or grasp the concept of technological progress in the years following the Industrial Revolution (1760–1860). After the Industrial Revolution and the advancement of medical science, the average life expectancy increased, and infant mortality decreased. At the same time, spending on education increased as parents began to place higher value on the quality of their children's education, which led to a decline in birth rates in most industrialized countries. With incomes rising faster than population growth, industrial economies significantly increased their per capita income over the next century. This is how the Malthusian conceptions were superseded.

1.3.2 *The Accumulation of Capital and Knowledge and the Contribution of Innovation*

The post-World War II period, in both developed and developing countries, was characterized by the need to develop quantitative economic models (using mathematical models beyond the theoretical approach). They were usually influenced by Keynesian conceptions of the lack of sufficient demand as a source of recessive influences.

A typical example of such a model is the one developed by R.F. Harrod (1939) and E. Domar (1946). The model was initially designed to interpret the function of economies in the short run, but then took the form of an interpretative model of growth. At its core is the attention it shows to the conditions under which investment and capital accumulation can be increased and, thus, the level of savings and productivity of capital. Accordingly, there may be a unique rate of increase in investment and income such as to maintain full employment for a significant period of time (steady growth). This takes into account both the classical notions of supply and the Keynesian demand concepts. The structure of the model as well as the policy proposals it generates imbue the model with an extrinsic character in terms of how it views growth evolving in the economy.

Important economic models developed in this period are neoclassical growth models (Solow-Swan, dynamic equilibrium models), endogenous growth models (AK, innovation models) and models characterized by increasing scale returns ("learning by doing").

The Solow-Swan model (Solow, 1956; Swan, 1956) is the most representative neoclassical general equilibrium model that attempts to explain long-term economic growth by focusing on productivity, capital accumulation, population growth and technological change. The micro-foundation of the model is based on a Cobb-Douglas production function with constant returns to scale. A key element of this model is its simplicity, which enables it to adequately describe the complex system of economics. Moreover, it does not "perceive" the economy as a multitude of people with different characteristics and preferences. Instead, it is a simple model of the economy of a commodity, of a representative agent and positive elasticity of substitution.

According to the model, the portion of disposable income saved is exogenously determined by external factors, for example, announcements by the government or the central bank. The behavioural rule of the fixed saving rate simplifies the determination of the dynamic equilibrium. Therefore, based on the neoclassical model, the only way to explain the long-term per capita production growth (observed in developed countries) is to accept that continuous technological change (increased productivity) outweighs the negative effects of declining returns on capital. In essence, the reduction in the ratio of production/capital (diminishing returns) is offset by technological progress. This applies until the economy reaches a steady state, where the two forces are mutually neutralized with the equilibrium point determined by the savings rate, depreciation rate and population rate.

In the long run, the pace of growth will return to the pace of technological progress. Therefore, for specific levels of technological progress, the neoclassical model of growth shows in a satisfactory way how the level of production, real wages and real interest rates are determined. Finally, if all economies had the same technology available, there would be convergence in long-term growth rates.

The Ramsey neoclassical growth model (Ramsey, 1928), also known as the Ramsey-Cass-Koopmans model, differs from the Solow model in the areas of optimizing individual behaviour as well as in the endogenization of savings, influencing behavioural preferences. It is widely used in several macroeconomic areas, such as fiscal policy, business cycles and monetary policy.

Dynamic equilibrium models refer to the overall flow of quantities and prices while households try to maximize their utility function. The problem in this process is closely linked to diachronic consumption choices (over time?) and to the time-varying rate of return.

Although the concept of expectations is not directly defined in the neoclassical model of growth, balance is determined by the interaction between investment and consumption, which in turn is determined by the discount rate.

Expectations and uncertainty affect capital and consumption through the discount rate, thereby affecting the equilibrium point. Uncertainty leads households to diversify their portfolio with less risky assets, such as government bonds. Government bonds also play an essential role in uncertainty models as they allow households to smooth out idiosyncratic shocks (Acemoglu, 2009).

The endogenization of savings in neoclassical growth is the main difference in relation to Solow's growth model, as savings, and in particular the discount factor, influence the rate of capital accumulation. In this way, a lower discount factor indicates higher savings, as it shows whether households are willing to substitute consumption with savings.

Younger generations are particularly sensitive to expectations of the future. The behaviour of young people in the first period (t_0) may be influenced by what they expect to happen in the future (second period, t_1). If expectations shift, then fluctuations in total demand may change the equilibrium. Regarding prices, new generations are influenced by expectations of future prices, which depend on the expectations of the next generation and so on. As a result, determining the equilibrium is subject to changes in expectations. Most of the time, equilibrium is not optimal by Pareto, as individuals do not correctly predict future fluctuations in prices and interest rates.

To analyse intergenerational choices, the analysis of growth has introduced two approaches: the hypothesis of representative agents, made known by Alfred Marshall in his work *Principles of Economics* (1890) and the Overlapping Generation Models (OGM) formulated in the leading work of Samuelson "An Exact Consumption-Loan model of Interest With or Without Social Contrivance of Money" (1958), which still influences economic thinking.

Overlapping generational models (a) are based on interactions between different generations (young and old) and (b) follow a never-ending process of introducing new generations into the model. The effects of the individuals' decisions are shaped in conjunction with the different stages of their lives. Interaction between consumption and savings depends on:

1. The motivation of a person to normalize consumption during their life. In the course of a life, a person is faced with different levels of income. Through savings, they can save when they are young, and use their savings when they are older.
2. The existence of uncertainty motivates the individual to save. Unexpected events, such as unemployment, can lead to fluctuations in income.
3. Through savings, one can purchase durable goods or invest in assets as well as debt repayments.

The main points of the OGM can be summarized as follows:

1. They constitute an alternative approach to representative agents' models.
2. They are different from neoclassical growth models.
3. They insert expectations into their analysis.
4. Interest rates are the mechanism of transition between different generations.

An important issue in establishing the neoclassical model of growth is the hypothesis of representative agents. Economics uses this term to simplify and homogenize the behaviour of economic agents in its models. However, it has received serious criticism. The criticism exerted (including by Lucas) is summarized in the fact that past events may ignore the consequent behavioural changes of economic agents, which may in turn alter the economic outcome. The problem can be solved only if we assume specific situations of decision-making by individual agents. In this case, policymakers can adjust their policies based on the response of each agent to each policy.

The introduction of new generations gives a new dimension to the models. In other words, there is a process of choosing between the "older" and the "younger" generations, which affects the equilibrium of the latter. Overlapping generational models introduce interactions between different generations. These models are particularly useful as they provide the nexus of intergenerational interactions, which was missing from the neoclassical model of growth. An important aspect of the OGM models is that in them, equilibrium, unlike the general equilibrium models, is not Pareto optimal. As the economy is made up of an infinite number of economic agents and the value of resources is infinite, the Pareto improvement can be achieved through the redistribution of available resources across generations. The effectiveness of the equilibrium depends on the interest rate as well as on the Cass criterion (competitive equilibrium is not Pareto optimal).[2]

Since about the beginning of the 1970s up to the mid-1980s, the focus of research on growth and development was on short-term fluctuations by incorporating rational expectations into Real Business Cycle (RBC) theory. This macroeconomic view focused on the mechanism of the economic cycles and the anti-cyclical effects of monetary and fiscal policy. By the mid-1980s, new research returned to the determinants of long-term economic growth.

Technological change, and the need to interpret and rationalize it in particular, has been the cornerstone of the further development of the theory of growth. All the focus on growth analysis has been on how to offset the diminishing returns on capital. Thus, after the neoclassical models of growth, the interest of economics has focused on the theory of endogenous growth (Acemoglu, 2009; Aghion & Howitt, 1988, 1992, 2009; Barro & Sala-i-Martin, 2003; Mankiw, Romer, & Weil, 1992) finding two main expressions:

1. AK models in which diminishing yields disappear because the model incorporates both natural and human capital.
2. Innovation-based growth models—essentially the second wave of endogenous growth—with two parallel subcategories:
   (a) Romer's Product Variety Model (1986, 1990) with multiple products, leading to the elimination of overall diminishing returns.
   (b) Schumpeterian Quality Improvement through Innovation, which builds on creative disaster and eliminates diminishing returns.

As endogenous growth models incorporate the concept of technological change, one may reasonably wonder on what this change depends. It is very reasonable to think that technological change depends on individual or collective decisions and is influenced by the current framework of incentives and institutional organization. If this framework is stable, the question that must be answered is how will people be motivated to develop new technology when they are in an environment with stable returns on capital and labour, so that everyone is rewarded in a competitive balance with their marginal product.

Arrow (1962) proposed a process that can generate increasing scale returns and thus create compensation opportunities for those developing technologies. This is the process of learning by doing.

So, when people accumulate capital, learning through practice creates technological advancement—creativity and innovation—that tends to increase the marginal product of capital, thus offsetting the tendency to reduce marginal product when technology remains unchanged.

The greater the accumulation of capital, the greater the potential for learning by doing. However, diminishing returns on capital can also be offset by improving the variety—quantity—of products, which in turn will destroy the previous ones by replacing them. Scale effects can be produced that work in such a way as to offset the diminishing returns on capital.

Romer's product variety model (1986, 1990) holds that innovation increases productivity by creating new, though not necessarily improved, products. Thus, it increases the capacity of the economy because it allows a given stock of capital to be allocated to a larger number of uses, each of which has diminishing returns. Thus, the existence of a variety of products becomes the parameter of economic productivity growth, and its growth rate is the long-term growth rate of the per capita product of the economy, that is, growth.

In addition, economic development is made up of innovations, which, when they emerge, render past innovations obsolete. Entering and leaving the market and the turnover of a business ensure continuous improvements in overall innovation and increased economy products. This is achieved by introducing the role of the "entrepreneur" who generates innovation by exploiting the results of the research they conduct. The more productive research, the higher the product growth. As a result, the more an economy spends on research, thereby increasing research productivity, the higher is the growth rate.

All of the above can be summarized in the Growth Paradigm of the following table (Table 1.1).

1.3.3 An Overview of the Evolution of Economic Thought on Growth and Development

Organizing analytical thinking around the modelling of growth and policy requires that several elements, which are typically identified in economic growth models, be considered together. In other words, all basic models and theories of growth incorporate certain features that exploit them one way or another, depending on the general context of the models. These key features should be taken into account when formulating economic growth and development policy. For instance, policy suggestions derived from a timeless growth model may have significant analytical utility, especially for how analytical thinking is developed. But they are very difficult to implement in practice and usually extend for more than a year without the required adjustments. Thus, it may be necessary to modify the original

Table 1.1 The growth paradigm

	Neoclassical paradigm	*AK models*	*Endogenous growth* — *Improving the quality and quantity of products*	*Long-term growth*
Reference case	Representative agent—maximization under restriction	Representative agent—maximization under restriction	Entrepreneur/innovator—maximization under restriction	Entrepreneur/innovator—evolutionary behaviour
Exogenous variables (Growth factors)	• Population change rate[a] • Technology change • Savings rate	• Population change rate[a]	• Population change rate[a] • Governmental actions	• Population change rate[a]
Critical variables	• Diminishing returns of inflows • Diminishing returns on capital	• Diminishing returns on capital • Increasing scale returns	• Diminishing returns on capital • Increasing scale returns	• Diminishing returns on capital • Increasing scale returns
Endogenous variables	• Capital accumulation • Real wages • Real rates, etc.	• Capital accumulation • Real wages • Real rates, etc.	• Capital accumulation • Real wages • Real rates etc.	• Governmental actions • Evolution of economic system • Capital accumulation • Real wages • Real rates etc.

(*continued*)

Table 1.1 (continued)

	Neoclassical paradigm	*AK models*	*Endogenous growth*	*Long-term growth*
			Improving the quality and quantity of products	
Growth rule	The pace of technological change offsets the declining returns on capital	Learning through doing integrates knowledge into the accumulation of capital and produces incremental returns of scale that in turn affect the diminishing returns on capital	• Research activities produce innovation that later leads to a monopoly power • Innovation generates increasing returns of scale that in turn affect the diminishing returns on capital	Entrepreneurial creativity generates innovation that leads to increasing returns of scale thus offsetting the diminishing returns on capital
Representative references	Solow (1956), Swan (1956), Ramsey (1928), Cass (1965), Koopmans (1965)	Romer (1986, 1987), Lucas (1988)	Aghion and Howitt (1992, 2002), Schumpeter (1934, 1950)	Schumpeter (1934, 1950), Nelson and Winter (1982), Pyka, Foster (2015)

Source: Authors' own creation

[a]In some models it may be endogenous

models so that they become dynamic. In such a case, it is possible, during these conversions, to also change these policy suggestions and therefore change the overall view of economic reality.

The structure of thinking about the leading issues in modelling the theory of economic growth and using it to produce policies is presented as follows:

1. Theoretical constructs usually include but also refer to some fundamental changes: These concern production and growth rate (intrinsic to consumption/saving/investment) money and credit, unemployment and inflation, and the openness of the economy. Finally, a particularly significant change is that of innovation.

2. Economic models and theories of growth have direct or indirect explicit references to the length of time we are referring to. There are usually two options for time length: short-term and medium- to long-term analyses.

It goes without saying that the reactions of the main actors—households and businesses—are immediate and have no secondary effects since time is not taken into account in the analysis. When, on the other hand, time enters the analysis and the concept of the future is formed in terms of the reactions of agents, two elements are most likely to be introduced: expectations and uncertainty. They are two conceptual categories that create behavioural frameworks for decision-makers. Uncertainty has been included in the analysis quantified either in the form of risk or in the form of alternative scenarios of the future.

Temporal models can have either neoclassical or evolutionary infrastructure. The first category mainly includes AK models and all other models with endogenous technology (Arrow, 1962; Frankel, 1962), which result in a steady-state equilibrium. By contrast, evolutionary models usually include the concept of evolutionary path dependence, which also defines evolution of growth (Fig. 1.1).

3. Usually, in the theoretical analysis of development and growth, there are two levels of analysis: the minor and the aggregate. The first refers to decision-making at the unit level—individual, household or business—and the second to the whole economy. A related approach is one that relies on the presence of agents/representative agents to analyse behaviours within models. The case of Dynamic, Stochastic, General Equilibrium (DSGE) models is typical of representative agents. When agents are introduced, they may be homogenous or heterogeneous.

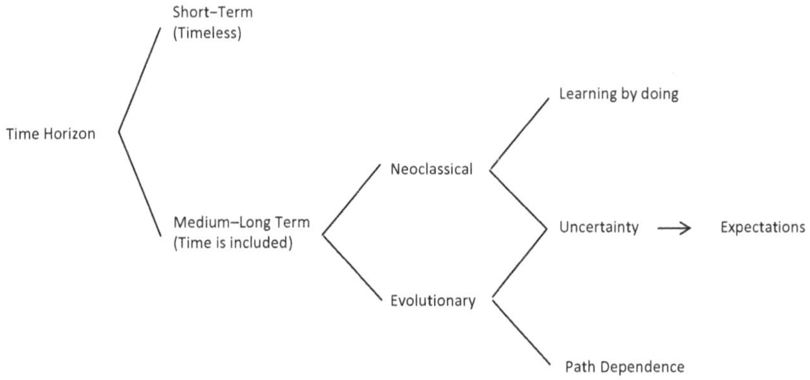

Fig. 1.1 The importance of time. (Source: Authors' own creation)

Evolutionary models are typical examples of how the reactions of an economic organization are considered algorithmically, if we consider that the agents involved are heterogeneous.

An important dimension of the degree of analysis, corresponding to the minor and the aggregate, relates to the micro- and the macro-level. The first relates to an analysis based on the agent, the business and the market. In this version, the general equilibrium analysis is referred to as the Walras equilibrium analysis. Such a system could have an auctioneer or no auctioneer to clear the markets. In this case, two concepts can play a crucial role in the analysis: transaction costs and institutions.

One of the many well-known versions of the aggregate economy analysis is, of course, the neoclassical IS-LM composition. But after the 1980s, economic science developed micro-/macro-analysis, with the emergence of the New Classicals and the New Keynesians. In this analysis, there is no distinction between the micro- and the macro-level, but economic thought as a whole is analysed as a single system of decisions (Fig. 1.2).

4. The way consumers and producers' preferences are expressed is described under the general heading "preferences". Preferences are expressed within specific assumptions. One could classify these frameworks of assumptions, as they move between two ends, that is, rational behaviour and natural human behaviour.

In between these two extremes, there are the well-known behavioural systems of which the best known are those referring to the degree of bounded rationality.

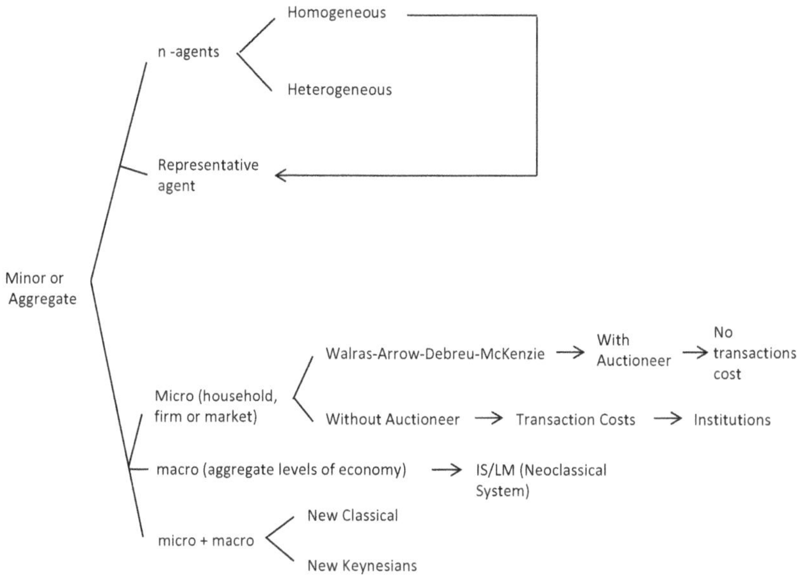

Fig. 1.2 The level of analysis. (Source: Authors' own creation)

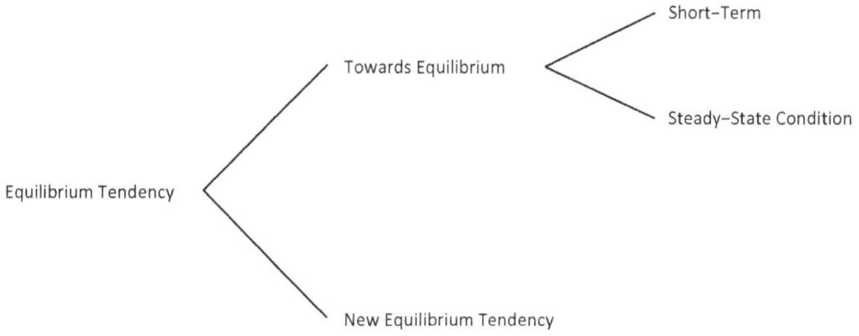

Fig. 1.3 Equilibrium or disequilibrium. (Source: Authors' own creation)

5. Economic systems tend to move either towards equilibrium or not. In the first case, when the system approaches the equilibrium point, this can happen automatically in the short run. If the time factor is present in the analysis, then it is common for the system to converge at a steady state (Fig. 1.3).

6. One of the major issues raised by growth modelling theorists concerns how the product, labour and capital markets function.

The important question is whether the signals needed to clear markets, that is, any form of pricing, are either flexible or rigid. Consequently, the analysis extends to whether information is available and how markets are organized, that is, the degree of market perfection (Fig. 1.4).

7. One of the major issues in modelling growth theory is whether technological change is endogenous or exogenous. Related to this is the question of the role of entrepreneurship (Fig. 1.5).

Moreover, the problem of time and space is of critical importance in analysing economic development and growth. When time and space are considered, social and distributional conflicts come into play. Time and space, then, will necessarily be at the centre of the dynamics of economics, contributing to the shaping of the evolutionary path dependence presented by the economy. Usually, concepts of time and space are not dealt with at the same time (Corpataux & Crevoisier, 2007), as we focus only on the role of time in economics (Davidson, 1996; O'Driscoll & Rizzo, 1985) or on the role of space (Crevoisier, 1996; Martin & Sunley, 1996).

The various schools of economics take a different approach to the concepts of space and time. Without necessarily naming these concepts, the way they are approached is a particularly important indication of the explanatory frameworks they use to simulate reality and interpret different theoretical frameworks (Corpataux & Crevoisier, 2007).

General equilibrium approaches perceive the concepts of space and time as exogenous, unchanging and objective, while non-equilibrium

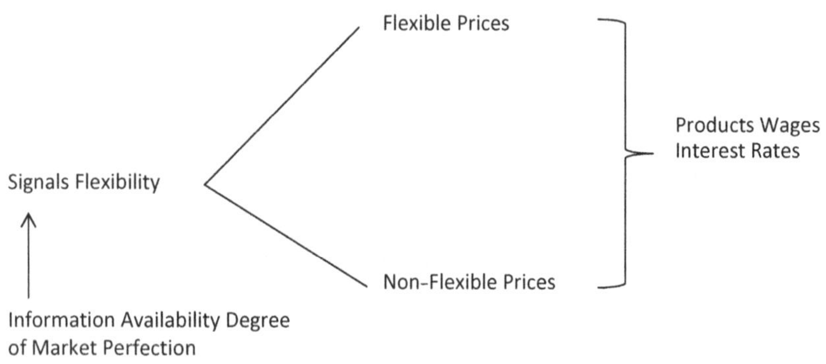

Fig. 1.4 Signals. (Source: Authors' own creation)

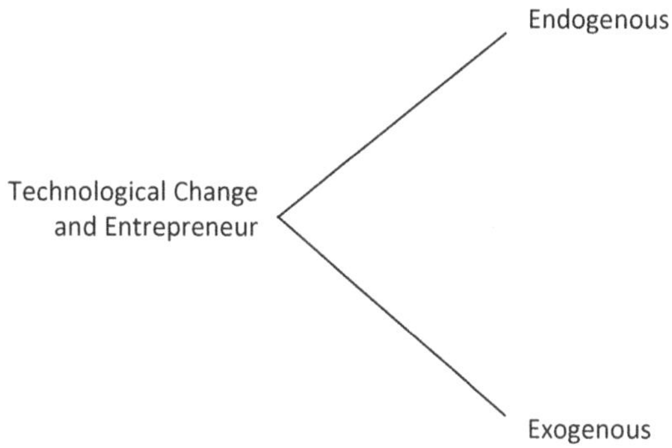

Fig. 1.5 Technology and entrepreneurship. (Source: Authors' own creation)

approaches do not distinguish between exogenous and endogenous time and space and consider the two concepts to be endogenous, variable and subjective.

The treatment of space and time in economic theories has critical implications not only for the development of economic policy but also for the theoretical background. The issue is particularly important when considering: (a) the interaction between theory and reality, (b) the relationship between equilibrium and evolutionary path dependence and (c) the effects of economic policy on different productive patterns and economies.

Developing an example of how the existence of different production and economic patterns—temporal and geographical—plays an important role in the economic policies applied, we can refer to European economies and, in particular, to the exit from the 2008 crisis. The economic policies to exit the crisis took quite a different form, depending on the country in which they were implemented, although they all had the same theoretical background in terms of their planning.

In conclusion, time and space matter. However, the issue of introducing these two concepts into the analysis is directly related to whether equilibrium or non-equilibrium theories are used, since equilibrium models are spaceless and timeless.

The economic policies that can be adopted to improve the growth of the economic system can have two main implementation horizons: a short- to medium-term and a medium- to long-term one. When we talk about implementation time, we mean the time needed to design, implement and display the results of the relevant policies.

It is a fact that literature, when referring to economic policy, often assumes automatic planning, immediate implementation and automatic display of results. The reason is that it is very difficult to accurately calculate the "gaps" in the various stages of policy implementation. It is noteworthy that often economic policy in the interims of planning, announcement and implementation has quite different results from those of the net implementation phase. In other words, it is likely that the "announcement" will lead to different results than the "implementation". The "announcement" can vary between one, three or five years, and the "implementation" can last up to maybe 30 years. Even if the policies under discussion relate to crucial institutions and behaviours, their implementation time can be extended from 50 to 100 years (see Chap. 7).

At the same time, alongside the importance of time in our analysis, we must also consider the circumstances of the economy: that is, whether it is below or above its potential production capacity. If the economy is below the potential output, then we usually describe it as being in the recessionary phase of the economic cycle. This is also the privileged area of macroeconomic policy that is exercised either through monetary or fiscal policy. When it is above the potential output, we consider it to be in the upward phase of the economic cycle, and policies may be required to expand the potential output of the economy. That is, growth policies should be put into effect.

Medium-term policies are usually linked to macroeconomic policies, while medium-to-long-term policies are linked to growth policies. But the relationship between timing and policy types is not exclusive as we shall see later in the chapter.

In conclusion, on the issue of GDP development and growth, the economy is either below the potential output—so there is a question of macroeconomic policies—or above the potential output, so it is a growth issue; the theoretical analytical capabilities we have acquired lead us to a time categorization of policy tools at our disposal: to the medium to long-term horizon that could—to a degree arbitrarily—be set to five years and to the medium- and long-term horizon beyond that horizon.

Many non-structural policies are exhausting their effectiveness in different reporting periods—one to two years—but extend their action to more than two years. It is particularly noteworthy that macroeconomic policies are often characterized as short term because they face short-term fluctuations.

1.4 The Deep Roots of Development and Growth

Identifying the underlying causes of economic growth answers an age-old question that concerns economics and is as follows: Why is GDP per capita higher in some societies than others? For decades now, exogenous growth models have emphasized the accumulation of capital and the identification of technological progress exogenously. By contrast, endogenous growth models have focused on the accumulation of human capital, investment and knowledge as key parameters of economic growth. Beyond that, however, a more modern approach places the institutional framework at the heart of the debate about the differences in wealth between countries.

At the beginning of the twentieth century, a divide in theories emerged as many scientists had assumed that natural selection could apply, not only at the level of individuals but also at the level of populations and ecosystems. This viewpoint changed after the 1960s and 1970s, when scientists began to see genes as the fundamental unit of choice (Dawkins, 1976) rejecting group selection.

On the contrary, according to the choice in groups, individuals do act altruistically and can sacrifice anything for the benefit of a group. At this level, the groups with the strongest bonds of cooperation are those that will be able to survive and reproduce. Similarly, economic growth is influenced by traits that are passed down from generation to generation over the years.

We could analyse the deep roots of economic growth on three levels: (a) at the level of geographical factors, (b) at the level of biological factors and gene transmission and (c) at the level of the cultural background, that is, all values, stereotypes and human behaviour.

Nevertheless, the above-mentioned approaches fail to fully explain the process of economic growth. Thus, we suspect that current economic growth is the result of a number of mechanisms that affect the wealth of nations; these are discussed as follows:

Individuals have a fund of information and data due to the cultural and institutional background of the societies in which they live (Petrakis & Kostis, 2014). These two types of backgrounds are deeply rooted in the subconscious and the environment of individuals and are responsible both for shaping human behaviour and for dealing with different aspects of daily life. Their formation is essentially based on the historical and cultural heritage of each nation. Individuals are able to use these elements to structure their cognitive background or reasoning processes (Douglas, 1987).

In this way, the cultural and institutional background offers a set of characteristics and rules that the individual uses as a model when confronted with problem-solving (Hodgson, 1988).

Apart from these, however, geographical factors are also directly related to economic growth. Yet, while it is easy to see that geography works directly on productivity, the indirect mechanism is not discernible. An important issue concerns whether historically transmitted characteristics affect economic development directly through productivity or act indirectly as an obstacle to the diffusion of knowledge and institutional innovation among populations (Spolaore & Wacziarg, 2013). As the relationship seems plausible, the direction of causation is not clear. Also, the climatic conditions and the relief of the environment have influenced the speed of transition of societies to the Neolithic era, a transition that is responsible for more efficiently organizing production through the development of agriculture.

Kamarck (1976) claims that geographical factors have a direct and simultaneous impact on productivity and growth. Diamond (1997) and Olsson and Hibbs Jr (2005) argue that geography indirectly influences growth, through history, including the analysis of prehistoric and biological factors that have contributed to the development of agriculture and the domestication of animals. The evolution of the European economy, for example, is due to more profound geographical advantages that developed during the Prehistoric era (Diamond, 1997). Finally, geographical factors continued to influence economic growth conditions, even after the development of agriculture (Ashraf & Galor, 2011).

Acemoglu, Johnson, and Robinson (2002), attempting to identify the causal direction between GDP per capita and geography, claim that the institutional framework interacts with economic growth. They believe that institutions exert either inhibitory or beneficial effects on the process of economic growth (Acemoglu, Johnson, & Robinson, 2004; Acemoglu & Robinson, 2012). This is why some institutions are encouraging investment in areas with low population density and low urbanization. By contrast, "extractive institutions" appear in areas where adverse geographical conditions prevail.

The quality of institutions may be beneficial to the process of economic development of societies; however, the broader characteristics of the population may be responsible for the trend in the economic performance of states. Institutions can be a characteristic of the population, but they are not a unique characteristic. Therefore, the comparison of the success of economies should not limit itself to focusing only on institutions but should examine the long-term characteristics of populations (Spolaore & Wacziarg, 2013).

Population characteristics are integrated and projected through human behaviour. The question arises as to how human behaviour can be transmitted. This can happen through two main mechanisms: (a) cultural transmission; and (b) genetic information transmitted from one generation to the next. By identifying the factors that shape human behaviour, we can understand the different performance of economies through those other than the widespread sources of growth—capital, technology, and so on.

Culture—the cultural background—is an essential cause of economic growth that can explain how human behaviour affects economic outcomes. The term "cultural background" incorporates all the beliefs, values, stereotypes and rules that characterize members of a society and differentiate it from others.

Cultural transmission and Darwin's theory, through the theory of natural selection, seeks to identify the mechanism of the evolution of human behaviour. Furthermore, cultural characteristics can be passed on from one generation to the next through social learning (Bandura, 1963, 1971). Finally, genetic transmission has its molecular basis in deoxyribose nucleic acid (DNA), through which the human species transmits biologically specific characteristics to subsequent generations (Spolaore & Wacziarg, 2013).

Cultural differences between humans and other species are universal. Behaviour is acquired through the process of social learning, so different behaviours are based on various social learning processes. Through social learning, a particular behaviour is adopted by the next generations and, therefore, great differences between populations persist without being due to genetic or environmental reasons.

The transmission of information between generations can take place through observation and the incentives generated by it (Boyd & Richerson, 1985). At the same time, individuals must retain the information available—perseverance—so as to pass it on to future generations. However, this process is not particularly easy, as interference by environmental elements may alter and differentiate one's available knowledge. Without the transmission and persistence of the cultural background, the development of social learning cannot be achieved.

On the other hand, human behaviour is embedded in genes and is therefore passed on to future generations. Boyd and Richerson (1985,

1988) focus on the evolution of persistence, assuming that transmission takes place with the evolution of genes, which influence the extent to which behaviour acquired through imitation is modified by individual learning. According to their findings, natural selection favours individuals who do not modify information acquired culturally, when individual knowledge is expensive and the environment unstable. Thus, natural selection can favour perseverance (Rogers, 1988). Investigating the causes that lead to the observed differences between the cultural backgrounds of societies is a crucial issue for social science, resolving which leads to particularly useful conclusions about the functioning of societies and, hence, their economic organization. However, to answer such a question would require the integration of many levels of analysis and would include social, economic, psychological, demographic, ecological and biological issues (Way & Lieberman, 2010).

In order to integrate most of these levels of analysis, the human brain is used in the operation of which all these influences are encountered (Chiao & Ambady, 2007). So, when the human brain is used as a means of differentiating the cultural background between societies, the role of genes seems to be important. Genes, by affecting brain function, can influence the creation and formation of cultural patterns, and, conversely, the cultural background can modulate gene expression and selection (Way & Lieberman, 2010). This is a two-way relationship.

However, we should not consider these two mechanisms of the transfer of human traits separately. According to the proponents of dual inheritance theory, both the evolution of the cultural background and the evolution of the gene have contributed to the evolution of societies and the establishment of institutions (Boyd & Richerson, 1985). Such changes take time; hence, we should not overlook the importance of historical legacy for economic performance through productivity.

The persistence of these deep causes and historical legacy impede the economic development of societies. The stages of economic growth consist in the transition from a low-income country to a middle-income country and, ultimately, to a high-income economy. Moving to the last stage is not an easy task, as there are many examples of countries that have managed to achieve high growth rates and improve their standard of living, but they have not been able to maintain sustainable growth for long enough to evolve into advanced economies.

1.5 The Short-, Medium- and Long-Term Horizons of Policies Affecting the Levels of Economic Activity: The Sources of Growth

Based on the preceding theoretical analysis, the medium- and short-term policies affecting economic activity fall under seven broad sections:

1. monetary policies;
2. fiscal policies,
3. policies aimed at human behaviour;
4. policies related to the policy area;
5. policies that refer to the general conditions of the economy;
6. redistributive policies; and, finally,
7. policies relating to systems of social security and intergenerational liability.

When referring to monetary and fiscal policies, we mainly distinguish areas of economic policy activity triggered in common by the notion of effective demand as formulated by Keynes in *General Theory of Employment, Interest, and Money* (1936), and by the New Classicals (Lucas Jr, 1972, 1976), the New Keynesians (Fischer, 1977; Phelps & Taylor, 1977; Taylor, 1980) and the Post-Keynesians (Davidson, 1984; Minsky, 1986).

In policies targeting human behaviour, we will distinguish four areas in which corresponding policies can be identified. These are (a) impact on expectations and well-known forward guidance (Woodford, 2013), (b) area of risk and uncertainty, (c) area of human and collective preferences, motivations and behaviours and, finally, (d) the area of goal setting and motives (Kahneman & Tversky, 1979; Knight, 1940; Maslow, 1943). This latter area also includes the development of policies that influence behaviour in the opposite way (see, e.g. instrument policies: change in interest rates, taxes or expenses).

The area of policy is not a field in which the economic policy of development and growth can be developed. However, it is now widely accepted that political stability has positive effects on growth rates (Aisen & Veiga, 2006; Alesina, Ozler, Roubini, & Swagel, 1996; Alesina & Perotti, 1996; Barro, 1989, 1991; Jong-a-Pin, 2009; Kormendi & McGuire, 1985), and the same happens with policies of political inclusivity. These are policies that increase the participation of the population in the joint economic effort.

In the area of policies pertaining to the general operating conditions of the economy, we can distinguish policies in five sub-areas: (a) The strengthening of external demand. These include exchange rate policies and some institutional improvements to any form of market inefficiency (information, functional, etc.). (b) Policies related to the transaction costs for the operation of economies (Williamson, 1975, 1985). (c) Policies related to structural change aiming (Lucas Jr, 1990) within a medium- to short-term framework, to increase the potential of the economy and ultimately its effectiveness. (d) The policies of deleveraging—reducing the financial burden—on individuals, businesses and the economy in general. (e) Finally, policies for the internalization of the externalities (Coase, 1960) are included, with a prime example being the pricing of environmental pollution. The internalization of externalities is related to the issue of development for economies of scale, which is central to the growth process, and finally to the depreciation policies of parallel economy linked to the policy for the creation of fiscal space. This is a structural issue to do with the possibilities of exerting fiscal policy.

The question of the relationship between income distribution and wealth, on the one hand, and growth on the other, is a pivotal one, which has a medium- to long-term effectiveness. However, some aspects, those of a mainly redistributive nature, may have a shorter implementation horizon (medium- to short term). The same applies to the system of social insurance and intergenerational liability.

In the medium- to long term, nine areas are identified where policies can be developed for the development and growth of the economy's potential productive capacity. There are obviously no macroeconomic policies within this temporal horizon. These policies can evolve in the following areas: the general conditions of operation of economies; the international position of the economy or business; the area of behaviours; the field of politics, human capital, entrepreneurship, redistribution, social insurance and intergenerational liability and, finally, in the area of geostrategic issues.

To be more specific, in the area of general economic conditions, we highlight nine sub-areas: the first includes policies that generate incremental returns of scale and measures related to the size of markets, and policies associated with managers and acquisitions at the operational level. The operational level contains the second area. It deals with the issues of competitiveness of businesses and products, including techniques of organization, of business management and so on.

The third includes policies concerning the utilization of primary sources of wealth in an economy, such as oil, minerals and so on. The fourth area covers the area of innovation through which new products or services can be produced for emerging needs of citizens and markets. The fifth area concerns the normalization and facilitation of the processes of creative disaster as a factor in renewing the productive pattern—bankruptcy proceedings, second chance and so on. The sixth area concerns the area of banking (inter)mediation, concerning the development of capital markets as a factor facilitating the growth process. The seventh area comprises a series of long-term structural changes and interventions in the institutional context. The eighth includes interventions on environmental issues. Finally, the ninth area includes policies referring to the demographic status of the population.

Five policy options can influence the international financial position of a country and the products produced therein—we recall that policies related to the external or internal depreciation of a currency are linked to the short- to long term. The first concerns participation of the economy in monetary or state unions. The second concerns participation in international trade agreements. The third concerns policies related to the position of the country or its products in international market sharing and the promotion of comparative advantages. The fourth concerns policy on the issue of the growth and marketing of new products and relates to innovation, copyright and other policies. Related are the policies relevant to the international competitiveness of businesses, their position vis-à-vis the international economic giants and finally the value chains that are developing worldwide.

The field of behaviour is privileged in pursuing policies that could affect it. This is because most of them usually change on an individual or collective level over the medium- to the long term. Influencing motivation and goals is an objective that can be adopted at this level.

Human capital defines a particular medium-to long-term space of interventions. There are usually no short-term yield policies in this area. Thus, improving the level of knowledge—the accumulation of human capital—learning by doing and capacity building are distinct areas regarding which individual policies can be developed.

The development of entrepreneurial creativity and business involvement is a field suitable for the implementation of development policies. In the area of long-term policies, we could include policy initiatives such as foreign exchange reforms.

Correspondingly, long-term redistributive policies include interventions involving, for instance, the interaction between capital and labour, the potential for absorption of wealth generated through mainly long-term tax policies—for example, taxation of real or other property. The same applies to matters of social insurance and intergenerational liability—for example, retirement thresholds or replacement rates for active work pay, retirement compensations and so on.

Finally, major geostrategic issues shape, in the long run, important conditions, whether positive or negative, for development and growth.

1.6 The Alternative Future of Growth

The speed of change in economic and social developments is a crucial feature of the twentieth century and especially so of the early twenty-first century. These changes affect all participants in the global economic situation, be it national economies, business entities or individuals.

Changes are observed that are almost impossible to avoid, which increase uncertainty about the future. Some of the factors that will determine the future change are already visible depending on the depth of the time horizon of the analysis. As a result, there are unavoidable trends that are expected to play an important role in the evolution of economic activity.

Developments in global economy and economic theory at the beginning of the twenty-first century raise new vital questions that need to be answered in the face of major economic developments. These questions are: What modern theoretical economic tools can be used to understand growth, forecast and control economic development? What is the evolution in the distribution of income and wealth and what is their relationship to growth? Is it possible in a socio-economic formation with a long historical evolution and structural barriers to development, to change the characteristics of the economy and release growth forces that had not appeared before?

The above-mentioned developments in global economy and economic theory provide signposts for the evolution of economies as these trends are very closely linked to the ensuing long-term economic reality in the world. In discussing the future, long-term, economic reality, we must take into account the conditions of long-term fluctuation. Kondratiev[3] waves (45–60 years) and shorter lasting fluctuations, such as Kuznets' infrastructure investment cycles (15–25 years) may be empirically identifiable in the evolution of economics, yet only a small amount of scientifically based information can be used for development of the future.

In predicting the future, it is impossible to take into account all the factors and relevant changes, which shape this future. One method that allows the observation of the course of these factors over time is trend analysis. This method offers the opportunity to develop hypotheses about which scenario for the future is most likely to become a reality.

However, the most common method of generating different possibilities for the future is to develop and analyse scenarios. Intuitive scenarios of how the future will be shaped are the most widely used. During the 1970s, scenario development was undertaken by only a few employees in a company—mainly senior executives, high in the company hierarchy. Over time, however, this method began to involve more employee groups and is implemented by hiring external teams, specialized in developing scenarios.

Moreover, intuition-based scenarios are more suited to the process of visualizing the future. This method mainly involves creating two or more different versions of the future, as the trends considered and the main questions that need to be answered through each scenario may be quite different. Through the development of scenarios, valuable conclusions are drawn about the functioning of companies and organizations.

In addition, detailed scenarios aimed at exploring the future (futuring) represent an alternative to the approach of intuition-based scenarios. These are mainly used for analysing different possibilities for the future, mainly in matters related to strategic thinking, and refer to cases where the future is influenced by events—long-term research, development programmes, technological acquisitions, new product development, and so on. They are also used to identify the most important trends, the interaction between them and the probability of linking specific trends to specific outcomes.

An equally important question is how to evaluate these scenarios as alternative approaches to the future. For example, when trend analysis takes place by using time series to predict the future, a specific size/number is obtained, which allows the comparison between estimated and actual values.

Scenarios are often shaped by behaviours and events considered to be expected. As a planning tool, a scenario must include multiple versions of the future, as even scenarios that are highly likely to be implemented, are associated with some level of risk (Fig. 1.6). Consequently, uncertainty

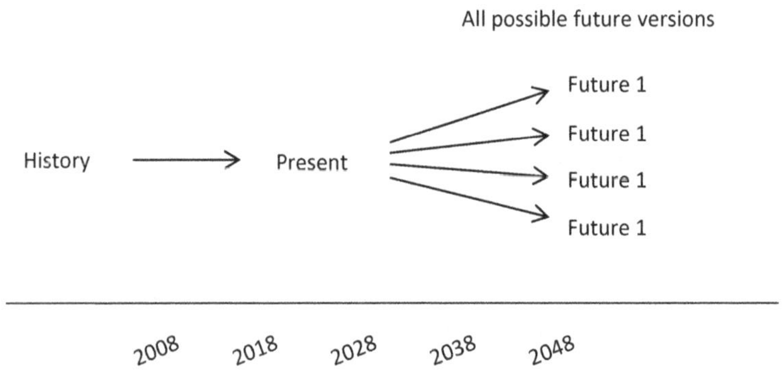

Fig. 1.6 Alternative visions of the future under different scenarios. (Source: Authors' own creation)

surrounding the future can be mitigated by using multiple scenarios over traditional quantitative forecasts or a single scenario (Van der Merwe, 2008).

Scenarios are considered to be effective tools for predicting the future because they include uncertainty. Scenario formation involves the adoption of specific hypotheses that can support a variety of scenarios that include events which (a) lead to the worst possible scenario, (b) significantly deteriorate the situation in the future, (c) continue to follow the present course without any significant changes, (d) improve the situation in the future and (e) eventually lead to a better situation. Finally, each scenario is associated with a probability of its implementation.

Notes

1. For a full analysis, the reader may refer to Part III by Petrakis (2017) *Economic Development and Growth: General and Integrated Approach*, Quaestor Editions.
2. The Cass Criterion, also known as the Malinvaud–Cass criterion, is the central result of the OGMs, named after David Cass (1965). An important feature of OGMs is that the first welfare theorem cannot be applied, that is, that competitive balance may not be Pareto optimal.
3. According to Schumpeter (1939), the Kondratiev circles, or, else, waves, is a phenomenon that suggests that economics follows a periodical pattern, named after Nikolai Kondratiev. According to this phenomenon, there is a period where high growth is followed by low, and the cycle is broken down into four phases named after the four seasons of the year.

- The first phase is inflationary growth and is described as "spring". It is the phase where the economy is at the bottom of the cycle and expanding steadily, with unemployment falling and productivity, wages and prices rising.
- Then comes the second phase, the "summer". It is the period of recession or, as it was initially called, stagflation. Initially at this stage the economy is expanding until it reaches the limit of its available resources—human and material. At this point, there is a shortage of resources and the product is starting to decline as unemployment increases.
- The third phase, the "autumn", also known as deflationary growth, is characterized by low growth. But quickly the imbalance—the sharp rise in prices—created in the previous period gives way to the rapid formation of excessive debt, eventually leading the economy into a sharp recession.
- The fourth phase, termed "winter", is one in which significant expenditure cuts are observed, leading to a sustained deflationary period. Finally, in this period, the innovation and technologies of the growth period are becoming cheaper and more widespread.

Yet, there is no specific model that fits Kondratiev's circles. Empirical work to support Kondratiev's hypothesis usually chooses a measure that describes the product and the data available on a log scale to detect yield and distribute data smoothly over time, using a mobile medium to eliminate accidental "noise" events. Another approach was supported by Metz (2011), who uses structural time series (STS) models to detect the hyper-cycles supported by Kondratiev. Finally, a reasonable estimate has been made by the Allianz Investors Group (2010) using the ten-year moving average returns of the S&P 500.

References

Acemoglu, D. (2009). *Introduction to Modern Economic Growth.* Princeton, NJ: Princeton University Press.

Acemoglu, D., Johnson, S., & Robinson, J. A. (2002). Reversal of Fortune: Geography and Institutions in the Making of the Modern World Income Distribution. *Quarterly Journal of Economics, 117*(4), 1231–1294.

Acemoglu, D., Johnson, S., & Robinson, J. A. (2004). Institutions as the Fundamental Cause of Long-Run Growth. *CEPR Discussion Paper* No. 4458.

Acemoglu, D., & Robinson, J. A. (2012). *Why Nations Fail: The Origins of Power, Prosperity and Poverty.* New York: Crown Publishing.

Aghion, P., & Howitt, P. (1988). *Growth and Cycles Through Creative Destruction.* Unpublished. University of Western Ontario.

Aghion, P., & Howitt, P. (1992). A Model of Growth Through Creative Destruction. *Econometrica, 60*(2), 323–351.

Aghion, P., & Howitt, P. (2009). *The Economics of Growth*. Cambridge, MA: MIT Press.

Aisen, A., & Veiga, F. J. (2006). Does Political Instability Lead to Higher Inflation? A Panel Data Analysis. *Journal of Money, Credit and Banking, 38*(5), 1379–1389.

Alesina, A., Ozler, S., Roubini, N., & Swagel, P. (1996). Political Instability and Economic Growth. *Journal of Economic Growth, 1*(2), 189–211.

Alesina, A., & Perotti, R. (1996). Income Distribution, Political Instability, and Investment. *European Economic Review, Elsevier, 40*(6), 1203–1228.

Allianz Investors Group. (2010). *The Sixth Kondratieff–Long Waves of Prosperity*. Frankfurt. Retrieved from https://www.allianz.com/content/dam/onemarketing/azcom/Allianz_com/migration/media/press/document/other/kondratieff_en.pdf

Arrow, K. (1962). The Economic Implications of Learning by Doing. *The Review of Economic Studies, 29*(3), 155–173. Retrieved from http://www.jstor.org/stable/2295952

Ashraf, Q., & Galor, O. (2011). Cultural Diversity, Geographical Isolation, and the Origin of the Wealth of Nations. *NBER (National Bureau of Economic Research) Working Paper* No. w17640.

Bandura, A. (1963). Behavior Theory and Indemnificatory Learning. *American Journal of Orthopsychiatry, 33*(4), 591–601.

Bandura, A. (1971). *Social Learning Theory*. New York: General Learning Press.

Barro, R. J. (1989). A Cross Country Study of Growth, Saving and Government. *NBER (National Bureau of Economic Research) Working Papers* No. 2855.

Barro, R. J. (1991). Economic Growth in a Cross Section of Countries. *Quarterly Journal of Economics, 106*(2), 407–443.

Barro, R. J., & Sala-i-Martin, X. (2003). *Economic Growth* (2nd ed.). Cambridge, MA: MIT Press.

Boyd, R., & Richerson, P. J. (1985). *Culture and the Evolutionary Process*. Chicago: University of Chicago Press.

Boyd, R., & Richerson, P. J. (1988). An Evolutionary Model of Social Learning: The Effects of Spatial and Temporal Variation. *Social Learning: Psychological and Biological Perspectives*, 29–48.

Cass, D. (1965). Optimum Growth in an Aggregative Model of Capital Accumulation. *The Review of Economic Studies, 32*(3), 233–240.

Chiao, J., & Ambady, N. (2007). Cultural Neuroscience: Parsing Universality and Diversity Across Levels of Analysis. In S. Kitayama & D. Cohen (Eds.), *The Handbook of Cultural Psychology* (pp. 237–254). New York: Guilford Press.

Coase, H. R. (1960). The Problem of Social Cost. *Journal of Law and Economics, 3*(1), 1–44.

Corpataux, J., & Crevoisier, O. (2007). Economic Theories and Spatial Transformations Clarifying the Space-Time Premises and Outcomes of Economic Theories. *Journal of Economic Geography, 7*(3), 285–309.

Crafts, N., & Mills, T. C. (2009). From Malthus to Solow: How Did the Malthusian Economy Really Evolve? *Journal of Macroeconomics, 31*(1), 68–93.
Crevoisier, O. (1996). Proximity and Territory Versus Space in Regional Science. *Environment and Planning A, 28*(9), 1683–1697.
Da Costa, P. N. (2015). *Ten Questions on Productivity, the Holy Grail of Economics.* Peterson Institute for International Economics. Retrieved from https://piie.com/blogs/realtime-economic-issues-watch/ten-questions-productivity-holy-grail-economics
Davidson, P. (1984). Reviving Keynes's Revolution. *Journal of Post Keynesian Economics, 6*(4), 561–575.
Davidson, P. (1996). Reality and Economic Theory. *Journal of Post Keynesian Economics, 18*(3), 479–508.
Dawkins, R. (1976). *The Selfish Gene.* London, Oxford: Oxford University Press.
Diamond, J. (1997). *Guns, Germs, and Steel: The Fates of Human Societies.* New York and London: Norton.
Domar, E. D. (1946). Capital Expansion, Rate of Growth, and Employment. *Econometrica, 14*(2), 137–147.
Douglas, M. (1987). *How Institutions Think.* London: Routledge & Kegan Paul.
Fischer, S. (1977). Long-Term Contracts, Rational Expectations, and the Optimal Money Supply Rule. *Journal of Political Economy, 85*(1), 191–205.
Frankel, M. (1962). The Production Function in Allocation of Growth: A Synthesis. *American Economic Review, 52*(5), 995–1022.
Groenewegen, P. D. (1977). Observations on a Paper by Saint-Péravy on the Subject of Indirect Taxation (1767). In P. D. Groenewegen (Ed.), *The Economics of A.R.J. Turgot* (1st ed., pp. 109–122). Dordrecht: Springer.
Harrod, R. F. (1939). An Essay in Dynamic Theory. *The Economic Journal, 49*(193), 14–33.
Hodgson, G. M. (1988). *Economics and Institutions, a Manifesto for a Modern Institutional Economics.* Cambridge: Policy Press.
IMF. (2017). *Seeking Sustainable Growth: Short-Term Recovery, Long-Term Challenges.* World Economic Outlook. Retrieved from https://www.imf.org/en/Publications/WEO/Issues/2017/09/19/world-economic-outlook-october-2017#top
Jong-a-Pin, R. (2009). On the Measurement of Political Instability and Its Impact on Economic Growth. *European Journal of Political Economy, 25*(1), 15–29.
Kahneman, D., & Tversky, A. (1979). Prospect Theory: An Analysis of Decision Under Risk. *Econometrica, 47*(2), 263–291.
Kamarck, A. M. (1976). *The Tropics and Economic Development: A Provocative Inquiry into the Poverty of Nations.* Baltimore and London: The Johns Hopkins University Press.
Keynes, J. M. (1936). *The General Theory of Employment, Investment, and Money.* London and New York: Macmillan.

Knight, F. H. (1940). *Risk, Uncertainty, and Profit.* London: London School of Economics and Political Science.
Koopmans, T. C. (1965). On the Concept of Optimal Economic Growth. In (Study Week on the) *Econometric Approach to Development Planning*, chap. 4, pp. 225–87. North-Holland Publishing Co., Amsterdam.
Kormendi, R. C., & Mcguire, P. G. (1985). Macroeconomic Determinants of Growth: Cross-Country Evidence. *Journal of Monetary Economics, 16*(2), 141–163.
Krugman, P. (1994). *The Age of Diminishing Expectations: US Economic Policy in the 1990* (3rd ed.). Cambridge, MA: MIT Press.
Lucas Jr., R. E. (1972). Expectations and the Neutrality of Money. *Journal of Economic Theory, 4*(2), 103–124.
Lucas Jr., R. E. (1988). On the Mechanics of Economic Development. *Journal of Monetary Economics, 22*, 3–42.
Lucas Jr., R. E. (1990). Supply-Side Economics: An Analytical Review. *Oxford Economic Papers, 42*(2), 293–316.
Lucas Jr., R. E. (1976). Econometric Policy Evaluation: A Critique. *Carnegie-Rochester Conference Series on Public Policy, 1*(*1*), 19–46.
Malthus, T. R. (1798). *An Essay on the Principle of Population, as It Affects the Future Improvement of Society, with Remarks on the Speculations of Mr. Godwin, M. Condorcet, and Other Writers.* London: J. Johnson.
Mankiw, N. G., Romer, D., & Weil, D. (1992). A Contribution to the Empirics of Economic Growth. *Quarterly Journal of Economics, 107*(2), 407–437.
Marshall, A. (1890). *Principles of Economics.* London: Macmillan.
Martin, R. L., & Sunley, P. (1996). Paul Krugman's Geographical Economics and Its Implications for Regional Development Theory: A Critical Assessment. *Economic Geography, 72*(3), 259–292.
Maslow, A. H. (1943). A Theory of Human Motivation. *Psychological Review, 50*(4), 370–396.
Metz, R. (2011). Do Kondratieff Waves Exist? How Time Series Techniques Can Help to Solve the Problem. *Cliometrica, 5*(3), 205–238.
Minsky, H. (1986). *Stabilizing an Unstable Economy.* New Haven: Yale University Press.
Nelson, R., & Winter, S.G. ([1982] 2005). *An Evolutionary Theory of Economic Change.* Cambridge, Mass.: Belknap Press of Harvard University Press.
O'Driscoll, G. P., & Rizzo, M. J. (1985). *The Economics of Time and Ignorance.* Oxford and New York: Basic Blackwell.
Olsson, O., & Hibbs Jr., D. A. (2005). Biogeography and Long-Run Economic Development. *European Economic Review, 49*(4), 909–938.
Petrakis, P. E. (2017). *Economic Development and Growth: General and Integrated Approach.* Athens: Quaestor Editions.

Petrakis, P. E., & Kostis, P. C. (2014). Medium Term Effects of Culture, Transactions and Institutions on Opportunity Entrepreneurship. *Journal of Innovation and Entrepreneurship, 3*(1), 11.

Phelps, E. S., & Taylor, J. B. (1977). Stabilizing Powers of Monetary Policy Under Rational Expectations. *Journal of Political Economy, 85*(1), 163–190.

Pyka, A., & Foster, J. (Eds.) (2015). *The Evolution of Economic and Innovation Systems*, Springer.

Ramsey, F. P. (1928). A Mathematical Theory of Saving. *The Economic Journal, 38*(152), 543–559.

Ricardo, D. (1817). *The Principles of Political Economy and Taxation*. London: John Murray.

Rogers, A. R. (1988). Does Biology Constrain Culture. *American Anthropologist, 90*(4), 819–831. https://doi.org/10.1525/aa.1988.90.4.02a00030

Romer, P. M. (1986). Increasing Returns and Long-Run Growth. *Journal of Political Economy, 94*(5), 1002–1037.

Romer, P. M. (1987). Growth Based on Increasing Returns Due to Specialization. *The American Economic Review, 77*(2), 56–62.

Romer, P. M. (1990). Endogenous Technological Change. *Journal of Political Economy, 98*(5), 71–102.

Samuelson, P. A. (1958). *An Exact Consumption-Loan Model of Interest with or without the Social Contrivance of Money 66* (pp. 467–467). Chicago: University of Chicago Press.

Schumpeter, J. A. (1934). *The Theory of Economic Development*. Cambridge: Harvard University Press.

Schumpeter, J. A. (1939). *Business Cycles: A Theoretical, Historical and Statistical Analysis of the Capitalist Process*. New York: McGraw-Hill.

Schumpeter, J. A. (1950). *Capitalism, Socialism, and Democracy*. New York: Harper.

Smith, A. (1776 [1981]). An Inquiry into the Nature and Causes of the Wealth of Nations. In R. H. Campbell & A. S. Skinner (Eds.), *The Glasgow Edition of the Works of Adam Smith, 2*. Indianapolis: Liberty Fund.

Solow, R. M. (1956). A Contribution to The Theory of Economic Growth. *The Quarterly Journal of Economics, 70*(1), 65–94.

Spolaore, E., & Wacziarg, R. (2013). How Deep Are the Roots of Economic Development? *Journal of Economic Literature, 51*(2), 325–369.

Swan, T. W. (1956). Economic Growth and Capital Accumulation. *Economic Record, 32*(2), 334–361.

Taylor, J. B. (1980). Aggregate Dynamics and Staggered Contracts. *Journal of Political Economy, 88*(1), 1–23.

Van der Merwe, L. (2008). Scenario-Based Strategy in Practice: A Framework. *Advances in Developing Human Resources, 10*(2), 216–239.

Way, B. M., & Lieberman, M. D. (2010). Is There A Genetic Contribution to Cultural Differences? Collectivism, Individualism and Genetic Markers of Social Sensitivity. *Social Cognitive and Affective Neuroscience*, *5*(2–3), 203–211.

Williamson, O. E. (1975). *Markets and Hierarchies: Analysis and Antitrust Implications: A Study in the Economics of Internal Organization*. Illinois, USA: University of Illinois at Urbana-Champaign's Academy for Entrepreneurial Leadership Historical Research Reference in Entrepreneurship.

Williamson, O. E. (1985). *The Economic Institutions of Capitalism*. New York: The Free Press.

Woodford, M. (2013). Forward Guidance by Inflation-Targeting Central Banks. *CEPR Discussion Papers* No. 9722.

CHAPTER 2

Modern Growth Theory Arguments

2.1 Introduction

The modern approach of economic growth is required to analyse the sources of economic growth and to formulate the policy tools needed to utilize them effectively. Thus, modern economic science is called upon to revise its basic parameters and assumptions, adapt to new conditions and present a new framework of theory and policies that will be more effective than previous ones.

Section 2.2 of the chapter presents the basic theoretical approach of development economics with regard to the "Big Push Concept" and the distribution of investments, as a policy for growth. Section 2.3 presents the theories of international trade and the concepts of comparative and absolute advantage. Section 2.4 discusses the macro-debate on growth. Section 2.5 presents the New Classical School of economics. Section 2.6 of the chapter presents the New Keynesians under the light of the behavioural approach, while in the Sect. 2.7, reference is made to heterogeneity. The core of the New Keynesians, by adding the case of bounded rationality, allows for the implementation of fiscal policy, while also allowing room for monetary policy, even under zero interest rates.

Section 2.8 presents the Phillips Curve from the perspective of the New Keynesians and its adoption to supply-side policies. Section 2.9 presents the DSGE models, which form the theoretical core of the New Keynesians.

In Sects. 2.10 and 2.11, respectively, the Schumpeterian and the evolutionary approach are analysed.

P. E. Petrakis et al., *Economic Growth and Development Policy*,
https://doi.org/10.1007/978-3-030-43181-5_2

The chapter concludes with the Sect. 2.12 on the ideology bias regarding the construction of economic models and their customization.

2.2 The Development Argument

The approach of the Big Push Theory (Rosenstein-Rodan, 1943) as balanced growth (Nath, 1962; Nurkse, 1971) influenced the thinking of development economics thinkers as it sought to answer the question of how underdeveloped countries could compensate for the handicap and catch up to developed economies. At the same time, it provided a structuralist approach to developmental economics.

The post–World War II period was marked by extreme poverty in underdeveloped countries, creating space for the implementation of new economic practices, in particular "Development Economics". While the development process approach for underdeveloped countries was nothing new, the emphasis of development economics has been on modernizing the developing world to "catch up" with more advanced nations (Kartika, 2014). But unlike Classical economics or Keynesian economics, development economics did not have a specific theoretical model on which to base its analysis.

Rosenstein's idea of Big Push (Rosenstein-Rodan, 1943) is often marked as the beginning of development economics. Further contributions were made later on by Murphy, Shleifer, and Vishny in 1989. Analysis of this theory usually involves the use of game theory. Rosenstein emphasized the importance of the complementarity of industries to justify his proposal for a balanced development strategy. The Big Push Theory emphasizes that underdeveloped countries require large-scale investments to begin their path to economic growth, given current conditions. The theory proposes that an investment programme cannot affect the development process as it would in developing countries. In fact, small-scale fragmented investments alone are not capable of leading to economic growth and close the gap with developed countries. On the contrary, such investments lead to a sub-optimal use of financial resources, with results falling short of the mark.

Nurkse (1971) assumes that underdeveloped countries need to make significant investments in many industries at the same time. This will expand the market size, increase productivity and encourage the private sector to invest. According to Nurkse, expanding market size is crucial to increasing investment incentives. Only then can the vicious cycle of poverty be broken.

Big Push Theory's strategy, as balanced growth, has focused on investing in infrastructure and all economically productive sectors, as the "complementarity" of different industries is so large that it requires a concurrent investment strategy.

In particular, Rosenstein-Rodan (1943) proposed three forms of investment indivisibility:

1. Indivisibilities in Production Function: When there is a multitude of different industries in the economy, conditions for the concentration of production factors, goods, services and production techniques are created. In addition to the above, if social capital is added, they all contribute directly and indirectly to development.
2. Indivisibilities of Demand: The main feature of developing countries is the low demand due to low incomes. Indivisibilities of demand require a portfolio of investments in a variety of sectors of economic activity so that they can mutually support one other. Therefore, the problem of the small market could be tackled by the creation of businesses that would lead to increased income through increased employment and stimulated demand.
3. Indivisibility in Supply of Savings: The amount of savings could be seen as a form of indivisibility. A certain amount of savings is needed to achieve a specific investment. However, in the case of developing countries, due to lower incomes, savings remain low.

In the presence of these indivisibilities and the lack of external economies, only a big push can lift the economy out of the trap of poverty. This means that a specific level of investment is needed to remove obstacles to economic growth.

Hirschman (1958) later questioned the feasibility of a balanced growth strategy and instead advocated unbalanced growth, for achieving industrialization. Criticism of balanced and big push theory questions both the need for balanced growth as a prerequisite for economies of scale, as well as its feasibility and realism, as a theory of growth. On the contrary, unbalanced growth theory argues that because of imperfect knowledge, which is indirectly endorsed by balanced growth theory, with regard to constraints, as well as the possibility of modifying them through the growth process, it is not possible to formulate a priori any unique maximum development path (Bhatt, 1964).

Market size was central to the views of Nurkse (1953) who, along with Rosenstein, were supporters of the concept of balanced growth. Large-scale investment in many sectors simultaneously induces demand complementarity across sectors. Therefore, the size of the market is expanding, as is the willingness of the economy to invest.

According to Nurkse (1953), market size is determined by a number of factors where productivity plays a dominant role. Low productivity reduces real purchasing power, so the Keynesian perceptions of boosting active demand do not have a significant response at least in developing economies. On the contrary, concepts such as population and geographical area of economic activity are not as important determinants as transport costs and non-tariff barriers to trade. On the other hand, an increase in productivity increases the flow of goods and services into the economy, thereby increasing consumption and economic growth.

2.3 International Trade and Comparative Advantage

In *The Wealth of Nations* (1776 [1981]), Smith first argued that the wealth of nations derives from the role of international trade, a concept also used by Ricardo (1817) to develop his theory of comparative and absolute advantage.

The dimension of productivity as a source of growth derives from the Ricardian theory of comparative advantage. The term "comparative" is used to analyse the ratio of labour productivity between two countries. In his classic work, *Principles of Economic and Taxation Policies* (1817), Ricardo described a model by which international trade between two countries can be beneficial to both if each country exports the products to which it has a comparative advantage.

The basic idea behind comparative advantage is that every economy, no matter how advanced or non-advanced, in terms of productivity of its labour compared to other economies, is able to trade profitably with others. The Ricardian model contains a factor of production, namely labour, and is based on the comparative advantage of countries, that is, country-by-country labour productivity. This concept defines the international division of labour.

It should be noted that Ricardo's theory of comparative advantage has been, from its creation until today, a very important tool in the intellectual toolkit of any economist (Irwin, 2017). Although more than 200 years have elapsed since the emergence of this theory, sophisticated models of international trade (Dornbusch, Fisher, & Samuelson, 1977; Eaton & Kortum, 2002) are significantly influenced by the basic framework of comparative advantage theory, as its design is highly structured, and the knowledge it affords is not restricted by time.

According to this model, international trade leads to growth—increasing global production—as each country specializes in producing goods with comparative advantage. Thus, for products of the same quality, one country has a comparative advantage in producing a product if the relative opportunity cost, in terms of production costs (labour costs), is lower than that for the product of the other country. So, if this country produces more and consumes less of this product, given the external demand—given that other countries are willing to trade with it—it would improve its production, that is, its development and growth. Ultimately, the pattern of international trade depends on differences in labour productivity.

In more recent works, the Ricardian model is extended to the case of many products (Deardorff, 2007; Dornbusch et al., 1977; Wilson, 1980). In its new version, the Ricardian model continues to examine the case of the open economy and the benefits of trade for both countries involved.

The concept of comparative advantage was developed in opposition to the absolute advantage of Smith (1776 [1981]). Based on absolute advantage, international trade takes place when one country exports products with higher labour productivity to another with lower labour productivity, that is to say, not by comparison to its trading partner. So, in a world with only one factor of production and a country lagging behind in terms of labour productivity, there should be no foreign trade.

In the field of trade theory, a further evolution of Ricardo's theory is the factor endowment theory by Heckscher (1919) and Ohlin (1933), who, using neoclassical logic, formulated the theory that international trade would develop between two different countries, even if they had the same technology, but differed in the available production factor portfolio—land, labour, capital.

The Heckscher-Ohlin model differs from the Ricardian model for two reasons. First, it adopts a more realistic framework than the Ricardian model, allowing a second factor of production in the form of capital. Second, in the Heckscher-Ohlin model, the comparative advantage is determined by differences in the factors between countries and not by technological differences, as in the Ricardian model. In the Heckscher-Ohlin model, countries have the same production technologies. The first innovation of the model shows that the production capacity limit will be concave and, thus, will result in increased opportunity costs. Therefore, full specialization, as in the Ricardian model, is not particularly likely. Furthermore, trade will cause a redistribution of income between labour and capital. The second innovation of the model shows that a country will export goods which make intensive use of the factor that is abundantly available.

In the 1970s–1980s, economic thought on international finance and international trade elements were added coming from the field of strategic advantage development at the level of enterprises and businesses with international frontiers.

Two approaches have played a significant role in the above-mentioned development: the product life cycle (Vernon, 1970) and the natural competitive advantage (Porter's Advantage)—a new, mature and standard product—(Porter, 1980). Product life-cycle theory assumes that the required development of innovations for the early stages of new product development will take place in developed countries by proposing a model for geographical innovation development. The products are then moved to join international trade flows. This theory is consistent with the 1960s model of innovation and economics in the United States.

The pre-existing theoretical constructs, based on the potential for international equilibrium of comparative advantage, were not able to interpret the development models of international trade and the movement of capital observed internationally (Vernon, 1966). By contrast, shifting attention to the timetable for the development—the accumulation of knowledge—and the release of new products, along with the role of economies of scale and uncertainty, can better interpret international models.

This approach, of course, fits in more with the first 20–30 post-war years and less so with recent years, with the rapid growth of developing countries, although they, too, now have research activities and at a much lower cost.

Porter's (1980) theory of national competitive advantage is a much more sophisticated view of the interpretation of international trading patterns if we compare it with the classical and neoclassical concepts of comparative advantage. Porter identified four determinants that influence the development of competitive advantage at the enterprise level and, then, at the economy level: (a) domestic resources and capabilities (factor conditions), (b) local market conditions, (c) domestic suppliers and complementary industries (effective support from related industries) and (d) domestic business characteristics, including business strategy, industry structure and so on. In addition, the government can play an active role in increasing the competitiveness of local industries.

The New Trade theory, developed mainly by Krugman (1979), has focused its attention on multinational companies and their efforts to develop a competitive advantage over other similar global companies. In order to develop a global competitive advantage, barriers to entry must be removed. To do this, multinationals can optimize research and development, copyright ownership, economies of scale, exclusivity in modes of production and knowledge and, finally, ascribe a central role to the necessary raw materials and production resources.

2.4 The Macro-Debate on Growth

The emergence of major economic crises at any time raises questions about the effectiveness of macroeconomic theory, creating the need for its reconceptualization. Typical examples are the Great Depression of 1929 and the period of high inflation in the 1970s, when the micro-foundation revolution took place (Vines & Wills, 2018). These two periods can help understand what actions are needed in order to change the theoretical background of macroeconomic thinking. At the same time, they are food for thought about how economic science should learn from the 2008 economic downturn and revise its assumptions.

Before the 1930s, economists had to rely on Alfred Marshall and the partial equilibrium model to interpret the functioning of the economy. The Great Depression of 1929 led John Maynard Keynes to intervene in the Marshallian model and add nominal rigidities in an attempt to explain why the economy does not immediately return to a state of full employment. Subsequently, Keynes devised the consumption function, the multipliers and the preference of the financial actors for liquidity. In this way, Keynes proceeded to change the content of macroeconomic theory. At the same time, a methodological change in macroeconomics was under way (Vines & Wills, 2018): the kind of general equilibrium analysis provided by IS-LMs.

Thus, Keynes through General Theory was able to state the reason why the flexible prices in the market for goods, cited by Marshall, do not necessarily provide equilibrium conditions. The crucial methodological difference is that Keynes began to think of the general equilibrium of the economy as a result of the interaction of markets with each other, assuming rigidity in nominal wages. Unless wages are adjusted to the labour market, flexible prices in the market for the goods on which the Marshallian model is based, cannot guarantee the equilibrium of the quantity of goods offered. In addition to the rigidity of nominal wages, Keynes added four more points to his methodological approach: (a) If wages are not adjusted after a decline in investment, then there will be a decrease in aggregate demand for the product market. (b) A decrease in aggregate demand, in turn, will lead to a decrease in consumption and savings—through the consumption function. (c) The consumption function can influence the size of the multipliers to show how much output should be reduced after investment is reduced, so as to rebalance savings with investment. (d) The preferences of economic agents for liquidity explain why interest rates will not fall sufficiently to prevent a decline in aggregate demand.

In the 1970s, the oil crisis and high inflation have triggered a renewed debate on changing the theoretical background of macroeconomic thinking. The consequence of this situation was the inability of the IS-LM curves in the fixed price system to provide an appropriate economic policy framework. This gave rise to two schools of thought: on the one hand, there were supporters of the view that existing macroeconomic models should evolve, and, on the other, they were supporters of more radical perceptions of how to model economic science.

The first school argued that the Keynesian effort to achieve full employment was responsible for rising inflation. In doing so, they have given precedence to monetary policy, questioning the effectiveness of fiscal policy. This school incorporated the Phillips Curve (Phillips, 1958), adaptive expectations and the nominal anchor, while the supply side was endogenized in the models.

The second school of thought supported the micro-foundations of macroeconomic models as well as the concept of optimization and future orientation with expectations being model-compatible (random error term). Significantly, a second element they introduced concerned the concept of equilibrium, as they argued that the economy is in a stable equilibrium, and therefore economic policy intervention is not required.

To this school of thought belongs the "Lucas critique" (Lucas, 1976), criticizing existing models in terms of the effectiveness of economic policy. In particular, he emphasized the role of rational expectations because if economic agents form expectations about the future and modify those expectations in response to a new policy, then the models could be acceptable, and expectations would be compatible with the model's predictions.

Based on the "Lucas critique", Lucas and Sargent (1979) attempted to incorporate rational expectations into economic models but, at the same time, to describe the behaviour resulting from optimizing agents under specific expectations. In this way, models could understand the way households and businesses react to possible changes in economic policy.

The global financial crisis of 2008 has in turn also triggered discussions among economic policymakers, prompting them to reconsider the effectiveness of existing macroeconomic policy. The collapse of Lehman Brothers in 2008 initially brought to light the weaknesses of the financial system and the mistaken assessment of existing risks. At the same time, it made clear the limits of monetary policy. Subsequently, the debt crisis in the Eurozone countries triggered a new debate on the functioning of monetary unions and the pursuit of fiscal policy. Therefore, economic policymakers had to improvise using unconventional monetary policies, fiscal incentives, the choice of speed of fiscal adjustment policies and the use of macroprudential instruments (Blanchard, Dell'Ariccia, & Mauro, 2013).

The above-mentioned concerns led the International Monetary Fund (IMF) in 2011 to organize a conference on "Macro and Growth Policies in the Wake of the Crisis" in which both academics and policymakers expressed the view that the global economy has entered a "brave new world" (Blanchard et al., 2013) with the questions outnumbering the answers. Many of these concerns persisted. Nevertheless, there has been definite progress, both theoretically and empirically.

Concerns about monetary policy were centred on the central banks and the rule of maintaining inflation through interest rates (Taylor's rule). It was realized that this rule would have to be diversified and set new goals using a multitude of tools to achieve them. (Woodford, 2013).

While monetary policy appeared to be in trouble due to the liquidity trap and low interest rates, policymakers were initially led to fiscal expansion policies to tackle the crisis. However, the outcomes were not those expected. Many economies were over-indebted and had high deficits resulting in no fiscal space. At the same time, the crisis has reduced the revenues of state budgets, and the focus has shifted to fiscal consolidation issues. Concerns surfaced about what levels of government debt can be considered safe for an economy, along with questions about the extent and speed of fiscal adjustment.

Finally, the third response of economic policymakers was the use of macroprudential policies (Borio & Shim, 2007), to maintain financial stability and address potential systemic risks. Macroprudential policies prevent excessive accumulation of risks due to external factors and failures of the market mechanism so as to smooth the financial cycle—time dimension. At the same time, they make the financial sector more resilient by limiting the dissemination of negative effects—(cross-sectoral dimension), and they encourage a system-wide view of regulating the financial system in order to provide appropriate incentives to market participants—(structural dimension.)

2.5 The New Classical on Growth

During the period of strong inflation and low growth (1970–1980), in response to the failure of the Keynesian economists to explain the inflationary crisis, the New Classical economics emerged, which quickly became the dominant school of economic thought. The New Classical Economics appeared in the early 1970s with main proponent economists from the Universities of Chicago and Minnesota and, in particular, Robert Lucas, Thomas Sargent, Neil Wallace and Edward Prescott.

The main characteristic of the New Classical economics is the analysis of the general equilibrium and mainly of price and market clearance based on rational expectations and price flexibility. Although they made an effort to bring back the ideas of Classical economics, the original aim was to provide a microeconomic background for the labour market, as Keynes had initially approached it. In contrast to the classics, Keynes believed that even without market imperfections, aggregate demand may be less than the total production capacity of labour and capital. In such a case, the workforce is not employed, although it may be willing to work at a salary lower than the salary paid to those already employed.

By contrast, Lucas and Rapping (1969), based on the concept of market equilibrium, leave no room for involuntary unemployment. According to Keynes' theory, recessions are the result of weak demand and, as a result, businesses are producing below their maximum potential production, leading to a decline in employment. For the New Classics, the existence of involuntary unemployment, that is, the over-supply of labour, ensures that businesses reduce their labour costs and increase their profits by following an optimizing behaviour. We note, therefore, that in the New Classical thinking, micro-foundational elements are inserted that consider individuals and businesses to work to maximize their usefulness, given their prices, wages and capital. At the same time, the price system is adjusted, thereby changing the motives and, hence, the choices of individuals.

Of particular interest is the New Classical approach to the effectiveness of economic policy. At this point, we can focus on the business cycles and the importance they attach to the emergence of unexpected shocks to the economy. For the New Classical economists, productivity and in particular its changes are a source of fluctuations in the economy. Fluctuations in aggregate demand cannot usually be predicted in changes in monetary or fiscal policy. Supply disturbances are generally caused by changes in productivity that may arise, for example, from changes in technology, raw material prices or production management. Ideally, businesses will choose to produce more and pay workers more when the economy is affected by positive shocks and less when affected by adverse disturbances. Similarly, workers will be willing to work more when productivity and wages are higher, and want to have more free time when their pay is lower. Employment, like the product produced, will increase with positive shocks and decrease with adverse disturbances.

However, the fact that the economy is facing good and bad phases is not enough to explain the business cycle. An adequate theory must take into account the fact that business cycles usually have long periods of prosperity, followed by shorter but significant periods of recession. The New Classical economists, who view demand disorders as dominant, argue that shocks are slowly spreading throughout the economy. This is because any adjustment to new conditions is expensive. If new capital is needed during economic boom, it takes a long time to create it. And when lower production makes existing capital redundant, it takes time to depreciate.

The New Classical features of the school of Real Business Cycle consider productivity change as the driving force of business cycles. Since technological changes may also occur over time, fluctuations in favourable or adverse effects on productivity or technology may be part of the existence and maintenance of economic cycles. Relying on the neoclassical model micro-foundation, the RBC models captured the impact of technological changes on the economic activity evolution and the unemployment rate, therefore, minimizing the influence exercised by the modifications occurring in goods and services or the money market (Hudea, 2015).

An important step in the analysis of the New Classical was the introduction of rational expectations. Muth (1961) was the one who first introduced rational expectations and then Lucas (1972) developed and consolidated the case of rational expectations (Rational Expectations Hypothesis), setting aside the previously dominant adaptive expectations. Building on this hypothesis, the New Classical economists grounded their theory on the predictive ability of economic models and the rationality of economic agents.

Based on this hypothesis, they have formed the core of their theory regarding the effectiveness of economic policy. Keynesian economists of the 1960s often cited the Phillips curve to emphasize that monetary or fiscal policy, while lowering the unemployment rate, could also lead to higher inflation rates. The interesting question, in terms of policymaking, lies in the relationship between inflation and unemployment. By contrast, the New Classical economists rejected the idea that there was some useful interaction between inflation and employment. They claim that the increase in aggregate demand reduces unemployment because price increases cannot be predicted. Both the rise in output and the reduction in unemployment are temporary, since neither the returns on business nor the purchasing power of workers are adjusted for inflation. Once they realize the "mistake", businesses and workers return to their old levels of production and labour supply, respectively.

In his article *Econometric Policy Evaluation: A Critique* (1976), Lucas argues against the effectiveness of economic policy because the latter changes the structure of the economic system. The criticism of Lucas (1976) necessitated a revision of Keynesian economics by reinforcing the introduction of microeconomic principles into macroeconomic models.

The quantitative change in policy objectives affects the coefficients of the estimated behavioural equations, as business and household expectations depend on the policy instruments under consideration. Lucas' criticism has helped economists change their view of the large-scale macroeconomic models of the 1960s and early 1970s.

According to Lucas' critique, econometric analysis, based on past experience, cannot be used to examine and predict the impact of economic policy in advance. Lucas (1976) criticizes market efficiency for failing to take into account the extent to which estimates differ from reality. Lucas, in this text, does not necessarily assume that economic agents are rational; however, in his critique of the macroeconomic models of the Keynesian tradition, he uses the framework of rational expectations. The problem for Lucas stems from the fact that the behaviour of households and businesses often depends on the rules of government policy that are ignored by the models under discussion.

2.6 New Keynesians with a Behavioral Approach

The weakness itself of the theories of the early 1980s (Ball, Mankiw, & Reis, 2005)—and not necessarily the non-verification of Keynesian theory through empirical data—made space for the development of new ideas and thoughts with the emergence of the New Keynesian Economics school.

New Keynesian economics is the school of macroeconomic thinking that seeks to align Keynesian economics with microeconomic bases, market imperfections and nominal wage rigidities. The emergence of New Keynesian economics came in the 1980s as a result of the strong criticism of New Classical economists on many aspects of the Keynesian revolution. Fischer (1977) is one of the first to contribute to New Keynesian economics, focusing on nominal rigidities, because of the existence of labour market contracts. He examines the role of monetary policy, which may influence the behaviour of the actual product produced. Fischer (1977) and Taylor (1980) argue that labour market contracts are a factor of wage rigidity.

The New Keynesians, as mentioned earlier, are based on the concept of individual rationality. However, there are reasons to believe that individuals do not always act rationally and to adopt the idea of bounded rationality (Sent, 1997; Simon, 1996). Incorporating behavioural data into the New Keynesian models could provide answers to several theoretical questions, such as whether low interest rates are responsible for rising inflation.

Xavier Gabaix develops a macroeconomic theory in his article *A Behavioral New Keynesian Model* (2017), which attempts to provide a different perspective on the way macroeconomic theory is structured.

Innovation in Gabaix's model is the introduction of a new parameter, M, which quantifies the underperformance of economic agents in terms of both future policies and their impact. This myopic parameter, in turn, affects the effectiveness of fiscal and monetary policy in a generalized macroeconomic equilibrium. In essence, the M parameter represents a degree of behaviourism. Economic agents cannot entirely focus on prospects that will arise when thinking about current consumption and price levels. For example, if the M parameter equals 0.5, a 10% increase in consumption means that consumers will only increase consumption by 5% next year. At the same time, making consumption and product output less sensitive to expectations (M > 1), Gabaix makes the equilibrium path of future consumption and inflation more sensitive to initial conditions.

In addition, it attempts to explain what it calls "forward guidance puzzle". The forward guidance puzzle summarizes the policies that need to be taken to address the imbalances in the economy; however, these policies have a more significant impact in the now, in terms of GDP and inflation, the further ahead they occur. However, this puzzle stems from the unrealistic assumption of full information and unlimited mental capacity of individuals. The fact that forward guidance is projected to be so strong, according to New Keynesians, is a paradox, as it is impossible to accept that policies in the distant future are more powerful than policies in the near future. To counteract this paradox, Gabaix introduces bounded rationality in which the effect of forward guidance over the long term is dramatically attenuated.

To interpret the relationship between interest rates and inflation, Gabaix argues that when interest rates or outputs change, individuals are not sufficiently aware of the difference. At the same time, their forecasts and their planning are rather short-sighted. The farther into the future an event (e.g. a recession) is likely to occur, the less concerned people are about it. Despite the simplicity of thinking, it is a radical step in macroeconomic theory, as many economists are advocates of perfect rationality. If the economy is driven by behaviours that are not rational, the explanation that economists are asked to give about what went wrong in the economy often goes astray, so the actual problem is not addressed.

The contribution of the behavioural approach to New Keynesians was crucial as it contributed to the concern raised by the emergence of zero-inflation conditions in Japan for 20 years, as well as in contemporary US history, where interest rates were stuck at zero since 2009. One easy interpretation, one might argue, would be to claim that interest rates can no longer keep up with inflation, and that the economy has to follow a "passive" monetary policy. Nevertheless, Gabaix's approach was able to get out of the theoretical impasse the New Keynesians, who could neither interpret nor solve the low-powered monetary policy effectiveness under conditions of zero interest rates and low inflation.

2.7 New Keynesians and Heterogeneity

New Keynesian models, like their predecessors, the RBCs, are based on the assumption that the economy consists of a representative household that exists in perpetuity. Although this case is unrealistic, simplification helps macroeconomic issues to be addressed. For example, a key question in macroeconomic theory is how to explain in a simple and understandable way the fluctuations of the economy and its interactions with monetary policy. However, it is not apparent why the assumption of the existence of the household in perpetuity is necessary for the creation of such models. Similarly, individuals are heterogeneous in their behaviour in many aspects of life, such as wealth, income, education, risk aversion, and so on. In order to simplify financial complexity, a model may not take into account the above-mentioned factors. In this light, it may be possible to argue that the case of a representative household is a good starting point for a macroeconomic model (Galí, 2018).

A major problem arising from the representative household case is that, in equilibrium, there is no separation of individuals into savers and borrowers, even if there are no financial frictions, as they are all identical. Thus, in order to understand whether the presence and nature of frictions have a non-trivial impact on economic fluctuations and monetary policy, it is necessary to relax the case of representative households.

A recent version of New Keynesian models, known as Heterogeneous Agent New Keynesian (HANK) models, incorporates heterogeneous individuals and financial frictions in their analysis (Guerrieri & Lorenzoni, 2017; McKay & Reis, 2016; Oh & Reis, 2012). A key feature of HANKs, which distinguishes them from traditional New Keynesian models, is the assumption of idiosyncratic shocks to labour productivity and therefore wages. Such shocks are often assumed to follow a stochastic process, which is consistent with key features of the micro-data.

It is also assumed that only a small number of assets can be traded, and that there is a limit on external lending. As a result, households cannot be fully protected from idiosyncratic risk. In addition, a changing portion of households is facing a binding debt restraint, which makes consumption highly influenced by current income fluctuations. The preceding features indicate that there is no simple dynamic IS equation that can be derived. However, the other two elements of the key New Keynesian framework—the New Keynesian Phillips curve and the interest rate rule—are not directly affected by the introduction of heterogeneity.

2.8 The New Keynesians Versus Supply-Side Theorists

The idea of a positive relationship between inflation and output was well known almost from the foundations of economics, but its contemporary theoretical background dates back to the late 1950s with A.W. Phillips documenting the statistical relationship between wage growth and unemployment in the UK. The Phillips curve subsequently appeared to be "working" for the relationship between inflation and unemployment in other economies as well, as an integral part of the Keynesian theory of the 1960s.

However, the power of the Phillips curve later received much criticism with M. Friedman as the dominant critic. Friedman (1968), in his article "The Role of Monetary Policy", focuses on how Keynesian economics treats human expectations. The Keynesian model tacitly rests on the idea that unemployment could be kept at a low level, "allowing" high inflation to lower real wages and thus increase labour demand. But Friedman pointed out that if policymakers try to keep the output above potential levels, then workers will demand higher real wages to adjust nominal wages to inflation levels. The result would be higher inflation rates without keeping unemployment low. The 1970s, with the prevalence of stagflation, confirmed Friedman's claims.

The response of the Keynesians to criticism was based on their attempt to construct models that would incorporate rational expectations by providing a microeconomic interpretation of monetary policy strength, at least in the short term. Thus, they introduced the rigidity of nominal prices according to the theoretical approach of what we know as New Keynesians. The rigidity of prices may explain why the economy is sometimes below its maximum production capacity. Also, in conditions of price rigidity, an increase in the money supply can lead to a short-term increase in purchasing power and thus stimulate production.

The rigidity of the nominal wages introduced in this New Keynesian approach introduces a different view of the Phillips curve, providing the ground for economic policy development. The New Keynesian Phillips curve (NKPC) essentially correlates inflation and expected inflation not with unemployment, but with a measure that expresses the aggregate marginal cost of firms. The NKPC is based on the theoretical contributions of Taylor (1980), Rotemberg (1982) and Calvo (1983) who use the nominal price rigidity assumption to explain inflation.

As prices do not adjust to the market, the question arises of how nominal prices are initially set. Almost all approaches to the rigidity of nominal prices are based on monopolistic competition, where the price of the product is determined by maximizing the monopoly's profits. As the price of a product depends on the prices of its substitutes, the monopolist, who can continuously adjust the price, will equate its marginal cost with its marginal benefit, with price being above marginal cost. However, if the nominal prices cannot be adjusted continuously, then the monopolist will choose the current nominal price, which equates the expected present value of the marginal revenue and marginal costs, as long as the price remains constant.

Using Calvo's (1983) methodology for modelling the price adjustment mechanism, Woodford (2003) derives an NKPC with structural features where current and expected inflation, as well as marginal costs, are given by the equation:

$$\pi_t = \gamma f \, E\pi_{t+1} + \lambda \, mc_t + \xi_t$$

where γf and λ are structural parameter functions, mc_t the aggregate marginal cost in period t and ξ_t a random variable (e.g. an exogenous shock). By solving the above-mentioned differential equation, we can find out how current and expected marginal costs are driven by current inflation.

The theoretical microeconomic foundation and the intrinsic role of future price expectations make the NKPC a useful tool in monetary policymaking (Abbas, Bhattacharya, & Sgro, 2016). Nominal market rigidities reflect non-monetary neutrality, making the NKPC particularly useful in pursuing monetary policy. In the past two decades, a great number of works has empirically examined its validity (Fuhrer, 1995; Gordon, 2011; Rudebusch & Svensson, 1999).

In addition to the potential offered by Phillips curve's theoretical approach and, in particular, its modification by the New Keynesian, it has again been at the centre of attention since the outbreak of the global financial crisis in 2008, and, in particular, in countries implementing fiscal adjustment programmes. The logic of its supply-side economics that prevailed was intended to "shift" the Phillips curve of troubled economies so that budgetary measures could be applied at a lower cost.

The logic of supply-side economic policies is based on theoretical considerations that form an organized economic policy platform called

"Austerity Policies". These views can be summarized in the following points:

1. Public or private debt (as a percentage of GDP) needs to be reduced because, after a certain level, they pose a threat to medium- and long-term growth.
2. Implementation of structural reforms (including internal devaluation) is needed, in order to liberalize production and increase confidence in the economic system. In such a case, future taxes will be reduced, current consumption will increase and the problems caused by fiscal adjustment will be addressed.
3. If current tax or debt increases (and, hence, taxes in the future), the level of demand will remain unchanged, reflecting a Ricardian equivalence: increasing savings to pay future taxes imposed to pay off debt and, thus, reducing consumption. That is why expansionary fiscal policy is not a viable solution.
4. Monetary policies that encourage excessive investment lead to increased inflation risks and debt costs (i.e. a threat to growth).
5. Reducing the deficit of Net Foreign Investment Position is a top priority. Budgetary and external deficits will need to be reduced. This is the reason for imposing an internal devaluation, if there is no option for an external devaluation.

Implementing a supply-side policy programme requires several structural reforms related to production, to consumption economies and to consumer sensitivity to price changes. Structural reforms are based on adjusting the current account balance and aim at restoring sustainability. More specifically, structural reforms need to address three main directions (Goldman Sachs, 2012a): (a) increasing market share of production, (b) improving price elasticity between non-marketable and marketable products and (c) labour market reforms to change the slope of the Phillips curve or shift it to the right. Structural adjustment may occur through changes in demand between marketable and non-marketable goods. The higher the production of marketable goods in a peripheral country, the easier it is for it to make the necessary adjustments to its current account balance and recover its lost competitiveness (Goldman Sachs, 2012b).

Implementation of structural changes in the labour market is expected to help reduce the cost of fiscal adjustment in terms of both lost product output and employment. As we know, the Phillips curve illustrates the relationship between inflation and the product based on specific parameters (marketable-to-non-marketable product ratio, elasticities, etc.), but this relationship is not linear. As a result, the declining GDP is not compounded by a corresponding reduction in inflation, nor does it not bring the expected benefits for regaining competitiveness. A change in the cost of macroeconomic adjustment can occur (a) by changing the inclination of the Phillips curve or (b) by shifting it (Goldman Sachs, 2012c).

Structural changes at labour market can change the slope of the curve and improve the "exchange" relationship between unemployment and inflation. For a given level of loss in terms of output or unemployment, improving competitiveness (reducing inflation) is higher. Accordingly, shifting the curve down and to the right implies a higher product for a given level of inflation.

2.9 The DSGE Models

Lucas' criticism served as an impetus for economists in the 1980s and 1990s to begin building macroeconomic models aiming at a sufficient microeconomic foundation. This process led to the development of Dynamic Stochastic General Equilibrium (DSGE) models.

Two schools of thought make up the main body of DSGEs: Classic RBC models and New Keynesian DSGEs, which are based on a structure similar to RBC models, but they assume that prices are set by monopolistic competitors and cannot be adjusted instantaneously and without cost (Rotemberg & Woodford, 1997).

The design of DSGE begins by identifying the economic agents in an economy, their preferences, their capacity and their possible institutional constraints. The basic premise is that each agent makes his or her own choices perfectly, provided there is sufficient information available about the prices and the corresponding choices of the rest of the economy in the present and for the future. So, when all these behaviours are concentrated, it is possible to strike a balance in which there are specific prices that equate supply with demand in each market.

The term "dynamic" refers to the fact that DSGE models describe the evolution of the economy over time, as opposed to the static equilibrium models of the Walrasian economy. The term "stochastic" refers to their ability to include random shocks that affect the economy, such as a technological change. At the same time, the fact that they are based on microeconomic foundations enables them to incorporate in their analysis the preferences of economic agents. Preferences, technology change and extrinsic influences are key sources for the evolution of economic variables over time. The DSGE models assume that the market is cleared through supply and demand adjustment. Their main advantage is that, at least on a theoretical level, they can predict the evolution of the economy as they "know" existing preferences, technology and institutional background. Forecasts of the evolution of the economy in traditional economic models are likely to be unreliable, given that these models are based on past values of macroeconomic variables.

DSGE models are widely used in macroeconomics to explain economic behaviours in a wide range of areas, such as fiscal and monetary policy, business cycles and economic growth. The utility of DSGEs lies in the fact that they can assess the evolution of key economic variables as a tool for implementing economic policy. DSGE models apply to two competing schools of thought: New Keynesian Economics and Real Business Cycle (RBC) (Kydland & Prescott, 1982). DSGE models of some New Keynesians (Rotemberg & Woodford, 1997) follow the structure of RBC models, but they assume non-competitive markets, while prices are adjusted at no cost.

DSGE models are complementary with and, in some cases, have replaced the macroeconomic models used by central banks. The Fed, for example, has developed DSGE models, which coexist with more traditional models such as Federal Reserve System (FRB)/US and FRB/Global (Brayton, Levin, Tryon, & Williams, 1997).

Scepticism about the credibility of DSGEs lies in the fact that they were less useful than their supporters claimed when Lehman Brothers collapsed, and the 2008 financial crisis broke out. There are several reasons why DSGEs have been criticized in terms of their credibility (Gerlach, 2017). Supporters of DSGEs stressed the structural parameters and the process of optimization at a small level, believing that the models would be stable, even in the event of a major negative shock to the economy. However, this has not been empirically confirmed, with these models exhibiting limited stability (Dotsey, 2013; Hendry & Mizon, 2014).

Moreover, as the economy is a complex system of many parameters and variables, the fact that DGSEs focus on only a handful of key chronologies generates debate and criticism on the part of policymakers. Creating role models for policy is certainly a challenge, as policymakers are constantly confronted with unexpected shocks (e.g. migration flows, war, Brexit). The above require quick thinking and continuous adjustments. However, many economists argue that DSGEs, with their insistence on logical purity and underlying principles, are unable to alter their analysis as their redesign is time consuming once a novel situation presents itself (Wren-Lewis, 2013).

2.10 The Schumpeterian Approach with Cultural and Institutional Dimensions

Schumpeterian models, expressed primarily by Aghion and Howitt (1992), are a particular type of growth models, in which growth is the result of conceiving of innovation as an endogenous process, while at the same time incorporating Schumpeter's concept of creative destruction. Schumpeterian models have also been developed by Grossman and Helpman (1991), while early versions of them were developed by Segerstrom, Anant, and Dinopoulos (1990) and Corriveau (1991). Schumpeter's theory of growth evolved in the early 1990s, influenced by emerging divergences in national growth rates, the challenge by Japan of the technological hegemony of the United States and the inability of neoclassical development theory to account for the long-term causes of technological progress (Dinopoulos, 2006).

Aghion and Howitt's (1992) model focuses on three basic ideas:

1. Long-term growth depends on innovation. These are innovations that increase the productivity of the factors of production, innovations that lead to new products and innovations that promote a more effective combination of the factors of production. The idea fully agrees with Solow's conclusion that long-term development is a consequence of continuous technological evolution.
2. Innovations can come from business investment—in research and development, business investment in skills and so on. Entrepreneurs are influenced by economic policies and institutions and respond accordingly to the various emerging economic incentives, positive or negative. At the same time, the role of the state in enhancing business knowledge and investment in research and development (R&D) is considered particularly serious, especially in times of recession, periods of imperfections in financial markets that limit lending, so that private companies tend to invest less in R&D and in training the workforce.

3. Creative destruction, as developed by Schumpeter (1942), with the central idea that new innovations tend to override earlier innovations, technologies and skills. The idea of creative destruction essentially focuses on the creation of barriers by existing businesses to those seeking to enter the sector. Hence, there is something called "the political economy of growth". A distinct prediction of the Schumpeterian growth model is that firm or job turnover should be positively correlated with productivity growth. Another distinctive implication of the model is that innovation-led growth may be excessive under laissez-faire. Growth is excessive under laissez-faire when the business-stealing effect associated with creative destruction dominates the intertemporal knowledge spillovers from current to future innovators (Aghion, Akcigit, & Howitt, 2014).

This contribution by Aghion and Howitt (1992) to Schumpeterian growth models is a perspective that focuses both on the macroeconomic structure of growth and on the analysis of microeconomic issues related to growth motives, policies and organizations (Aghion et al., 2014). It also focuses on issues related to the impact of innovation (who wins-who loses), while also highlighting the role of protecting property rights, competition, knowledge and so on in each country or even in sectors that are at different stages of development. In recent years, a new generation of Schumpeterian models has emerged, with main contributors being Klette, J.T. and Kortum, (2002), Lentz and Mortensen (2008), Akcigit and Kerr (2010), and Acemoglou, Akcigit, Alp, Bloom, and Kerr (2013). These models focus on firm dynamics and the reallocation of resources among incumbents and new entrants. These models are easily estimable using micro-firm-level data sets, which also bring a rich set of existing tools from other empirical fields into macroeconomics and endogenous growth (Aghion et al., 2014).

Competition and free entry into a market should be elements that promote greater growth of business leaders, which means that they should promote growth in developed economies to a higher extent, insofar as these economies have a greater number of business leaders. Acemoglu, Aghion and Zilibotti (Acemoglou, Aghion, & Zilibotti, 2006) add that the average growth rate should decrease more rapidly as a country approaches the world technology frontier, when the degree of openness is low. Also, high barriers to entry are becoming increasingly detrimental to growth as a country approaches its optimum world technology frontier.

Moreover, the closer to the optimal world technology frontier an economy is, the more growth in that country is based on research and education. Finally, the correlation between democracy and innovation/growth is more positive and statistically significant for economies close to the optimal world technology frontier.

2.11 The Evolutionary Approach

Evolutionary economic theory aims to interpret and confine the mainstream economics' weaknesses in the course of shaping the economic system through business development and strategic decision-making under conditions of uncertainty.

The main difference between economics and evolutionary science comes from the fact that the proponents of evolutionary theory have declined to take a particular path to equilibrium. Economists believe that the economy follows a "natural law" behaviour that leads it to a point of natural evolution. Any event or situation that causes the system to deviate is considered a "disturbance factor", which Veblen (1899) named a standpoint of ceremonial adequacy. As he said, "evolutionary economics must be the theory of a process of cultural development, as defined by economic interest, a theory of the cumulative sequence of economic institutions, which are referred to in terms of the process itself" (Veblen, 1899).

Veblen (1899) developed a new conception regarding the focus of economic science, namely man as a complex being, characterized by instinctive behaviour and by habits, that is, culture. Based on Smith's perspective (1776 [1981]) on the "invisible hand", and the view that the economy is moving towards equilibrium, he identifies the "difference of mental attitude or view" by drawing a parallel with the science of taxonomy of animal or plant species ("a system of economic taxonomy"). He considers that the equilibrium provides an overview of what reality is, but it does not provide any information about the process of change. The "system of economic taxonomy" may be considered as a result of the economic process in technological terms. In essence, Veblen rejects the notion of equilibrium of the classic economists, by advocating an evolutionary aspect of economic science, whereby the system can be brought to any situation, without this being necessarily good or bad in terms of social welfare. Drawing from Darwin and others the urgent need to explain the causal origin of all evolutionary phenomena, he addresses the future evolution of society and the economy as a result of the collective change of society and its institutions rather than as the result of change at the individual level.

Of particular interest is the theory of evolution in economic science and, in particular, as regards the role of entrepreneurship in the theory of growth (Nelson & Winter, 1982). Thus, evolutionary theory has attempted to provide answers to the way firms develop an ever-changing economic environment. Key to this was the contribution of Alchian (1950) who developed an evolutionary approach to describe the behaviour of firms, incorporating the principles of biological evolution and natural selection. Drawing on Alchian (1950), Nelson and Winter (1982) use the concept of natural selection to describe business behaviour in the light of evolutionary theory, emphasizing that evolutionary theory is based on learning and adaptation, and, on this account, it may be superior to other theories of business.

Subsequently, new models of evolutionary economic thought were developed in light of the consideration that evolutionary models, as pioneered by Nelson and Winter (1982), are driven by a Schumpeterian core with endogenous innovation, although they largely neglect to account for any demand-related driver of the macroeconomic activity. Based on this theoretical background, Dosi, Grazzi, and Moschella (2015) present some Keynes + Schumpeter (K + S) (Dosi, Fagiolo, Napoletano, & Roventini, 2013; Dosi, Fagiolo, & Roventini, 2010) evolutionary, individual-based models that study the effects of a broad set of innovations, industry dynamics and macroeconomic policies on the long-term growth and short-term fluctuations of the economy. They emphasize that the K + S models incorporate the Schumpeterian growth model into a complex system of incomplete coordination between heterogeneous, interacting businesses and banks, where demand-related Keynesian and Minskian credit-related cycles feed macroeconomic dynamics. These models are capable of generating endogenous long-term growth along with business cycles and major crises. Moreover, they reproduce a long list of macroeconomic and microeconomic stylized facts.

Evolutionary economics was able to establish itself as a field of economics that can provide new insights into many other fields of economics (Cantner & Hanusch, 1993; Nelson & Winter, 1982; Witt, 2001). However, what is not often considered in evolutionary economics is economic policymaking. This may be due to a rather controversial assessment of the effectiveness of policy interventions (Gerybadze, 1992; Hayek,

1978; Metcalfe, 1994; Pelikan, 2003), although political interventions are widespread in all modern economies and cannot be ignored.

Witt (2001) points out that from an evolutionary perspective, both during the policymaking process and after the implementation of economic policy, the positive and normative knowledge that informs individual actions can be modified through experience and induced inventive learning. At the same time, at each of the different levels of the theory of economic policymaking, the time horizon in tracking causes and effects and in assessing means-ends relationships needs to be extended to account for the repercussions of the modifications induced in the agents' knowledge constraints.

The link between evolutionary economics and economic policy is based on the fact that research and development (R&D) is at the core of evolutionary theory, focusing on the spending associated with the accumulation of knowledge and the development of know-how, that is, factors that increase the chances of businesses to survive in the face of intense competition and also enable them to grow further (Helfat, 1994; Nelson & Winter, 1982). Focusing on research and development spending has been the basis of restructuring economic theory through a more evolutionary approach, which contributes to decision-making by business executives, under uncertainty. The terms "technology", "organization" and "change" are highly featured in management and the theory of evolution and offer business executives a different, more interesting and useful way of thinking. Evolutionary theory is based on certain basic principles, particularly important, and also useful for business executives to move to more efficient decision-making regarding the advancement of their business plans. Initially, it is preferable to use an indicator that links R&D spending with the amount of business sales, thereby showing the intensity of R&D spending as well as its effective use. Also—based on evolutionary theory—business decisions on R&D spending are shaped by previous decisions and the results of those decisions. Finally, it is observed that significant and persistent differences accrue between different sectors in terms of the intensity of R&D spending, with existing pressures from the economic and technological environment playing an essential role in highlighting these differences.

Also, from the perspective of management theory, evolutionary theory focuses on businesses and on the problems faced when operating in a competitive environment. It does not merely suggest but, rather, urges extensive research into corporate processes and functions, on how the business is organized, the type and quantity of products it can produce and the services it can provide; the way of distribution and evaluation of expenditures; and the promotional price and the direction towards which research and development costs ought to be effectively driven to create a model of growth. It also leads to the tracing of future paths, especially if there is concern about whether the company has the potential and can operate and successfully cope in an open economy. Finally, it believes that entrepreneurs and executives who possess high skills, experience and are open to challenges can prove very useful in making decisions under conditions of uncertainty.

Dosi, Napoletano, Roventini, and Treibich (2014) argue that the newer Keynes + Schumpeter (K + S) evolutionary, individual-based models (Dosi et al., 2010, 2013, 2015) can be used to evaluate the short-term and long-term effects of various experiments which pertain to the role of innovation policy, industry dynamics, aggregate demand and income distribution. Their analysis concludes that there is a strong complementarity between Schumpeterian (technological) and Keynesian (demand-related) policies, which aim to assure that the economic system is on a sustainable path of growth. In addition, increasing income inequality has detrimental effects on the short- and long-run performance of the economy, thus supporting the case for redistributive fiscal policies. Also, Dosi (2012) argues that a proper investigation of the above-mentioned mechanisms requires that we go far beyond the Schumpeterian separation between coordination and change, and ought to be based on models capable of accounting jointly for both business cycles arising from effective demand failures (Leijonhufvud, 1973) and long-term growth potential. However, this is not the case, as even Schumpeterian models, including evolutionary models rooted in Nelson and Winter (1982) and equilibrium models originating with Aghion and Howitt (1992), have focused on technological and industrial dynamics, without considering the possible role of aggregate demand on the evolution of technology, let alone macroeconomic performance (Aghion et al., 2014; Aghion, Algan, Cahuc, & Shleifer, 2010; Ciarli, Porto, & Savona, 2010).

2.12 Ideology Bias, Macro and Growth

The development of economic theories and modelling, as well as their customization, are products of human mental processing. This entails the existence of defects, which result from both the limited mental capacity of the human brain and the presence of biased situations. The latter could be described as ideological bias. If, however, there is biased behaviour in the creation of macroeconomic models, it is reasonable to question their reliability and predictive capacity. At the same time, we might attribute less accountability to the science of economics for its credibility if we focused more on the extent to which the human factor may be affected.

That is, could ideological biases infiltrate the development of economic models and act so that the prevailing models remain consistent with the data of macroeconomic variables? Such biases can explain the current controversy between the various schools of economic thought (Saint-Paul, 2018), such as the size of fiscal multipliers, the slope of the aggregate supply curve and the nature of the risks responsible for business cycles. It is noteworthy that, following the onset of the Great Recession of 2008, numerous publications by prominent economists of different ideological positions approached the problem and made proposals that were often diametrically opposed.

That is, individuals appear to adopt views about the parameters they will use in their models which favour their policies based on their ideology (Fuchs, Krueger, & Porterba, 1998). Left-wing economists indeed adopt a "flat" Phillips curve, while more conservative ones adopt a vertical or more inclined one. In the 1980s, with the advent of RBC models, proponents of "fresh waters" economics placed a strong emphasis on supply-side shocks, while the "salt waters" considered demand shocks to be the driving force behind economic changes.

Concerning the political factors, Eichengreen and Panizza (2014) identify a positive effect of a left-wing government on the emergence of surpluses—a 7.7% increase in the likelihood of a surplus. From a political point of view, the emergence of surpluses is accompanied by pressure to distribute it to the lower social groups. But the paradox that emerges from the analysis of Eichengreen and Panizza (2014), in contrast to what one would expect, is that a leftist government is more likely to achieve multi-year high primary surpluses than other governments. The emergence of surpluses is also more likely to occur in countries with proportional representation, and it also depends on the ruling party's electoral strength. Beyond that, however, surpluses are associated with high growth rates.

Although much of the literature focuses on the economic consequences of the social models of individuals, such as social capital and confidence (Petrakis, 2014), other dimensions of social rules, such as political ideology, receive less attention. This lack of interest may stem from the fact that ideology can affect the business cycle in the short run, but not the long-term trend of economic growth. As Alesina (1987) argues in theory, the political ideology of governments affects the short-term economic fluctuations through citizens' expectations without affecting social rules. However, institutional economics argue that ideology plays an essential role in the long-term return of economies through individual behaviour and public policy choices (North, 1990, 1998). Indeed, ideology can directly influence growth through people's preferences for work and savings. Voters' ideology can also work indirectly in the process of growth, through the policies they vote for.

According to Piketty (1995) and Benabou and Ok (1998), societies can adopt ideologies that can lead to ineffective public policies and the failure of the function of markets. Bjørnskov (2005) develops a theoretical framework, which argues that people with a strong acceptance of value for effort and reward are more productive, and thus encourage economic growth. In addition, people with these values are in the conservative right ideological space and seek a stronger legal system, indirectly promoting development.

References

Abbas, S. K., Bhattacharya, P. S., & Sgro, P. (2016). The New Keynesian Phillips Curve: An Update on Recent Empirical Advances. *International Review of Economics and Finance, 43*(C), 378–403.

Acemoglou, D., Aghion, P., & Zilibotti, F. (2006). Distance to Frontier, Selection, and Economic Growth. *Journal of the European Economic Association, 4*(1), 37–74.

Acemoglou, D., Akcigit, U., Alp, H., Bloom, N., & Kerr, R. W. (2013). *Innovation, Reallocation and Growth*. NBER Working Paper No. 18993. Retrieved from http://www.nber.org/papers/w18993

Aghion, P., Akcigit, U., & Howitt, P. (2014). What Do We Learn from Schumpeterian Growth Theory? In P. Aghion & S. Durlauf (Eds.), *Handbook of Economic Growth* (pp. 515–563). Amsterdam: Elsevier.

Aghion, P., Algan, Y., Cahuc, P., & Shleifer, A. (2010). Regulation and Distrust. *Quarterly Journal of Economics, 125*(3), 1015–1049.

Aghion, P., & Howitt, P. (1992). A Model of Growth Through Creative Destruction. *Econometrica, 60*(2), 323–351.

Akcigit, U., & Kerr, W. R. (2010). *Growth Through Heterogeneous Innovations*. NBER Working Paper No. 16443. Retrieved from http://www.nber.org/papers/w16443

Alchian, A. A. (1950). Uncertainty, Evolution and Economic Theory. *Journal of Political Economy, 58*(3), 211–222.

Alesina, A. (1987). Macroeconomic Policy in a Two-Party System as a Repeated Game. *The Quarterly Journal of Economics, 102*(3), 651–678. https://doi.org/10.2307/1884222

Ball, L., Mankiw, N. G., & Reis, R. (2005). Monetary Policy for Inattentive Economies. *Journal of Monetary Economics, 52*(4), 703–725.

Benabou, R., & Ok, E. A. (1998). *Social Mobility and the Demand for Redistribution: The POUM Hypothesis.* Centre of Economic Policy Research Discussion Paper Series No. 1955.

Bhatt, V. V. (1964). Theories of Balanced and Unbalanced Growth: A Critical Appraisal. *Kyklos, 17*(4), 612–626. https://doi.org/10.1111/j.1467-6435.1964.tb01844.x

Bjørnskov, C. (2005). Does Political Ideology Affect Economic Growth? *Public Choice, 123*(1), 133–146.

Blanchard, O. J., Dell'Ariccia, M. G., & Mauro, M. P. (2013). *Rethinking Macro Policy II: Getting Granular.* IMF Staff Discussion Paper SDN/13/03. Retrieved from https://www.imf.org/external/pubs/ft/sdn/2013/sdn1303.pdf

Borio, C., & Shim, I. (2007). *What Can (Macro)-Prudential Policy Do to Support Monetary Policy?* BIS Working Papers No. 242. Bank for International Settlements. Retrieved from https://www.bis.org/publ/work242.htm

Brayton, F., Levin, A., Tryon, R., & Williams, J. C. (1997). The Evolution of Macro Models at the Federal Reserve Board. *Carnegie-Rochester Conference Series on Public Policy, 47*(1), 43–81.

Calvo, G. (1983). Staggered Prices in a Utility Maximizing Framework. *Journal of Monetary Economics, 12*(3), 383–398.

Cantner, U., & Hanusch, H. (1993). Process and Product Innovations in an International Trade Context. *Economics of Innovation and New Technology, 2*(3), 217–236.

Ciarli, T., Porto, S., & Savona, M. (2010). *Conflict and Entrepreneurship Activity in Afghanistan.* United Nation University, Shibuya Working Paper 8/2010.

Corriveau, L. (1991). *Entrepreneurs, Growth, and Cycles.* Doctoral dissertation, University of Western Ontario, Ontario, Canada.

Deardorff, A. V. (2007). *The Ricardian Model.* RSIE (Research Seminar in International Economics) Discussion Paper No. 564. University of Michigan.

Dinopoulos, E. (2006). Growth in Open Economies, Schumpeterian Models. In K. Reinert & R. Rajan (Eds.), *Princeton Encyclopedia of the World Economy* (pp. 576–580). Princeton, NJ: Princeton University Press.

Dornbusch, R. S., Fisher, I., & Samuelson, P. (1977). Comparative Advantage, Trade and Payments in a Ricardian Model with a Continuum of Goods. *American Economic Review, 67*(5), 823–839.

Dosi, G. (2012). *Economic Coordination and Dynamics: Some Elements of an Alternative "Evolutionary" Paradigm*. LEM (Laboratory of Economics and Management) Working Paper Series 2012/8.

Dosi, G., Fagiolo, G., Napoletano, M., & Roventini, A. (2013). Income Distribution, Credit and Fiscal Policies in Anagent-Based Keynesian Model. *Journal of Economic Dynamics & Control, 37*(8), 1598–1625.

Dosi, G., Fagiolo, G., & Roventini, A. (2010). Schumpeter Meeting Keynes: A Policy-Friendly Model of Endogenous Growth and Business Cycles. *Journal of Economic Dynamics & Control, 34*(9), 1748–1767.

Dosi, G., Grazzi, M., & Moschella, D. (2015). Technology and Costs in International Competitiveness: From Countries and Sectors to Firms. *Research Policy, 44*(10), 1795–1814.

Dosi, G., Napoletano, A., Roventini, A., & Treibich, T. (2014). *The Short- and Long-Run Damages of Fiscal Austerity: Keynes Beyond Schumpeter*. LEM (Laboratory of Economics and Management) Working Paper Series 2014/22.

Dotsey, M. (2013). DSGE Models and Their Use in Monetary Policy. *Federal Reserve Bank of Philadelphia Business Review, Q2*, 10–18.

Eaton, J., & Kortum, S. (2002). Technology, Geography, and Trade. *Econometrica, 70*(5), 1741–1779.

Eichengreen, B., & Panizza, U. (2014). *A Surplus of Ambition: Can Europe Rely on Large Primary Surpluses to Solve Its Debt Problem?* CEPR Discussion Paper No. 10069.

Fischer, S. (1977). Wage-Indexation and Macro-Economic Stability. *Carnegie-Rochester Conference Series on Public Policy, Elsevier, 5*(1), 107–147.

Friedman, M. (1968). The Role of Monetary Policy. *American Economic Review, 58*(1), 1–17.

Fuchs, V., Krueger, A., & Porterba, J. M. (1998). Economists Views About Parameters, Values, and Policies: Survey Results in Labour and Public Economics. *Journal of Economic Literature, 36*(3), 1387–1425.

Fuhrer, J. C. (1995). The Phillips Curve Is Alive and Well. *New England Economic Review* (March), 41–56.

Gabaix, X. (2017). *A Behavioural New Keynesian Model*. NBER Working Paper No. 22954. https://doi.org/10.3386/w22954

Galí, J. (2018). The State of New Keynesian Economics: A Partial Assessment. *Journal of Economic Perspectives, 32*(3), 87–112.

Gerlach, S. (2017). DSGE Models in Monetary Policy Committees. In R. S. Gürkaynak & C. Tille (Eds.), *DSGE Models in the Conduct of Policy: Use as Intended* (pp. 31–37). London: CEPR (Centre for Economic Policy Research).

Gerybadze, A. (1992). The Implementation of Industrial Policy in an Evolutionary Perspective. In U. Witt (Ed.), *Explaining Process and Change* (pp. 151–173). Ann Arbor, MI: University of Michigan Press.

Goldman Sachs. (2012a). *Achieving Fiscal and External Balance (Part 1): The Price Adjustment Rewired for External Sustainability.* European Economics Analyst.

Goldman Sachs. (2012b). *Can the Euro Area Adjust?* European Economics Analyst.

Goldman Sachs. (2012c). *Achieving Fiscal and External Balance (Part 4): Escaping the Vicious Circle.* European Economics Analyst.

Gordon, R. J. (2011). The History of the Phillips Curve: Consensus and Bifurcation. *Economica, 78*(309), 10–50.

Grossman, G. M., & Helpman, E. (1991). *Innovation and Growth in the Global Economy.* MIT Press.

Guerrieri, V., & Lorenzoni, G. (2017). Credit Crises, Precautionary Savings, and the Liquidity Trap. *Quarterly Journal of Economics, 132*(3), 1427–1467.

Hayek, F. A. (1978). *New Studies in Philosophy, Politics, Economics, and the History of Ideas.* Chicago, IL: University of Chicago Press.

Heckscher, E. (1919). The Effect of Foreign Trade on the Distribution of Income. *Ekonomisk Tidskriff,* 497–512.

Helfat, C. E. (1994). Firm-Specificity in Corporate Applied R&D. *Organization Science, 5*(2), 173–184. Retrieved from https://www.jstor.org/stable/2635013

Hendry, D., & Mizon, G. (2014). *Why DSGE Models Crash During Crises.* Vox Eu, CEPR (Centre for Economic Policy Research).

Hirschman, A. (1958). *The Strategy of Economic Development.* New Haven: Yale University Press.

Hudea, O. S. (2015). Classical, Neoclassical and New Classical Theories and Their Impact on Macroeconomic Modelling. *Procedia Economics and Finance, 23,* 309–312.

Irwin, D. A. (2017, May/June). The False Promise of Protectionism: Why Trump's Trade Policy Could Backfire. *Foreign Affairs, 96*(3), 45–56.

Kartika, D. M. (2014). *The Big Push: Early Development Economics (1945–1975).* MPRA (Munich Personal RePEc Archive) Paper No. 72115.

Klette, J. T., & Kortum, S. (2002). *Innovating Firms and Aggregate Innovation.* NBER Working Paper Series No. 8819. Retrieved from http://www.nber.org/papers/w8819

Krugman, P. R. (1979). Increasing Returns, Monopolistic Competition, and International Trade. *Journal of International Economics, 9*(4), 469–479.

Kydland, F. E., & Prescott, E. C. (1982). Time to Build and Aggregate Fluctuations. *Econometrica, 50*(6), 1345–1370.

Leijonhufvud, A. (1973). Effective Demand Failures. *Swedish Economic Journal, 76*(3), 27–48.

Lentz, R., & Mortensen, T. D. (2008). An Empirical Model of Growth Through Production Innovation. *Econometrica, 76*(6), 1317–1373.

Lucas Jr., R. E. (1972). Expectations and the Neutrality of Money. *Journal of Economic Theory, Elsevier, 4*(2), 103–124.

Lucas Jr., R. E. (1976). Econometric Policy Evaluation: A Critique. *Carnegie-Rochester Conference Series on Public Policy, 1*(1), 19–46.

Lucas Jr., R. E., & Rapping, L. A. (1969). Real Wages, Employment and the Price Level. *Journal of Political Economy, 77*(5), 721–754.

Lucas, R. E., Jr & Sargent, T. (1979). After Keynesian Macroeconomics. *Quarterly Review, Federal Reserve Bank of Minnesota, 3*(Spring), 49–72

McKay, A., & Reis, R. (2016). The Role of Automatic Stabilizers in the U.S. Business Cycle. *Econometrica, 84*(1), 141–194.

Metcalfe, L. (1994). International Policy Co-ordination and Public Management Reform. *International Review of Administrative Sciences, 60*(2), 271–290.

Murphy, K. M., Shleifer, A., & Vishny, R. W. (1989). Industrialization and the Big Push. *Journal of Political Economy, 97*(5), 1003–1026.

Muth, F. J. (1961). Rational Expectations and the Theory of Price Movements. *Econometrica, 29*(3), 315–335.

Nath, S. (1962). The Theory of Balanced Growth. *Oxford Economic Papers, 14*(2), 138–153. Retrieved from http://www.jstor.org/stable/2661956

Nelson, R. R., & Winter, S. G. (1982). *An Evolutionary Theory of Economic Change*. Cambridge, MA and London: The Belknap Press of Harvard University Press.

North, D. C. (1990). A Transaction Cost Theory of Politics. *Journal of Theoretical Politics, 2*(4), 355–367.

North, D. C. (1998). Institutions, Ideology, and Economic Performance. *The Revolution in Development Economics, 2*, 95–108.

Nurkse, R. (1953). Problems of Capital Formation in Underdeveloped Countries. *The Economic Journal, 63*(252), 897–899. https://doi.org/10.2307/2226663

Nurkse, R. (1971). The Theory of Development and the Idea of Balanced Growth. In A. B. Mountjoy (Ed.), *Developing the Underdeveloped Countries. Geographical Readings*. London: Palgrave Macmillan.

Oh, H., & Reis, R. (2012). Targeted Transfers and the Fiscal Response to the Great Recession. *Journal of Monetary Economics, 59*(S), 50–64.

Ohlin, B. (1933). *Interregional and International Trade*. Cambridge, MA: Harvard University Press.

Pelikan, P. (2003). Why Economic Policies Require Comprehensive Evolutionary Analysis. In P. Pelikan & G. Wegner (Eds.), *The Evolutionary Analysis of Economic Policy* (pp. 15–45). Cheltenham: Edward Elgar.

Petrakis, P. E. (2014). *Culture, Growth and Economic Policy; From the Question to Exploration*. New York and Heidelberg: Springer, ISBN 978-3-642-41439-8, p. 250.

Phillips, A. W. (1958). The Relationship Between Unemployment and the Rate of Change of Money Wage Rates in the United Kingdom, 1861–1957. *Economica, 25*(100), 283–299.

Piketty, T. (1995). Social Mobility and Redistributive Politics. *The Quarterly Journal of Economics, 110*(3), 551–584.

Porter, M. E. (1980). *Competitive Strategy: Techniques for Analyzing Industries and Competitors.* New York: Free Press.

Ricardo, D. (1817). *The Principles of Political Economy and Taxation.* London: John Murray.

Rosenstein-Rodan, P. N. (1943). Problems of Industrialization of Eastern and South-Eastern Europe. *The Economic Journal, 53*(1), 202–211.

Rotemberg, J. J. (1982). Sticky Prices in the United States. *Journal of Political Economy, 90*(6), 1187–1211.

Rotemberg, J. J., & Woodford, M. (1997). An Optimization-Based Econometric Framework for the Evaluation of Monetary Policy. *NBER Macroeconomics Annual, 12*, 297–346. https://doi.org/10.2307/3585236

Rudebusch, G. D., & Svensson, L. E. O. (1999). Policy Rules for Inflation Targeting. In J. Taylor (Ed.), *Monetary Policy Rules* (pp. 203–262). Chicago: University of Chicago Press.

Saint-Paul, G. (2018). The Possibility of Ideological Bias in Structural Macroeconomic Models. *American Economic Journal: Macroeconomics, 10*(1), 216–241.

Schumpeter, J. A. (1942). *Capitalism, Socialism and Democracy.* New York: Harper.

Segerstrom, P. S., Anant, T. C. A., & Dinopoulos, E. (1990). A Schumpeterian Model of the Product Life Cycle. *American Economic Review, 80*(5), 1077–1791.

Sent, E.-M. (1997). Sargent Versus Simon: Rounded Rationality Unbound. *Cambridge Journal of Economics, 21*(3), 323–338.

Simon, H. A. (1996). *Models of My Life.* Cambridge, MA: The MIT Press.

Smith, A. (1776 [1981]). *An Inquiry into the Nature and Causes of the Wealth of Nations.* In R. H. Campbell & A. S. Skinner (Eds.), *The Glasgow Edition of the Works of Adam Smith, 2.* Indianapolis: Liberty Fund.

Taylor, J. B. (1980). Aggregate Dynamics and Staggered Contracts. *Journal of Political Economy, 88*(1), 1–23.

Veblen, T. (1899). *The Theory of the Leisure Class: An Economic Study of Institutions.* New York: Macmillan.

Vernon, R. (1966). International Investment and International Trade in the Product Cycle. *Quarterly Journal of Economics, 80*(2), 190–207.

Vernon, R. (1970). *The Technology Factor in International Trade.* New York: Columbia University Press.

Vines, D., & Wills, S. (2018). The Rebuilding Macroeconomic Theory Project: An Analytical Assessment. *Oxford Review of Economic Policy, 34*(1–2), 1–42. https://doi.org/10.1093/oxrep/grx062

Wilson, C. A. (1980). On the General Structure of Ricardian Models with a Continuum of Goods. *Econometrica, 48*(7), 1675–1702.

Witt, U. (2001). Learning to Consume – A Theory of Wants and the Growth of Demand. *Journal Evolutionary Economics, 11*(1), 23–36.

Woodford, M. (2003). *Interest and Prices.* Princeton, NJ: Princeton University Press.

Woodford, M. (2013). Macroeconomic Analysis Without the Rational Expectations Hypothesis. *Annual Review of Economics, 5*(1), 303–346.

Wren-Lewis, S. (2013, May 29). *Data, Theory and Central Bank Models.* Mainly Macro Blog. Retrieved from https://mainlymacro.blogspot.com/2013/05/data-theory-and-central-bank-models.html

CHAPTER 3

Growth Prototypes and Economic Policy

3.1 Introduction

It is clear that in the development and implementation of an economic policy, the actual basis upon which it is to be applied, that is, the economic reality to which it refers, is crucial. The policy applied is always linked to the particular circumstances prevailing in an economy, which makes it unique each time. Different parameters can lead to different results and generally raise issues of economic efficiency. Essentially, an economic policy is effective in a perfectly competitive production context, whereas in a hierarchically structured productive model where administrative decisions play an important role, this is not the case. Different economic policies also apply depending on the prevailing growth prototype.

This chapter analyses the concept of growth prototype. For many decades in economic thought, the model of growth, which was the main subject of economic thought, was a given. This prototype was based on Walras' economic principles and its further delineation by Arrow-Debreu-McKenzie (ADM model), with crucial assumptions including the absence of frictions in trading systems, and the existence of an optimal institutional framework for decisions. Nevertheless, economic thought over time has been enriched by the observation and evolution of economic reality as well as by the advancement of economic science itself.

Section 3.2 of this chapter discusses the issue of the first-, second- and third-best theory for policy making. Section 3.3 analyses the optimum growth prototype, while Sect. 3.4 presents the institutional and cultural

P. E. Petrakis et al., *Economic Growth and Development Policy*,
https://doi.org/10.1007/978-3-030-43181-5_3

background deviations from the optimum growth prototype. The concepts of the poverty trap and cultural trap, stagnation and acceleration of economies are discussed in Sect. 3.5, while Sect. 3.6 analyses the concept of multiple equilibrium points to be found in an economy. This is directly related to the economic policy being implemented, as it has both theoretical and practical implications.

3.2 First-, Second- and Third-Best Theory: Generality Against a Concrete Framework

The first fundamental theorem of welfare economics proposes that the market will move towards a forced equilibrium when the economy has two key features that make up a weak Pareto optimum:

1. There are complete markets without transaction costs and perfect information.
2. Price-taking behaviour prevails. In other words, there are no monopolies nor is there entering and exiting markets.

When to these two features a third is added (the local non-satiation of preferences), where for each complaint or service portfolio there is always another which is very close to the first, but preferable to it, then, an equilibrium point can be achieved, which is weakly Pareto optimal.

The crucial second theorem states that amongst all the possible Pareto optimal equilibrium points, we can select and achieve some of them by performing a lump-sum wealth redistribution, and then allowing the economy to operate without further intervention.

Thus, the general equilibrium theories, such as those of Walras (1874) and Arrow and Debreu (1954) and McKenzie (1959), in the presence of the first and second fundamental theorems of welfare economics, propose a general and extremely released concept of the functioning of economies.

This framework is general, it has market dominance as its critical feature and is characterized by first-best conditions. Economic policy proposals are deduced accordingly. The first-best conditions for optimum allocation of resources are derived from a static model that fulfils several well-known and stringent requirements, including that all firms be price takers, and that there be neither externalities nor unexploited ranges of increasing returns. It is generally agreed that the model's full set of conditions is so stringent that it would be impossible in practice to adopt policies that would achieve most, let alone all of them (Lipsey, 2017).

The most well-known shift from this general framework of analysis involves the analysis of externalities in economies with incomplete markets and incomplete information (Greenwald & Stiglitz, 1986). However, this is only one reason, however dominant and general, for departing from the theories of general equilibrium. Other causes are related either to the cultural background or to specialized aspects of the institutional background or, finally, to the dependence of the economy on the past (path dependence) (Hoeffler, Ariely, & West, 2006).

This creates second-best (or higher-order) conditions, which in turn shape more than one different set of economic conditions. Lipsey and Lancaster's (1956) original second-best theory demonstrated that the necessary conditions for maximizing any function do not provide piecemeal guides for increasing the value of that function when all the necessary conditions cannot be satisfied. Under these conditions "one-size-fits–all" policies (Stiglitz, 2002) prove to be extremely controversial. This is how context specificity conditions (Lipsey & Ng, 2017) are formulated, which can create real-world policies. The usual situation in the real world is to be objective with cases in which individual policies are applied rather than in a general situation that is ideal.

In order to form a body of economic policy implemented under second-best (or higher order) policies, it is necessary to "conquer" the present state of the market under consideration and the first-best conditions for the real market. This brings to the fore those policies that are capable of eliminating these disturbances.

"The General Second-Best Theories" (Lipsey & Lancaster, 1956) state that the "piecemeal satisfaction" of any one first-best optimality condition is not sufficient to increase community welfare in a world in which "first-best conditions are not achieved globally". This proposal may be general in nature and argues that individual conditions, which satisfy only certain first-best conditions, do not lead to an increase in the value of any utility function.

In essence, the second-best theory concludes that there are very few situations where general economic policy rules may always be applied. Instead, this requires particular knowledge of the individual markets and their interaction. The second-best theory, therefore, supports the need for individual policies that are context-specific.

But what causes the "departure" of the economic prototype from first-order to second-order conditions? What are the conditions that hinder an efficient resource allocation? We are talking about the conditions that could follow "constraints" or "distortions". This is anything that can prevent the acquisition of a perfectly competitive, price-taking equilibrium that would be characterized as Pareto efficient.

3.3 The Optimal Growth Prototype

Each society is characterized by a specific institutional background which, together with the prevailing set of cultural values,[1] functions at times to inhibit and at other times to promote the process of economic growth (Petrakis, Valsamis, & Kafka, 2017). In an ideal environment, we would like to have an excellent network of institutions. However, the existence of such an institutional structure related to an optimal grid of cultural values can only exist at a theoretical level and is used only for the sake of simplification and to improve analytical tools of understanding. In this sense, defining an optimal prototype of economic growth is a theoretical construct, which is expounded according to the particularities of different economies in order to apply the optimal economic policy.

Institutions in society and the economy are human constructs and act as precepts and constraints in shaping human economic and social behaviour (Chang, 2007; Greif, 2006; North, 1990). As a result, they organize the context of the incentives for human transactions, whether at a political, social or economic level. In essence, the institutional framework reduces the uncertainty that accompanies everyday life by providing a structure for its functioning—not a necessarily effective one. Besides, it is clear that the same transaction in different parts of the world is surrounded by different types of institutional set-ups. The institutional background of transactions mainly concerns the matter of property rights and the terms of trade-related contracts (North, 1990). The cultural background is a crucial component of the institutional set-up and comes from a basic matrix of behaviours and structures: the human mind. The human mind processes information and understands situations. However, that information is incomplete, and the processing capacity is limited. Thus, there is no equilibrium point or level, but only multiple equilibrium levels or points, if we take into account the costs of processing information and the operation of transactions.

Walras (1874) developed a general equilibrium model for the microfoundation of price formation. The key assumptions underlying Walras' paradigm are (a) the existence of perfect competition, (b) the Pareto optimal allocation of resources, (c) the institutions that foster growth, (d) the absence of systemic risk and (e) the non-idiosyncratic character of the preferences of individuals and firms; in other words, the growth-oriented dimensions of the cultural background. The basic assumption of perfect competition combined with the Pareto optimal allocation of resources in Walras' paradigm, and in neoclassical theory overall, ensures a specific framework of behaviour and preferences, shaping the operation of financial institutions. At the same time, under conditions of perfect information, markets are cleared, and there are no transaction costs due to the complete contracting hypothesis.

As Walras' paradigm rejects the interactions between economic agents, the price mechanism is unable to integrate the available information, since some aspects of transactions are not expressed in enforceable contracts (Bowles & Gintis, 2000). However, the role of entrepreneurship and innovation in Walras' example is rather weak. This makes the Schumpeterian framework necessary.

Schumpeter (1921, 1939) has based his analysis on the existence of a perfectly competitive economy and a perfectly competitive balance, without profit, interest rates, savings and, unintentionally, unemployment. But a capitalist economy never remains stagnant. Innovation is the element that creates the imbalance and, at the same time, makes the economy evolve. For Schumpeter (1939), equilibrium is a concept introduced to explain the imbalance created by innovation. The above describes the transition to dynamic economic growth, which has been detached from the increase in production factors.

According to Schumpeter, the role of institutions is important and is responsible for the emergence of specific behaviours. Thus, institutions can be seen as a partial reflection of individual behaviours (Festré & Garrouste, 2008). Schumpeter pointed out that "economic sociology deals with institutions", as opposed to economic theory which deals with purely economic mechanisms and phenomena. In the Schumpeterian competitive landscape, innovation plays a prominent role in economic change by increasing the effectiveness of economic and institutional structures (Ülgen, 2014). Swedberg (2002) argues that, for Schumpeter, institutions are a necessary condition for a dynamic capitalism.

In addition, Schumpeter argues that societal preferences are incomplete and that education, experience, innovation and the social environment shape the needs of society. He also deals with how to set preferences and concludes that, given the ignorance of what the benefits of some results will be, we may not only rely on past experiences but may seek guidance from revealed preferences of other, more experienced, consumers (Jonsson, 1994). In the field of consumer behaviours and preferences, Schumpeter adopts a very categorical view that the behaviours and activities of producers are essential because they have the potential to influence and change consumer preferences (Croitoru, 2012).

In attempting to determine the optimal institutional framework of an economy, we could argue that its constituent features depend, among other things, on how markets operate, the use of information available by economic actors, the limited presence of systemic risk and the absence of dependence on the past. The existence of these characteristics, though not unique, forms the institutional framework that favours the prevalence of an optimal model of growth.

Table 3.1 presents the characteristics of an excellent institutional mode of operation compared to an idiosyncratic institutional framework.

The description of the basic dimensions of the institutional framework, in terms of geography and time, proves that in different situations of space and time, different institutional conditions may prevail. It is therefore important to have a concrete picture of the prevailing institutional framework within which we are called upon to analyse a problem of development and growth in a way that is also applicable.

In order to form a corresponding picture of the cultural value framework, Table 3.2 presents the optimal operating economic framework of

Table 3.1 Optimal and idiosyncratic institutional framework

Optimal institutional framework	*Idiosyncratic institutional framework*
• Perfect market allocation of resources	• Non-market allocation of resources
• Effective coordination	• Coordination failures
• Full access to information	• Information asymmetry
• History does not play a role	• Dependence on the past
• Creating new wealth	• Rent-seeking activities
• Non-systematic risk	• High systemic risk

Source: Authors' own creation

Table 3.2 Optimal and idiosyncratic cultural values framework

Optimal cultural values framework	*Idiosyncratic framework of cultural values*
• Differentiated investment attitudes	• Undifferentiated investment attitudes
• Moderate avoidance of uncertainty	• High uncertainty avoidance
• Individualism	• In-group collectivism
• Moderate discounting of time	• High time discount
• High levels of confidence	• Lack of confidence
• Desire to earn profits	• Loss aversion

Source: Authors' own creation

the economy—Optimal Cultural Values Framework—compared to the Idiosyncratic Cultural Values Framework.

The above-mentioned distinction between two prototypes of the organization of economies corresponds to the distinction of applying them to two distinct spatial production structures. They may also reflect the evolution of the same production system over time.

It should be understood that there are many versions of the peculiar/stagnated framework of institutions and cultural values. By contrast, the optimum frame approaches what is quite typically described in a Walras system.

3.4 Deviations of Institutions and of the Cultural Background from the Optimal Prototype

The optimal growth prototype is an ideal situation that can rarely be realized due to the existence of idiosyncratic institutions (Petrakis et al., 2017). It can, however, exist on a theoretical basis and be used for simplification purposes and to improve analytical comprehension tools. Thus, in reality, institutions and the cultural background diverge from the optimal phase of co-evolution (Petrakis et al., 2017). A similar perspective has been adopted by the neoclassical view.

3.4.1 When Institutions Deviate from the Optimal Prototype

The prevalence of extractive institutions may create divergence from the optimal growth prototype (Acemoglu & Robinson, 2012). Economies dominated by such institutions are characterized by a lack of established relationships among members of the economic system, giving rise to situations that could be characterized as idiosyncratic (Petrakis et al., 2017) and which are discussed as follows:

1. Non-market allocation of resources. Hierarchies exist "mainly because of uncertainty and opportunism, though bounded rationality is involved as well. They exist when the real underlying circumstances relevant to the transaction, or set of transactions, are known to one or more parties but cannot be costlessly discerned or modified by others" (Williamson, 1973). When hierarchies are spread along the whole range of economic activities, they increase the uncertainty and the systematic risk. High transaction costs lead to market failures and thus limit the efficient utilization of resources, consequently increasing the chances of systematic risk.
2. Coordination failures, are responsible for the emergence of externalities, resulting in the creation of a cost in economic terms.
3. Information asymmetry, similar to coordination failures, generates an economic cost as its elimination requires contractualization between the principal and the agent, thereby making more difficult the achievement of market efficiency.
4. Path dependency (historical legacy) in the sense that "history matters" in everyday aspects of human activity, such as preferences, decisions and behaviours. To the extent that preferences are formed by initial experiences, latter preferences are path-dependent (Hoeffler et al., 2006). Both the institutions and the mode of operation of the economy are the outcome of a path-dependent procedure, with elements of historical legacy. On the basis of this theorization, the existence of high levels of systematic risk is favoured in societies that maintain historical elements, which distort the smooth operation of the economy and create disincentives in the undertaking of entrepreneurial action and, generally, in market efficiency.
5. Rent-seeking activities. These activities involve seeking to increase one's share of existing wealth without creating new wealth. Rent-seeking results in reduced economic efficiency through poor allocation of resources, reduced actual wealth creation, lost government revenue and increased income inequality.
6. High systemic risk. High systematic risk can prevail with exogenous origin or after huge internal shocks that have long-lasting

implications. The existence of transaction costs misallocates resources, thereby violating the optimal allocation of resources.

3.4.2 *When Culture Deviates from the Optimal Prototype*

The factors that divert the cultural background from the optimal prototype vary and may be due to the external environment and to human behaviour. According to Petrakis et al. (2017), the factors that may lead the cultural background to deviate from the optimal model are the following:

1. An idiosyncratic cultural background, characterized by the existence of some specific characteristics that act in a peculiar manner, shaping human behaviour and preferences. This kind of cultural background may be represented through the analysis of several cultural dimensions that deviate significantly from the optimal pattern: (a) prevalence of high systematic risks in the economy creates the need among individuals to protect themselves against the risk by adopting uncertainty avoidance behaviours, (b) incorporation of individuals in teams (in-group collectivism) so that they feel more secure, protect themselves against uncertain conditions and secure material resources and social support (Triandis, Bontempo, Villareal, Asai, & Lucca, 1988), (c) high time discount preferences due to the fact that in uncertain environments, the members of a society tend to be cautious over their future decisions, avoiding to commit resources and effort for a long period of time and (d) lack of trust since under conditions of high systematic risk, individuals lose their trust in the institutions that surround them, while the level of interpersonal trust towards individuals, who are outside the groups to which an individual belongs, is also reduced.
2. Non-diversified investment attitudes: The economies, whose production and investment are highly concentrated in a few sectors, fail to eliminate the systematic risk and attain to an optimal growth pattern. Kuznets (1971) suggests that a country's economic growth may be defined as a long-term rise in capacity to supply increasingly diverse economic goods to its population. This argument is further strengthened by the view of Grossman and Helpman (1992) who claim that for an economy to grow, it has to produce an ever-

increasing quantity, quality and variety of goods and services. Thus, the stagnated prototype possesses a special characteristic of non-diversification of investment activities in line with the idiosyncratic cultural background (see earlier) and probably with loss aversion behaviour (see later). Non-diversification investment behaviour may take the form of holding cash or investing in specific sectors such as housing.

3. Loss aversion behaviour: The loss aversion assertion (Kahneman & Tversky, 1979) is one of the elements of prospect theory (Kahneman & Tversky, 2000), which implies that people are twice as sensitive to risks as to gains. That is, the absolute subjective value of a specific loss is larger than the absolute subjective value of an equivalent gain (Ert & Erev, 2010). Loss aversion behaviour is correlated with the existence of high levels of systematic risk and an idiosyncratic/stagnated cultural background.

3.5 Traps, Stagnation and Acceleration of Economic Growth

The process of shifting economies to different levels of income[2] (low, medium, high) is not an easy task. In most cases, this transition is accompanied by obstacles and a lack of necessary resources (Petrakis, 2014). For example, on the path to economic growth, developing countries first face the poverty trap and then the middle-income trap. Thus, there are many examples of countries that have experienced high growth rates, significantly increasing their standard of living, but failing to grow into developed economies.

But what are the characteristics of the transition of economies to different levels of income? In the first stage of economic development, low-income countries rely on agriculture, with their labour force characterized by low levels of specialization and productivity. Therefore, the scope for improvement is such that it is particularly easy to improve the production process. The strong growth of low-income countries is mainly due to the mobility of surplus labour from low-productivity activities—primary sector—to industrial production but also to activities with higher productivity.

Low wages, due to labour excess, make low-income countries competitive so their exports flourish. Their goods and services become attractive to developed countries, as they can be procured at lower prices than if they were produced locally. Through the inflow of foreign currency from third countries, low-income economies find the resources needed to develop infrastructure, introduce new technologies and thereby improve their productivity. In addition to capital accumulation, incoming resources are also directed towards improving living standards and human capital.

The strategy pursued in the first stage cannot be applied to the new conditions, which are beginning to develop in the next stage of growth, which characterizes middle-income countries. The economy must now face new challenges from the environment, both internally and externally. Growth tends to be more capital intensive in industry, while an increase in the services sector is needed to serve the new interconnections created in the production process.

Increased production and labour demand lead to increased wages and reduced competitiveness. As a result, exports do not have the same demand as they did before. The problem that arises at this stage has two sources of origin: On the one hand, middle-income countries, due to higher production costs, cannot compete with low-income economies, while, on the other hand, the low-quality products they produce cannot compete with those of the developed countries. Nevertheless, recovering the share of lost exports can be offset either by producing quality products and services or by increasing domestic demand.

The middle class can play a decisive role in boosting domestic demand, by increasing consumption due to its increased incomes, offsetting the reduced demand for exports. Also, improving institutional efficiency will help reduce uncertainty by freeing up resources for the production process and giving incentives for doing business.

The process of transitioning economies, from middle to high income, fails several times, as transition economies are caught in what is called a "middle-income trap". The term "middle-income trap" (Gill, Kharas, & Bhattasali, 2007) is used to describe the situation in which an economy manages to overcome the poverty trap and reach middle-income countries, but it does not manage to reach high-income countries. Thus, the economy, taking advantage of its benefits, does achieve a certain level of per capita income, but it stagnates (Kharas & Kohli, 2011).

An additional feature in this process is the "Cultural Growth Trap". This term was introduced by Petrakis (2014) to describe the phenomenon where the failure of middle-income countries to maintain economic growth and evolve into developed economies is due to the prevailing cultural values that impede this process. According to this theory, the cultural background can explain the deeper causes of low-income countries' growth rates unless low productivity is the main cause of the "middle-income trap". Table 3.3 shows how the model of cultural values delineated between middle- and high-income countries, reveals significant differences that can interpret countries' disparities in terms of economic performance.

The characteristics of the transition of economies to different income levels are shown in Fig. 3.1, which illustrates the necessary changes for middle-income countries to escape the trap of this stage and become more developed. In order to make the last transition, it is requisite for middle-income countries to improve their infrastructure, strengthen property rights, reform the labour market, improve their total factor productivity (TFP), the role of governance and institutions, and acquire characteristics of high-income economies.

Table 3.3 The cultural model of middle- and high-income countries according to Hofstede

	Power distance	*Individualism*	*Uncertainty avoidance*	*Masculinity*	*Long-term orientation*	*Indulgence*
Middle-income countries	44.67	46.56	62.06	45.75	47.24	49.22
High-income countries	30.36	44.72	43.41	31.73	34.70	37.06

Source: Hofstede, Hofstede, and Minkov (2010), and authors' calculations

Note: Middle-income countries: Argentina, Brazil, Bulgaria, Chile, China, Colombia, El Salvador, India, Indonesia, Iran, Latvia, Lithuania, Malaysia, Mexico, Morocco, Pakistan, Peru, the Philippines, Romania, Russia, Serbia, Thailand, Turkey, Venezuela and Vietnam. High-income countries: Australia, Austria, Belgium, Canada, Croatia, Czech Rep., Denmark, Estonia, Finland, France, Germany, Greece, Hong Kong, Hungary, Ireland, Italy, Japan, South Korea, Luxembourg, Malta, the Netherlands, New Zealand, Norway, Poland, Portugal, Singapore, Slovak Rep., Slovenia, Spain, Sweden, Switzerland, Trinidad and Tobago, United States and Uruguay

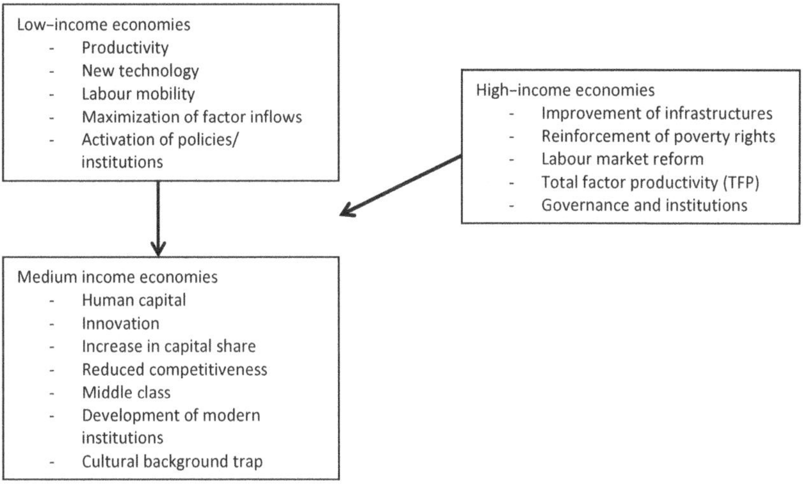

Fig. 3.1 Characteristics of transition stages to different income levels. (Source: Authors' own creation)

From the foregoing, it is clear that the steady increase in per capita income over time, to an even higher level, is the pattern that is followed by every steadily growing economy. Conversely, middle-income countries do not follow this pattern, as periods of high growth are followed by periods of stagnation or recession. The interaction of the characteristics of the idiosyncratic institutions—non-market allocation of resources, coordination failures, information asymmetry, dependence on the past, rent-seeking activities, high systematic risk, including that of an idiosyncratic cultural background, non-diversified investment attitudes, high aversion of uncertainty, in-group collectivism, high time discount, lack of trust and damage aversion—leads to a perpetual stagnant growth prototype (Fig. 3.2).

The preceding analysis of the different growth traps helps us expand our thinking one step further and question why there should be "traps" and "accelerations" in economic growth. Avoiding the traps and accelerating the process of economic growth in a sustainable way are the most

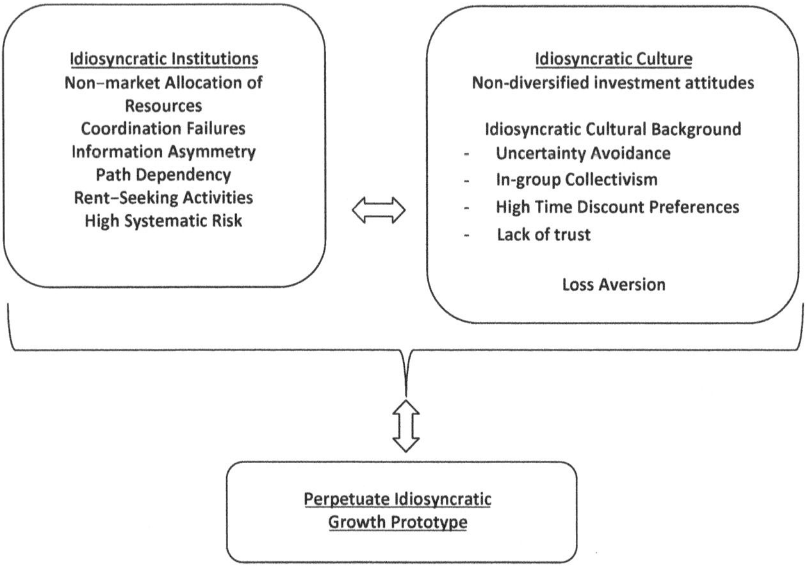

Fig. 3.2 Stagnated idiosyncratic growth prototype. (Source: Authors' own creation)

critical issues in economic science (Hausmann, Pritchett, & Rodrik, 2005), insofar as the growth process appears to be quite unstable (Easterly, Kremer, Pritchett, & Summers, 1993). After all—as we have seen before—there are not many countries that have attained consistently high growth rates for several decades.

This observation is also the point where conventional growth theory or endogenous models (cf. Chap. 1, Sect. 1.2) fail to provide satisfactory answers on how to achieve sustainable development. After all, growth models are inextricably linked to the particular conditions prevailing during the period in which they were developed. For this reason, they focus for the most part on identifying the factors of recession rather than the sources of growth, and, as such, do not provide a comprehensive grasp of the problem.

It is characteristic that since 1950, only 80 episodes of strong acceleration of the growth rate have been recorded (Hausmann et al., 2005), that is, cases where growth has been sustained for at least 8 consecutive years. Hausmann et al. (2005), attempting to answer the question of the causes of these episodes, argue that a change in the political regime increases the probability of growth acceleration by 5.3%, while economic reforms are not linked to these episodes.

It therefore appears that the acceleration of growth rates is influenced by a complex set of parameters with dependence on the past as their common starting point. In this context, the institutional background can affect the evolution of the economy either by creating growth-enhancing conditions or by creating barriers. Institutional differences, such as the establishment of property rights, the level of corruption, the quality of human capital, public infrastructure and the tendency to do business, highlight the contrast between countries in terms of growth experiences. If differences in the institutional background of countries can interpret the differences in their economic development, then we need to ask ourselves where these differences arise. The relevant literature focuses on the importance of persistent exogenous differences in religion or national heritage (Sokoloff & Engerman, 2000).

In other words, the dependence of institutional change on the past may be responsible for a country's economic performance. Consequently, improving the quality of institutions increases the likelihood of a country's moving to better economic performance (Jerzmanowski, 2006).

However, the above-mentioned improvement is not considered sufficient. At this stage, the contribution is required of structural reforms and structural changes to a range of economic system activities. Both of these can offer the tools to improve the supply-side economy and significantly eliminate the prevailing uncertainty.

3.6 Multiple Equilibrium Points

Thus far, we have seen in detail the trajectory of economies in the different stages of development of their income level. In these stages, different "traps" (poverty trap, middle-income trap) have been observed, which impede the process of economic growth and entrench the economy in one point of equilibrium (stagnation), without the ability to move into a better one point. But what if there is more than one point of equilibrium? Such a version is supported by De Grauwe and Ji (2012), and it has a significant impact on the economic policy to be applied. By contrast, Gaspar, Vasconcelos, and Afonso (2014) argue that this assumption is quite difficult to be substantiated.

According to De Grauwe and Ji (2012), the history of the Eurozone is characterized by systematic mispricing of debt, which leads to multiple equilibria. Typically, in the pre-crisis period (2001–2008), markets underestimated the pricing of the bond yields of peripheral countries in relation to those of Germany, considering the risk premium of Greek and German bonds to be the same, despite the high debt/GDP differences of the two economies. By contrast, after the crisis, the markets, driven by panic, overestimated the price differences of the peripheral countries' yields in relation to Germany, and thus overestimated the risk of bankruptcy of these economies.

The concept of risk, expressed through the high yields of bonds, does not just refer to these bonds as such. It automatically concerns the private sector bonds and lending opportunities, and generally the overall activity of the economy. Therefore, the price of bonds, and, hence, the risk, is critical in turning the economy's stagnation into growth. This point preserves stabilization but does not favour development momentum.

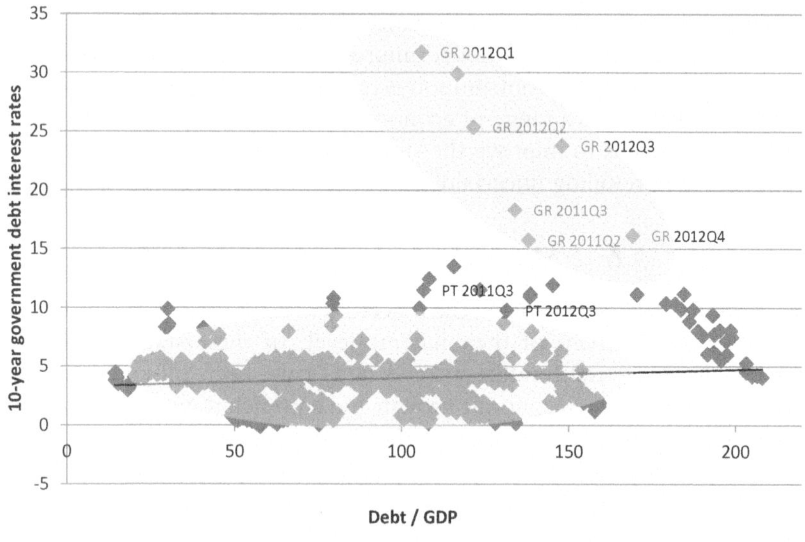

Fig. 3.3 A ten-year Eurozone government debt interest rates and debt/GDP growth (quarterly data). (Source: Oxford Economics and authors' calculations)

Economists understand that this way of analysing the evolution and significance of risk was completely unknown before the crisis.

It is noteworthy that after 2010, there has been a "detachment" of the differences between the peripheral bond yields and the German yields and of the fundamentals of these peripheral economies (such as debt/GDP and current account balance). Figure 3.3 shows the relationship between (a) interest rates on ten-year Eurozone bonds and (b) Eurozone debt-to-GDP rate evolution between 2000 and 2018. It is clear from Fig. 3.3 that after 2010, the yields of the peripheral countries (Greece, Portugal, Ireland) and mainly Greece were detached from the rest of the Eurozone.

Therefore, De Grauwe and Ji (2012) conclude that, after 2010, overestimating the pricing of bond yield differences has led the peripheral countries to a state of bad-equilibria, which erroneously motivates policymakers, as in times of economic growth, there is no incentive to reduce debt, while in times of economic crisis there is an incentive for countries to enter austerity policies.

On the other hand, Gaspar et al. (2014) argue that the assumption of multiple equilibria is far removed from reality. This conclusion is drawn from their empirical analysis,[3] where many equilibrium points appeared under the strict assumptions in the parameters used in their analysis, which render the analysis less realistic.

Notes

1. The term "cultural background" or "cultural values" reflects the behaviour of the individual who is influenced by other people through teaching, imitation and other forms of social dissemination. That is, it is the set of beliefs, preferences, skills, values, stereotypes and rules, which characterize members of a given society and differentiate them from those of other societies. The way a person behaves, perceives and reacts is shaped by the architecture of the human mind shaped by the ongoing action of organic evolution.
2. The different levels of income, based on GDP per capita, are classified as follows: low-income economies have GDP per capita of less than US$1025; middle-income economies have GDP per capita of between US$1026 and US$12,475 and high-income economies have a GDP per capita greater than US$12,476.
3. According to their analysis, in order to achieve two points of equilibrium in the economy, it is necessary to have high weightings in the discount factor and in the public health infrastructure. For this reason, they consider the analysis unrealistic.

References

Acemoglu, D., & Robinson, J. (2012). *Why Nations Fail: The Origins of Power, Prosperity and Poverty*. New York, NY: Crown.

Arrow, K. J., & Debreu, G. (1954). Existence of an Equilibrium for a Competitive Economy. *Econometrica, 22*(3), 265–290.

Bowles, S., & Gintis, H. (2000). Walrasian Economics in Retrospect. *Quarterly Journal of Economics, 115*(4), 1411–1439.

Chang, H.-J. (2007). *Institutional Change and Economic Development*. New York: Anthem Press.

Croitoru, A. (2012). A Review to a Book that Is 100 Years Old. *Journal of Comparative Research in Anthropology and Sociology, 3*(2), 137–148.

De Grauwe, D., & Ji, Y. (2012). Mispricing of Sovereign Risk and Multiple Equilibria in the Eurozone. *VOX, CEPR Policy Portal*. Retrieved from http://voxeu.org/article/mispricing-sovereign-risk-and-multiple-equilibria-eurozone

Easterly, W., Kremer, M., Pritchett, L., & Summers, L. H. (1993). Good Policy or Good Luck? *Journal of Monetary Economics, 32*(3), 459–483.

Ert, E., & Erev, I. (2010). On the Descriptive Value of Loss Aversion in Decisions Under Risk. *Harvard Business School Working Papers* 10-056. Retrieved from https://www.hbs.edu/faculty/Publication%20Files/10-056_0bf56e91-9c2d-4e3d-97e5-d22fbaa13b35.pdf

Festré, A., & Garrouste, P. (2008). *Self Determination and Incentives: A New Look at the Crowding Out Effect*. Mimeo ATOM. Retrieved from https://www.yumpu.com/en/document/read/23200198/locus-of-control-and-crowding-out-effect-cnrs

Gaspar, J., Vasconcelos, P. B., & Afonso, O. (2014). Economic Growth and Multiple Equilibria: A Critical Note. *Economic Modelling, 36*(C), 157–160.

Gill, I., Kharas, H., & Bhattasali, D. (2007). *An East Asian Renaissance: Ideas for Economic Growth*. Washington, DC: World Bank.

Greenwald, B. C., & Stiglitz, J. E. (1986). Externalities in Economies with Imperfect Information and Incomplete Markets. *The Quarterly Journal of Economics, 101*(2), 229–264.

Greif, A. (2006). *Institutions and the Path to the Modern Economy: Lessons from Medieval Trade*. Cambridge: Cambridge University Press.

Grossman, G. M., & Helpman, E. (1992). *Innovation and Growth in the Global Economy*. Cambridge, MA: MIT Press.

Hausmann, R., Pritchett, L., & Rodrik, D. (2005). Growth Accelerations. *Journal of Economic Growth, 10*(4), 303–329.

Hoeffler, S., Ariely, D., & West, P. (2006). Path Dependent Preferences: The Role of Early Experience and Biased Search in Preference Development. *Organizational Behaviour and Human Decision Processes, 101*(2), 215–229.

Hofstede, G., Hofstede, J. G., & Minkov, M. (2010). *Cultures and Organizations-Intercultural Cooperation and its Importance for Survival* (3rd ed.). New York: McGraw Hill.
Jerzmanowski, M. (2006). Empirics of Hills, Plateaus, Mountains and Plains: A Markov-Switching Approach to Growth. *Journal of Development Economics, 81*(2), 357–385.
Jonsson, P. O. (1994). Social Influence and Individual Preferences: On Schumpeter's Theory of Consumer Choice. *Review of Social Economy, 52*(4), 301–314.
Kahneman, D., & Tversky, A. (1979). Prospect Theory: An Analysis of Decision Under Risk. *Econometrica, 47*(2), 263–292.
Kahneman, D., & Tversky, A. (2000). *Choices, Values and Frames.* Cambridge: Cambridge University Press.
Kharas, H., & Kohli, H. (2011). What Is the Middle Income Trap, Why Do Countries Fall into It, and How It Can Be Avoided? *Global Journal of Emerging Market Economies, 3*(3), 281–289.
Kuznets, S. (1971). Prize Lecture (December 11, 1971), Modern Economic Growth: Findings and Reflections. *NobelPrize.org.* Retrieved from https://www.nobelprize.org/prizes/economic-sciences/1971/kuznets/lecture/
Lipsey, R. G. (2017). Generality Versus Context Specificity: First, Second and Third Best in Theory and Policy. *Pacific Economic Review, 22*(2), 167–177.
Lipsey, R. G., & Lancaster, K. (1956). The General Theory of Second Best. *The Review of Economic Studies, 24*(1), 11–32.
Lipsey, R. G., & Ng, Y. K. (2017). Concluding Comments to the Debate. *Pacific Economic Review, 22*(2), 213–228.
McKenzie, L. W. (1959). On the Existence of General Equilibrium for a Competitive Economy. *Econometrica, 27*(1), 54–71.
North, D. (1990). *Institutions, Institutional Change and Economic Performance.* Cambridge: Cambridge University Press.
Petrakis, P. E. (2014). *Culture, Growth and Economic Policy.* New York and Heidelberg: Springer.
Petrakis, P. E., Valsamis, D. G., & Kafka, K. I. (2017). From an Optimal to a Stagnated Growth Prototype: The Role of Institutions and Culture. *Journal of Innovation & Knowledge, 2*(3), 97–105.
Schumpeter, J. A. (1921). *The Theory of Economic Development.* Cambridge: Harvard University Press.
Schumpeter, J. A. (1939). *Business Cycles, A Theoretical, Historical and Statistical Analysis of Capitalist Process.* New York: McGraw-Hill.
Sokoloff, K. L., & Engerman, S. L. (2000). History Lessons: Institutions, Factors Endowments, and Paths of Development in the New World. *The Journal of Economic Perspectives, 14*(3), 217–232.
Stiglitz, J. E. (2002). *Globalization and Its Discontents.* New York: Norton.

Swedberg, R. (2002). The Economic Sociology of Capitalism: Weber and Schumpeter. *Journal of Classical Sociology, 2*(3), 227–255.

Triandis, H. C., Bontempo, R., Villareal, M. J., Asai, M., & Lucca, N. (1988). Individualism and Collectivism: Cross-Cultural Perspectives on Self-Ingroup Relationships. *Journal of Personality and Social Psychology, 54*(2), 323–338.

Ülgen, F. (2014). Schumpeterian Economic Development and Financial Innovations: A Conflicting Evolution. *Journal of Institutional Economics, 10*(2), 257–277. https://doi.org/10.1017/S1744137414000022

Walras, L. (1874). Principe d'Une Théorie Mathématique de L' Échange. *Journal des Économistes, 34*, 5–22.

Williamson, O. E. (1973). Markets and Hierarchies: Some Elementary Considerations. *The American Economic Review, 63*(2), 316–325.

CHAPTER 4

Economic Policy Formation and Decision-Making

4.1 Introduction

The theory and the policy of growth involve interpretations about past economic performance as a key human activity and provide an analytical framework regarding the future development of both the individual and social welfare. Therefore, particular importance is placed on understanding the conditions of past growth and the conditions that will shape the future. Economic policy is considered a broader category of development and growth policy.

This chapter presents the basic logical assumptions of an economic policy-making system in Sect. 4.2. Then, Sect. 4.3 analyses the relationship between economic analysis and theory with economic policy-making, emphasizing the existence of a twofold relationship of causality. Section 4.4 presents the concepts of historicism and serendipity as two conflicting forms of approaching and linking the present with the future, while half way between these two perspectives is found the perspective of path dependence. Next, in Sect. 4.5, the importance of the market mechanism versus the policy-making hierarchy is analysed followed by the four main types of economic systems: traditional, command, market economy and mixed (Sect. 4.6). There follows the neoclassical concept of economic policy-making as a single system of decisions (Sect. 4.7) along with a separate analysis of the importance of positive public choice and normative public choice. Finally in Sect. 4.8, the evolutionary perspective on economic policy-making and the role of learning are briefly discussed, while

P. E. Petrakis et al., *Economic Growth and Development Policy*,
https://doi.org/10.1007/978-3-030-43181-5_4

the fundamental issues of economic policy-making are treated from the evolutionary perspective.

4.2 Foundations of Economic Policy Goals

The fundamental issues relating to the formation of economic policy have always been at the heart of the social, political and, certainly, the economic sciences. These issues are the political economy for economic policy-making ("what policy does do"), the analysis of policy tools for specific goals ("what policy could do") and the debate over political goals and their legitimacy ("what policy ought to do") (Witt, 2003).

Whether the debate is about political reforms or gradual political change, the answer to the first question "what policy does do" requires the acceptance of certain assumptions (Sutton, 1937). These fundamental assumptions affect the decision-making process. They are:

1. Every human being always tries to choose between alternative actions in order to derive possible objective satisfaction from the limited resources available to them.
2. Subjectively, the objective satisfaction of each consumption unit can be measured and compared only with the resources and effort available to obtain it.
3. When two persons engage in a transaction, this transaction, compared to any other, can maximize their objective satisfaction from the existing resources available to them.
4. When through free trade, every rare product or service is allocated to the one whose active demand is higher, then the sum of the objective satisfaction of all persons together will be the greatest possible.

Of course, not all philosophers or social scientists, and certainly not all economists, agree that the above principles uniquely determine the incentives for a person's mobilization and action. There are different perspectives on the above-mentioned assumptions that could conceivably lead to very different policy conclusions. These are:

1. Individuals do not merely seek to maximize their subjective or cumulative social well-being. On the contrary, they also exhibit

altruistic behaviours, which do not fit into individual or social behaviours that maximize well-being.

2. Maximizing satisfaction may not be confined to the present and to the individual's position. Satisfaction of the group to which the individual belongs may be a significant factor in influencing behaviour. In addition, the balance of satisfaction may be the result of the interaction of the members of the group to which the individual belongs with other groups, within one or more strategy games.
3. Usually, all goals to be achieved include restrictive conditions of freedom for other members of society. Ignoring this fact reduces the rate of collective satisfaction.
4. There are concepts difficult to incorporate into the rationale of maximizing satisfaction: for example, stability, security and high levels of uncertainty.

These two opposed methodological systems dealing with key decision-making incentives also form two fundamentally different views of where economic policy should be targeted.

4.3 Economic Analysis and Theory and Economic Policy

The relationship between economic analysis and theory, and the formation of economic policy can only be complex. This is because the economic forces that shape the outcome interact with the institutional framework, with social and political norms of conduct/behaviour and, also, with political ideas and interests.

Indeed, the interaction between theory and policy is two way and of mutual influence. Many theoretical ideas of applied economic policy were first formulated through actual economic policy practice. They were then rationalized, within the bounds of the theoretical rules of economic theory, and finally accounted for and empirically tested according to its rules.

Two factors play an essential role in the way that theory and economic policy are interconnected: the ideas—theoretical conceptions—and people—economists in this case—that drive them (Bruno, 1989). Given that the "market" of economic ideas often overlaps with that of political views, the risk is likely of accepting only economic ideas that serve specific political ideas. This risk comes in two extreme forms: the first is an extreme attitude of accepting only ideas that are consistent with particular theoretical contexts and the second is the disregard of any theoretical dimension of the practical problem posed "as theoretical" by its very nature.

Economists who turn ideas into policies have an important role, depending on their position in producing new ideas: if they produce ideas which they publish, it makes a difference whether they are involved in the process of applying those ideas to policy proposals. There are many examples of great economists who either succeeded or failed to link their ideas to policies. One example of an economist who successfully participated in economic policy-making is Keynes, who played a major role in shaping economic architecture from World War I to World War II—although he failed to convince politicians of the consequences of high compensations (Keynes, 1919)—but also post–World War II international economic architecture.

Worldwide, there seems to be trends showing that politics is becoming less and less relevant in today's democracies because (a) political parties tend to converge at the centre and have similar government programmes as the effect of ideology is diminished, (b) globalization emphasizes certain shared economic values and (c) national governments are limited by the power of supranational structures, with the former often implementing policies in line with the latter's proposals. On the other hand, the political and economic "populism" that has brought to light several political goals—nationalism, anti-elitism and so on—seems to gain popularity as it disputes the above-mentioned trends.

In this political context, and as a consequence of factors both external—international organizations and globalization—and internal—structure of political parties—public policies seem to be defined by a mix of economic and political variables. These factors result from the interaction of ideas, interests, policies, preferences and, also, institutional and socio-economic dimensions.

4.4 Historicism, Serendipity and Path Dependence

The evolution of economics is a topic that concerns researchers beyond the narrow confines of economic science. To this end, two contradictory theoretical conceptions define the extremes of the evolution course of economies. The first perspective is related to historicism, while the second to serendipity. In between stands the view that what is happening now is the result of limitations and opportunities that "come" from the past (path dependence).

At the heart of historicist thinking is the view that societies and human activities are defined by the past and have a determined future. The opposite view, based on the role of serendipity, claims that evolution is the sum of the effects of random events without a predictable development.

Path dependence assumes that history plays a decisive role in a variety of everyday human activities, such as preferences, decisions and institutional behaviours. Consequently, a sequential evolutionary dependency is created. Thus, preferences, behaviours, decisions and institutions are shaped by initial experiences and constructs and are sequentially dependent (Hoeffler, Ariely, & West, 2006). The reasons why prior experiences can influence future preferences and constructs can be sought in mechanisms that promote anchoring and adaptation (Chapman & Johnson, 1999; Strack & Mussweiler, 1997).

Evolutionary sequential dependence brings out the problem of economic science—and especially neoclassical economics—about the efficient functioning of markets. By analysing an example, we find that in most cases, institutions do not guarantee property rights. However, property rights and how an economy operates greatly influence the process of evolutionary sequential perspective by introducing historical heritage elements. However, altering property rights creates disincentives for business initiatives and generally limits the effectiveness of the market. In other words, the dependence of institutional change on the past may be responsible for the economic performance of a country due to the problematic nature of the property rights system. Therefore, improving the quality of institutions increases a country's chances of achieving better economic performance (Jerzmanowski, 2006).

The serendipity perspective on the evolution of economies and societies is based on the existence of unpredictable events that may change the prevailing conditions of this process. Rasmus (2011) uses the term "Serendipity Economy" to describe "an emerging and unpredictable economic model that is unfolding in the future, not in a linear way, but by serendipity and circumstance". Knowledge economy ascribes particular importance to knowledge and cognitive abilities that shift the means of production from machines to individuals. In addition, investment in innovation and technological progress in general are at the heart of economic development, and technology is a primary means of improving productivity. However, in real terms, only knowledge and learning can bring improvement. In this way, an accidental technological development may lead to a marked improvement in the production process and a divergence from the evolutionary process of economic dependence. In actual fact, it is not easy to predict how conditions will evolve.

The term "historicism" was used by Karl Popper in *The Poverty of Historicism* (1957), which was widely criticized. Historicism is a perspective which explicitly or implicitly assumes that historical prediction is the main objective of the social sciences and can be achieved by recognizing the rhythms, patterns, laws or evolution trends of human history. Although Popper has repeatedly resorted to Hegel in his text, his objection to the supporters of historicism lies in the fact that the existence of a deterministic model in the development of things abolishes the free expression of the individual and, therefore, of society. Popper used the concept of knowledge as a supreme tool to overthrow the power of historicism (Popper, 1957). In other words, he argued that knowledge, whether of the past or knowledge in itself, is enough to reverse any future development anticipated by laws or trends.

Historical institutionalism approaches institutions as a construct, which does not necessarily serve functional reasons, but through which divergent historical trajectories can be sought (Amenta & Ramsey, 2010). This concept is closely linked to a distinct perspective of historical development (Hall & Taylor, 1996). Its supporters propose a process of evolutionary sequential dependence, arguing that institutions are generally the central factors driving historical evolution over a course. But how are these processes created by the institutions? In other words, how does the institutional framework create new structures? Literature focuses on the impact of existing state capabilities and of policy legacy on subsequent policy choices (Weir & Skocpol, 1985). At the same time, however, future policies and the evolution of institutions are influenced by the forces of society that promote specific actions (Pierson, 1994). In this context, historical institutionalism stresses the importance of the ineffective functioning of existing institutions (March & Olsen, 1984; North, 1990) and those forces that "resist" change in order to defend their interests.

The observed development trends can provide the basis for predicting the future. They rely on the general idea that "tomorrow" will be just like "today" because "today" is very much like "yesterday". They are based on the idea that the past never changes, and we can look back to it at any time to seek information. Thus, a picture is formed of the state to which development leads individuals and societies, as well as of the origin of events.

But even if the past cannot predict the future, it can provide an abundance of information about it (Millett, 2011).

The social structures that exist in any part of the planet are built on the historical events that shaped them. In short, the past is what has shaped the existing political and economic system, the social rules and cultural background in every society. The future as well is shaped based on these structures.

Using the past to preview the future usually leads to a situation where in some way history tends to repeat itself. Of course, conditions may not be the same as time and circumstances change, but there are undoubtedly future situations that very much resemble situations in the past. At the same time, knowledge of the past for shaping the future is important because knowledge of past achievements prevents the repetition of the same situations in the present and future. However, if the evolution of economies and societies in general is not an evolutionary sequential dependence process but, rather, the outcome of a series of random events, then the key consideration is how to manage future situations. The effort to manage the future is linked with identifying future needs, which is difficult as the future is considered unknown.

4.4.1 *Shaping the Future*

The passage of time necessitates changes. Changes generate uncertainty (Grunwald, 2013; Wernerfelt & Karnani, 1987), which is a key component of the future. Consequently, the future contains a combination of factors that cannot be easily identified and then controlled. They are described as "possibility", "opportunity", "luck" or "coincidence". However, through strategic planning, we can control or even minimize the negative effects that these variables may cause (Mintzberg, 1994; Olsen, 2012).

The term "Black Swan" is often used to describe events that cause sharp and sudden changes in the evolution of the economy (Taleb, 2007). These are events that have the following three characteristics:

1. They are outside the sphere of expectations and experience, while at the same time there were no indications in the past of their likelihood of occurrence.
2. They generate extreme effects and, in general, extreme conditions.

3. Despite the extreme conditions they generate, they may subsequently be described as explainable and considered to have even been predictable.

The fact is impressive that the majority of people act by disregarding the existence of such phenomena. The main characteristic of the "Black Swan" phenomena is that what we don't know is more important than what we know. These phenomena are unpredictable, and we need to adapt to them when they occur, not merely try to predict them.

New information and events which people either ignored or thought would never come to pass and were, as such, outside their prediction are usually more frequent and common. Their influence is not much more significant than we might imagine. Thus, the future must not be seen as a state characterized by predictability and continuity. The complexity of modern societies makes the occurrence of "Black Swan" phenomena more frequent than ever.

A basic assumption on which all methods of predicting the future are based is the assumption that the present—as opposed to the future—literally exists, and we experience it (Millett, 2011). The future, on the one hand, is not known, nor is there any way of its becoming known today, in the present. Nevertheless, we can theoretically have "access" to the future, albeit in an abstract way. Knowledge of the past and present, as well as the ability to use reasoning in conjunction with imagination, allow us to "shape" the possible future (Bartlett & Ghoshal, 2002).

Let it be noted that the future, when we do experience it, has only one, unique aspect, but when we prepare for it—while being in the present—we have to imagine more than one possibility for the future, imagine and prepare for more than one aspect of it. These will be the outcome of the different assumptions that will be formulated.

Both individuals and businesses need to try to "intervene" in the future in order to shape it—to what extent is possible—in accordance with their wishes. But to intervene, they need to be able to predict it. The endeavour begins by assessing potential changes in the environment in which they operate. Predictive failure is particularly accentuated when changes are fast and turbulent or when the information available cannot be described as useful—either because there is a lack of information or because there is too much information.

A key feature of modern societies is their attitude towards time, especially with reference to the future. For non-advanced societies, the future is something that would just happen. For contemporary societies, the future is something we have to reflect about and ideally, to the extent that it is possible, shape as we desire (Giddens, 1990, 1991). This can be accomplished through strategic planning. Strategic planning reduces the negative effects of events that take place beyond the control of individuals and contribute to a particularly adverse future. Therefore, the future may be the product of the interaction of factors that we are able to control—through strategic planning—as well as factors that cannot be controlled. So, the future cannot be controlled, but it can be "steered" in a particular direction.

4.4.2 Conclusions on Shaping the Future

In conclusion, the differentiation of the earlier perspectives, that is, historicism and serendipity, lies in the value they each give to the concept of learning and knowledge, which individuals accumulate over time. Historicists fail to understand and integrate these two concepts in their analysis and, thus, see evolution as a process that follows a particular path. On the contrary, serendipity in the unfolding of events—even it is not impossible to predict them—emphasizes knowledge, technological progress and innovation, explaining how an economy can diverge from a predefined trajectory of evolution. After all, if we agree that history is indeed a crucial issue, then sequential evolutionary dependence alone cannot explain how societies have evolved to date. We may have to look at the two perspectives as complementary rather than as piecemeal or contradictory.

The path dependence perspective is useful, as it gives us information on the evolution of economic phenomena. At the same time, it is a tool for comparing whether the economy's equilibrium is optimal or sub-optimal. Under optimal conditions, economy operates in perfect market conditions. On the other hand, sub-optimal equilibrium is associated with market failures (David, 2001).

Changing the institutional background as an evolutionary process leads to improved conditions in the different subsystems of the economy and, thus, enhances the dominance of a particular economic model over alternative choices. At the same time, the mechanism of evolutionary sequential dependence may answer the question of why the economy is following a particular path, in terms of the historical evolution, and how predetermined paths offer a set of potential equilibrium points. The introduction of new paths is quite feasible at the beginning of the process, but it becomes increasingly difficult over time (Henning, Stam, & Wenting, 2013). Existing institutional structures may not negate possible changes, but they do set the limits of these changes. Earlier paths define the structures and direction of future changes by affecting a number of parameters such as technological progress (Dosi & Nelson, 2010).

On the other hand, the assumption of rationality does not incorporate elements of the evolutionary process, since it does not take into account the factor of time. Conventional economic thinking is a static perspective, which does not include time in the functioning of the economic system. The simplification of reality, through the absence of time, provides a theoretical framework for a partial interpretation of how the economy operates at a given time, depriving it of its dynamic character.

The search for an equilibrium point in the economy through the process of evolutionary sequential perspective—by contrast to the rational perspective of neoclassical economics—does take into account the time factor in its analysis. However, time in every society is integrated into the cultural background, which is the product of long processes, as well as in the knowledge which its members acquire. Through knowledge, individuals form behaviours and reaction attitudes to the situations which they will be called to face. Of course, it is not certain that we always learn from our great mistakes (Popper, 1957). Popper argues that the gravest source of great collective mistakes—social experiments as he defines them—lies in the fact that while a central designer or government can possess all the power necessary to implement them, nevertheless, "it is impossible to concentrate all the knowledge necessary to manage the particular situation wisely". Lack of sufficient knowledge will lead to a forced simplification which will in turn lead those in power to exert pressure in attempting to control people's conscience; alternatively, if society and the wider framework are strong, it will lead to the downfall of the powers that be. Exercising pressure on people's conscience is incompatible with the free expression of critical thinking. Insofar as the latter is missing, it is impossible to assess significant mistakes.

4.5 Markets, Hierarchies and Economic Policy Formation

The economic system is responsible for ensuring the proper distribution of resources to society's members and their activities. Through the price system, prices are expressed in the form of money for the valuation and distribution of goods/services, and of the various production factors. A price system can be either free or fixed. The first characterizes Western economies—free markets of capitalist economies—in which prices are determined by the factors of demand and supply. The second is most common in centrally planned economies—communist economies—where prices are set by the government.

The price mechanism allows for "economic coordination" to take place as signals of price changes guide the production factors to their most efficient use. Hayek (1945) in his paper "The Use of Knowledge in Society" comments on the importance of the price system as follows: "one of these designs that individuals have learnt to use (though they are far from learning how to make the best use of it) after getting involved in it without ever understanding it".

The price mechanism in the free market raises questions about its effectiveness within a complex economic system. The reason is that information asymmetries and moral hazard issues necessitate the formation of bureaucratic structures. The structures are associated with the existence of transaction costs and their relevant contract signing. In addition, information asymmetries affect the allocation of resources within an economy and make it difficult to achieve market efficiency. Their elimination requires contract signing between the principal and the agent, which generates additional operating costs for the economy. Therefore, hierarchical structures and transaction costs alter the efficient allocation of resources and increase systematic risk (Petrakis, Valsamis, & Kafka, 2016).

Market distortions, however, lead to coordination failures, resulting in a division between markets—price mechanism—and firms—hierarchies. According to the theory of the firm, both markets and firms—hierarchies—are two alternative institutional forms governing transactions (Coase, 1937). In addition, businesses may replace markets when the transaction cost of the internal organization is lower than that resulting from the functioning of the market, while the existence of transaction cost adds inefficiency to the market (Coase, 1937). In this context, Williamson

(1985) defines transaction cost as the "operating cost of the economic system".

Market functioning involves cost for the transactors. The creation of companies by entrepreneurs reduces marketing costs by directing the resources of the economy to the production process (Coase, 1937). We can, however, reasonably ask why production is not concentrated in one big business. Coase stresses that concentrating production in one organization leads to efficiency problems, which in turn weaken the advantage of hierarchies over the price mechanism.

Williamson (1973) in *Market and Hierarchies* claims that hierarchies exist mainly because of uncertainty and opportunism, although bounded rationality is involved. They exist when the actual underlying circumstances, in relation to the transaction or to a set of transactions, are known in one or more parties but cannot be distinguished or modified by others at no cost. When hierarchies are present in the full range of economic activities, uncertainty and systematic risk increase. Moreover, the existence of transaction costs deprives the real economy of resources, and, consequently, the optimal allocation of resources is distorted. High transaction costs lead to market failures and, as a result, limit the effective use of resources and increase systematic risk. Therefore, hierarchies, transaction costs and income-seeking activities distort the allocation of resources and increase systematic risk. After all, in a free market regime, as has been said, the transaction cost is zero, and market transactions have a competitive effect. In general, any attempt to incorporate transaction costs into conventional economies—based on a general equilibrium framework—is out of equilibrium (Williamson, 1981).

Factors that enhance the formation of hierarchies and high transaction costs result in transaction failures, rent-seeking activities, information asymmetries and evolutionary sequential dependence. Coordination failures occur when the actions of an individual or a business create externalities to other members of the economic system. As a result, externalities, which have not been taken into account, entail some cost in economic terms, leading the economy to a point of equilibrium that deviates from the optimal model. Another crucial point is that the existence of information asymmetries also affects the allocation of the resources of the economy and, therefore, makes it difficult to achieve market efficiency.

The prevalence of hierarchical structures in the production process creates barriers to the orientation of available resources to more productive sector (Petrakis et al., 2016), so that economies do not adapt or delay adapting to the process of creative disaster, which is necessary for the regeneration of the economy.

In conclusion, if the market is the key mechanism—that is, if there are no hierarchies—the market price mechanism is the basic way of determining the equilibrium of the economy and how each batch of production activity is coordinated. Market rules provide the necessary coordination for allocating resources to an economy. Under these circumstances, it is governments that make decisions and exercise policy. However, according to Coase's analysis (1937), the main characteristic advantage of an enterprise, as an institutional and legal entity, is the ability to enable the transactor to decide, as applicable, whether to use the market for the production of an economic activity or to opt for completing the production process within the internal organizational structure of the enterprise. Each of these two options, according to Coase, has its cost. Which process will an enterprise ultimately decide to choose in each of its transactions depends on which transaction, is estimated to have the lowest cost, whether outside or within the organizational boundaries of the enterprise. If the entrepreneur decides to use the internal organizational structure of the enterprise, it is himself or the management who will proceed with decision-making and policy formation. Thus, in this case, hierarchically structured financial operations develop mechanisms that are ideally intended to "imitate" the efficiency of markets in resource allocation. However, hierarchies are associated with high transaction costs with the other economic agents, outside the enterprise, and with high uncertainty and lack of information, a fact which makes policy formation under these circumstances extremely difficult. When hierarchies prevail, the aim of those in power (government) and those implementing economic policy should be to deal with these conditions.

4.6 The Types of Economic Systems and Economic Policy

The analysis of economic systems traditionally focuses on the divisions and comparisons between market economies and centrally planned economies. The functioning of the economic system depends on how efficiently the price mechanism works and its substitution by non-market allocative mechanisms, while the degree of intervention/freedom of markets determines the types of economic systems. There are four main types of economic systems: traditional, command, market economy and mixed.

The traditional economic system is the oldest form of economic organization, which we may encounter today in Third World countries. The command economic system is characterized by the control of most of the economic activity by a central authority. Market economy is a capitalist or free market economy where the state has no control over the vital resources or any other major factors of the economy. In addition, the economy is free to determine the supply and demand for goods and services and can be regulated without government intervention. Finally, a mixed economic system is the most common form of organization of the economy. It combines key features of a free economy with state intervention to provide either a normative framework for the operation of markets or even for the complete control over certain markets.

The fall of the Berlin Wall and the collapse of the Soviet Union in 1989 have drawn the attention of scholars of comparative political economy to the varieties of the capitalist system. The approach to the varieties of capitalism (VoC: Varieties of Capitalism) (Hall & Soskice, 2001) addresses the fundamental differences in national political economies and examines how they affect economic performance, given the strong competitive pressures arising from globalization.

At the heart of VoC are those enterprises which determine the performance of the overall economy. The success of capitalism is a matter of co-coordinating a number of enterprise-related parameters: access to financing, finding and training the workforce in the appropriate skills, using new technologies, developing networks to market their products and so on. Thus, the most important problem of enterprises is the coordination problems relating to other "players" in the economy (Hall & Gingerich, 2004).

On the one hand, through competitive markets, enterprises cooperate with the other economic agents on the basis of predefined relationships (contract signing). In this case, the equilibrium point arises from both the relative prices and the market signals received by economic agents. On the other hand, coordination can be a matter of strategic decisions based on game theory. The equilibrium point, in this case, depends on institutional factors that contribute to the dissemination of information, monitoring, imposing sanctions and consultation (Ostrom, 1990).

Market coordination takes place in all capitalist economies. However, the way coordination occurs, whether from a competitive market or from strategic interactions, defines the varieties of capitalism. Thus, we can, in terms of varieties of capitalism, distinguish between Liberal Market Economies (LMEs), where the relationships of enterprises with the other "players" are defined by the markets, and Coordinated Market Economies (CMEs), where enterprises are in strategic interaction with the other "players" (Hall & Soskice, 2001). Subsequent surveys have extended this initial division, adding other groups of market economies, not readily identifiable as either LMEs or CMEs. Mixed Market Economies (MMEs), also known as State Capitalism, is the category proposed in the comparative political economy literature (Molina & Rhodes, 2007; Schmidt, 2002). Germany, Austria and Japan are typical examples of a Coordinated Market Economy, while the United States and Britain are examples of a Liberal Market Economy. Southern European countries could be classified as Mixed Market Economies.

The institutional framework formed in each of the above-mentioned differentiations of the capitalist system allows for assessments of how the economy responds to different situations over time and who is making policy implementation decisions. To the extent that the economic system supports institutional complementarity, enterprises, too, develop their own strategies. In other words, there must be a correspondence between the institutional structure of each sphere of the economy and the nature of coordination therein (Hall & Gingerich, 2004).

The functioning of economic systems also reflects the social model's mode of development in each case. The European social model is controversial. Some claim that it never existed as such, while others say it has collapsed. Many believe that there are three or four social models in Europe (Bertola, Boeri, & Nicoletti, 2001; Boeri, 2002; Ferrera, 1998; Sapir, 2006). Some compare it to the social model of the United States (Freeman, 2005; Hall & Soskice, 2001), while yet others consider it ought to be replaced by the Anglo-Saxon model. Some blame the European social model for its limited ability to achieve competitiveness, employment and growth, while others regard the presence of social cohesion and good conditions in the labour market as positive effects of its existence.

The model in Europe differs significantly from that of the United States. The US social model is characterized by the fact that a small proportion of society members is favoured to the detriment of the majority. In addition, the US model provides a very low degree of social and occupational security. According to Freeman (2005), the two models have many differences but similarities too. In particular, he argues that their main differences have to do with the emphasis they place on institutions and markets. The United States follows the neoclassical theory that the invisible hand of the market determines the economic results, while the market regulates wages and employment levels. Employees do not participate in determining the amount of wages, but they take them for granted, with only the option of whether to accept them or not. Finally, employment and access to healthcare services are the main forms of social protection. In terms of their similarities, according to Freeman (2005), both social models concern developed capitalist systems that make institutional changes and comply with the rule of law, protection of property rights, freedom of business mobility, social insurance and welfare.

In addition, the four social models that seem to exist in European society concern four different geographical areas (Bertola et al., 2001; Boeri, 2002; Ferrera, 1998; Sapir, 2006). These are the social model of the Nordic countries (Denmark, Finland, Sweden and the Netherlands: Nordics), the model of the Anglo-Saxon countries (the United Kingdom and Ireland), the model of the countries of Continental Europe (Austria, Belgium, France, Germany and Luxembourg) and that of the Mediterranean countries (Greece, Spain, Italy and Portugal).

The Nordic model is characterized by high spending on social protection and attempting to achieve high levels of well-being, with the focus on the individual members of society. It implements social interventions in the labour market, and there is extensive employment in the public sector. Ultimately, wages are significantly determined by trade unions, which also determine levels of unemployment.

The Anglo-Saxon model is half way between the American and the European social model. Transfer payments are observed, especially for members of the workforce. The labour market is characterized by weak labour unions, large wage gaps and significant levels of low-paid employment.

The social model of the countries of Continental Europe is mainly based on social insurance, pension schemes, unemployment and disability benefits programmes through transfer payments and income contributions. Labour unions have been particularly weak over the last 30 years, but they continue to influence the development of labour markets through adjustments and regulations that have come about through collective bargaining in the past (Boeri, Brugiavini, & Calmfors, 2001).

Lastly, the Mediterranean models focus on spending on pension schemes and are characterized by significant fragmentation of property rights and high social inequalities. Work protection is observed too, while efforts are being made to include new members into the labour market through an early retirement process for older employees, so as to enhance the participation of specific parts of the population in the labour market. Also, mainly in the official sector of economies, collective bargaining is observed between employees and employers, which leads to a strong suppression of wage structures.

The following question arises at this point: why do some economies pursue growth paths that lead them to perform better than others? To answer it, we need to consider how the institutional system of the economy, the State, policy, class conflicts and sources of crisis are organized. An additional question is, whether these institutional systems are capable of fostering and developing entrepreneurship and innovation, whether radically or even gradually with, simultaneously, a greater or lesser imbalance in the distribution of income and wealth?

At the same time, the question arises of the possibility of changing the economic system and of the effectiveness of implementing individual policies insofar as they may conflict with or enhance specific institutional aspects of the economies. In this context, it is important to consider whether the liberal type or the coordinated type of capitalist economy "matches" more specific short-term countercyclical macroeconomic policies or supply growth policies. In other words, can a liberal economy more efficiently pursue a demand-driven growth policy and coordinated economies pursue a supply growth policy? Do the differences in the types of capitalism adequately explain the sources of growth policies being implemented?

The great crisis of the early twenty-first century renewed the interest in exploring what type of capitalism accelerates growth and improves prosperity. The debate (Acemoglu, Robinson, & Verdier, 2012; Maliranta, Määttänen, & Vihriälä, 2012) focuses on whether economies are capable of achieving innovative production, such as the Nordics, without sacrificing social welfare programmes and the ensuing social equality. Even though these societies may have lower per capita incomes (e.g. compared to the United States), because of greater social cohesion, they ultimately have higher prosperity. The substantive argument focuses on whether a society with limited inequalities provides sufficient incentives for entrepreneurship and innovation.

Acemoglu et al. (2012) argue that, in the context of global equilibrium, some countries have greater incentives for innovation than others so that those countries which opt for a more aggressive type of capitalism ("cut-throat capitalism"), which generates greater inequality and more innovation, will become technological leaders, while other countries will opt for a more moderate ("cuddly") type of capitalism. Thus, technologically leading countries choose liberal institutions, while the follower countries adopt coordinated-type institutions. In other words, the diversity of institutions between countries can be explained not only as a historical outcome but, also, as a result of a mutually self-reinforcing asymmetric equilibrium.

Yet Maliranta et al. (2012) question the above-mentioned view by showing that more equal societies (Nordics) can also deliver better innovative returns and, therefore, aggressive capitalism is not the only path to an innovative economy.

4.7 The Neoclassical Perception of Economic Policy Formation as a Single Decision System

The main difference between political science and economic science may be that the former adopts a "what should be" normative perspective, while the latter has always been more of a positivist perspective, without containing many "what should be" (Mueller, 1976). At the same time, economic science highlights a lot more on the concept of economic efficiency, as a positivist concept, and as the core of policy-making, resulting from behaviours that are influenced by the functioning of markets, as opposed to more redistributive policies, which contain more normative policy proposals.

However, focusing on the functioning of markets is not a sufficient reason to develop systems of economic thinking that contain "public choice" features. Another notion of the assumption of "market failure" is required, as developed in the economic literature of the 1940s and 1950s (Buchanan, 1988). The concept of "market failure", in terms of economic efficiency, leads to the idea that there is a comparable, much better state of efficient economic operation than that of market failure, which can be ensured by governmental or political mobilization. This is precisely the core of economic policy in both its normative and positivist perspective. Thus, public choice can be defined as the economic study of non-market decision-making.

In the context of the positivist theory of public choice, some aspects seem to be of particular interest: the reasons imposing the existence of collective choice, the conditions for policy-making in direct democracy and representative democracy, how policy decisions about quasi-public goods are made, decision-making under revolutionary conditions and, finally, some aspects of the empirical dimension of decision-making methodology.

In examining the normative theories of public choice, Rawls' theory of justice is analysed, along with the importance of constitutional order and theoretical conceptions about social welfare function. Finally, some comparative comments are added on the different views.

4.7.1 Rational Choice Theories

Rational choice theories are based on assumptions according to which actors have a fixed type of preferences and act rationally to maximize the achievement of their preferences. Two examples of rational choice theories are considered: Game theory and agency theory.

Game theory is a mathematical approach that presents how individuals will act in a conflict in order to achieve their preferred targets (Firestone, 1989). It applies to many different areas of interest, such as political sciences, conduct of research and ecology. For example, in political science, game theory is considered particularly useful in analysing the formation of alliances, with the aim of applying items of legislation(s) that are in the interest of particular groups (Winter, 2003).

Agency theory—that is, the interaction of the principal-agent relationship and the authorization granted to the latter to make decisions on behalf of the former—applies to economics, political sciences and sociology (Kiser, 1999). Political science researchers have emphasized three points: third parties, administrative procedures and cases where there is more than one principal.

Rational choice theories provide a limited framework in which rational individuals aim to satisfy their preferences and interact strategically with others. However, according to John (2003), rational choice does not provide solutions in all contexts, as it gives an explanation of results only when preferences are already established, without identifying the sources of those preferences. Game theory provides an inductive approach, combining every approach where all relevant parties operate strategically but does not address issues such as uncertainty, and it provides a framework from which institutionalization is missing (O'Toole, 1995) and, consequently, so are institutionalization costs. On the other hand, agency theory leaves many questions unanswered, such as who exactly is the principal, who is supposed to control the actions of the agents and, finally, how agents are selected.

4.7.2 Positivist Public Choice

The premise of the public choice perspective to non-market decisions is based on three points, namely on:

1. rational behavioural assumptions (individuals acting in a rational and utilitarian manner),
2. an approach to economics similar to the political preferences perspective, where "voting" and "participating in behavioral groups" are fundamental and
3. answers to questions such as those posed by economic science: Are there equilibrium points? Are they constant? Are they Pareto efficient?

The analysis of the positivist theory of public choice is based on the fact that people, having exclusively selfish characteristics, can engage with each other in transactions that lead to the satisfaction of all. So, there are serious reasons for collective action and decisions (collective choice). This raises the following question: How are decisions made?

Collective decisions can be made in a political environment when there is direct democracy. In addition, it has been found that these decisions can be made when the Unanimity Rule applies, the rule that leads to Pareto-preferred quantities of public goods (Buchanan & Tullock, 1962; Wicksell, 1896 [1958]).

The simple majority rule method argues that at least the entire first integer over the $n/2$ percentage of voters is required to impose a decision on the community. However, when we attempt to defend the majority rule in decision-making, it is very likely that we resort to normative perspectives (Baumol, 1965; Rae, 1969). In addition, the majority rule limits the equilibrium points that can be chosen in the Pareto frontier, that is, the geometric location of points that are Pareto efficient, and it turns out that the equilibrium point may not exist, a phenomenon called "cycling" (Arrow, 1963). In this case, a solution can be given if we assume that people who vote have specific behaviours (e.g. voter preferences are single-peaked [Black, 1948]) or if we impose restrictions on voter preferences (such as those put forth by single-peaked condition) (Sen, 1966).

When the preferences of voters on a given issue are not the same, the profits for the prevailing majority may be less than the losses of the minority. The way in which this problem in decision-making can be overcome is by "logrolling"—the prior agreement of legislators to vote each other's bills (Stratmann, 2004)—namely "vote trading" (Tullock, 1970).

Finally, one way of discovering voters' preferences for public goods and public economic policies is to combine every public expenditure action with a specific way of financing (Wicksell, 1896). If this can be done technically, then the solution to the policy dilemma is quite clear. If, however, expenditure is financed by "general budgetary revenue", then, there are two separate decisions behind each such decision: (a) the allocation of the total budget and (b) the overall size of the budget.

However, when decisions are made under a representative democracy, as opposed to direct democracy, their characteristic properties and decision-making processes are quite different.

The presence of intermediaries (Members of the Parliament, Senators) between voters and decision-makers creates new conditions for efficiency. Here, we have to assume that the elected intermediaries will also be rational, as are their voters, but also aim to maximize their own benefit (e.g. to be re-elected).

Hotelling (1929) analysed the situation where there are two parties and one stake—a matter for voters to decide. If everyone votes for someone who is close to their views, then the candidate who has the views of the average voter wins the vote. Depending on the assumptions we make, cycling and logrolling phenomena may also occur.

Whether more than one party appears will depend on the voting rules. A candidate is elected when he receives more than 50% of the votes. In this case, the candidate is moving very close to the average voter. If more than one candidate can be selected, then one may be elected with fewer votes. This will remove the one who is elected by the average voter, and therefore more parties may emerge, as none of them necessarily represent the average voter. However, behaviours in a multi-party system can be analysed using gaming theory with essential applications in the case of redistributive policies, which redistribute a certain amount of available resources with a zero-sum game logic.

If we consider policy as a situation that is capable of dynamic analysis, with the ability to reposition the issues that are at stake and reorganize political alliances, we can get closer to reality, although the risk of increasing the complexity of the analysis is greatly enhanced.

The analysis of the different characteristic situations of public choice in a representative democracy concludes by examining the conditions of the voter's behaviour. When consumers buy a good, they do so with their purchasing power, which allows them to achieve the desired effect. When we move to the correspondence with voting power, then, the result depends on the behaviour of the other voters and, in the case of representative democracy, on the way of representation. The conditions for gathering the necessary information and the direct involvement of the voter in ongoing processes play a specific role.

"Classic" pure public goods are characterized by the inability to exclude massive and coordinated bidding. Consequently, revealing consumer preferences requires a common way of expressing them if we seek to enhance Pareto efficiency. There is no such need in private markets, as consumers can enter and exit them at will.

Between these two extremes, there is a multitude of private and public goods with a different composition of properties. Therefore, improving the efficiency of resource allocation comes from a combination of collective preference methods (public goods) and consumer entry-exit methods (private goods).

Finally, two main systems of collective expression of preference are mentioned: "voting with the feet" and club theory. In general, the "voting" held in the first way is carried out by moving voters where the best public goods are offered—better public education, better environment and so on. According to "voting with the feet", people come in and out of the communities that offer the goods, just as individuals come in and out of the private markets. This results in the formation of consumer clubs with homogeneous preferences. In the second case, that is to say, the formation of larger consumer clubs, the average cost of the goods is reduced, that is, economies of scale are created. If the average cost is constantly decreasing, then the club formed coincides with that of the population. Moreover, if the average cost reaches a minimum for a variety of reasons, then, preference clubs are formed that are smaller than the population at large (Buchanan, 1965).

Thus, the voluntary formation of consumer clubs with homogeneous preferences is a more effective way of revealing preferences than "voting with the feet", since transport costs are avoided. If either the ballot box is not functioning or clubs of homogeneous preferences cannot be formed, neither by "voting with the feet" nor by the voluntary formation of clubs, then conditions are present for overturning the preferences system through a revolutionary process.

4.7.3 *Normative Public Choice*

The normative public choice perspective relates to how the state or community can set economic policy targets, what they should be and how they may be achieved. The challenge of normative public choice is to develop a theory of the expression of community values based on generally accepted principles with interpretive and predictive power.

Perhaps one of the most influential theorists of the theory of normative choice is Rawls (1971), who likens participation in society to participation in a game of probabilities: individuals are born into a system of values, with given behavioural characteristics, and their happiness could be determined by adopting practices defined by the theory of positive public choice, that is, by placing themselves in the Pareto Frontier.

But if one's position in society is defined with serendipity, then the allocation of resources, and therefore happiness, may be arbitrary or unfair. But in that way, individuals could organize their participation and form institutions and distribution of resources, disregarding their original position in the system of values and allocation of resources. The formation of new institutions, that is, the social contract, will depend on the quality and quantity of information imposed, in "ethical terms", on individuals regardless of their original position. Thus, the social contract is fair and does not work in the direction of favouring certain groups of the population, since the initial posts in values and distribution of resources are disregarded.

These assumptions form the main body of the social contract, which is summarized in two principles: (a) everyone has the same right to freedom of choice as everyone else, and (b) there are fair and equal opportunities.

Buchanan and Tullock (1962) pointed at the situation where individuals choose constitutional rules by placing themselves in the position of future citizens.

The distinction between day-to-day decisions and a "social contract" that takes the form of a constitution helps us to understand the value of collective decisions that are medium to long term. This introduces the importance of time, future and uncertainty in public choice.

A different view of the organization of the constitution of society is to treat it as a “social welfare function”, which, in certain circumstances, is shaped by the individual preferences of citizens. In a similar logic, the social welfare function could be a cumulative result of the individual welfare functions.

The normative public choice perspective reached its peak with the contribution of Arrow (1963), who specified five axioms, expressing value judgements, individuals’ assumptions and collective rationality, as essential components of the social welfare function or the constitution of society. These are as follows: (a) all possible classifications of individual preferences are allowed, (b) Pareto ordering, (c) transitivity, (d) non-dictatorship and (e) independence of irrelevant alternatives (Arrow, 1963; Sen, 1970).

The problem is that all these five principles are impossible to apply together. Thus, the actual economic policy decision-making process evolves through the loss of one or more of the above-mentioned assumptions, leaving a gap in who can decide how economic policy decisions are made. In this case, a general consensus is needed. The ultimate question is who will decide whether or not there is general consensus on a topic. Politicians or economists?

Several collective choices lead to a selection of equilibrium points along the Pareto Frontier, in which case analyses of the positivist public policy perspective apply, whereas others, following the normative perspective, include distribution and redistribution of resources. The two perspectives may produce the same results if the Pareto conditions are true, and the equilibrium points are along the Pareto Frontier. However, in order to select one of these points, value choices must be included in the analysis. That is to say, choices that refer to justice and ethics and which define societies. Finally, the social welfare function, the social contract or the constitution reflect these values.

4.8 The Evolutionary Perspective on Economic Policy-Making

At the core of evolutionary perspective, economic policy-making is related to the learning process. This perspective refers to the process of changing thoughts or behaviours, which derives from the experience created through the achievement of specific policy targets.

Policy-related learning includes a series of categories, such as social learning (Hall, 1993), political learning (Heclo, 1972), policy-oriented learning (Jenkins-Smith & Sabatier, 1993), and leaves open issues such as who learns, what they learn and so on. At all events, the process of the impact of the learning perspective on political change covers periods of more than a decade.

As in the neoclassical conception of policy decision-making and policy change, there are three sub-areas that make up the knowledge of the predictions of evolutionary theory regarding economic policy-making (Witt, 2003): these are the political economy for economic policy-making ("what policy does do"), the analysis of policy instruments aiming to specific results ("what policy could do") and the debate on political targets and their legitimization ("what policy ought to do") (Witt, 2003).

4.8.1 Political Economy for Economic Policy Formation

The debate focusing on the neoclassical public choice, as regards the conditions of economic policy-making, is a particularly forceful analytic framework for economic policy-making. Of course, the persistent tendency of neoclassical thought to search for an equilibrium point, which encourages static comparisons—along with the dimension that does not include time and presumes complete information about the actions undertaken—define the claims of this approach.

The inclusion in this analysis of the concept of time allows for the introduction of education as a factor in shaping future development. The introduction of time and education is combined with the prevalence of more realistic assumptions of bounded rationality, which focuses on the extent to which the means for fulfilling policy-making conditions are available, the analysis of the interests of the various pressure groups/lobbies, the means available for achieving policy targets and so on.

An essential point in the evolutionary perspective concerns the way in which public opinion is formed and, in general, the ways in which social action is organized. Consequently, the way in which communication between stakeholders is organized is extremely important.

In conclusion, the factors that play a role in the process of economic policy-making are the conditions of communication, socio-cognitive learning and the restriction in the required positivist and normative awareness (Witt, 2003).

4.8.2 *Economic Policy Means and Targets*

The starting point in the search for economic policy means and targets is the conditions of bounded rationality and the cognitive constraints of policymakers and individuals, insofar as they influence the education process.

However, in order to have a concrete conception consistent with the evolutionary perspective, as regards the means for achieving the most effective implementation of the economic policy target, we need to stress the role of individual incentives as affected by the proposed policy. When incentives are affected, the reaction to policy measures is shaped accordingly. Thus, an increase in tax rates does not automatically lead to a proportional increase in tax revenue, as it is likely to increase tax evasion. In actual fact, the agitation of personal incentives contributes to the accumulation of knowledge about policy targets.

Consequently, the historical (temporal) analysis of economic policy implementation answers the evolutionary analysis of the implementation of means for achieving economic policy targets in order to (a) assess how learning and research incentives will be affected and (b) assess the potential long-term individual and social reactions to the implementation of policy measures.

The divergence between means and targets, that is, the relationship between the policy implementation instruments and the goals they are called upon to serve, is the next area of concern. In this context, two ways of approaching the effects can be distinguished: spillovers and temporal effects. That is, when a policy implementation instrument is activated, it usually does not only affect one sector or one single economic change. Results are diffused in different sectors and are often unrelated. Also, the implementation of a policy instrument has effects in different time horizons. Short-term effects are likely to offset long-term effects and vice versa. Even more difficult to analyse is that the medium- to long-term effects may be identified much later. Moreover, the analysis may be particularly complicated when we consider that the decisions to use the instruments for policy implementation and achieving their targets must be adopted after discussion in the political field. Political economy analysis of the use of policy instruments is often extremely complex and challenging for participants to accept.

4.8.3 *The Evolutionary Normative Foundations*

Particular importance is also given to the normative framework of economic policy targets—"what policy ought to do". This is the level of analysis of economic policy-making in which the outcomes or targets are discussed in the light of normative crises. Then, questions arise such as the following: Are the goals set legitimized? If so, on what basis and by what criteria? Are the targets comparable to each other? What is the impact of this comparison?

A key element of the evolutionary approach is that the use of the concept itself and of the evolutionary method does not ensure that the conclusions will be useful in any way. Thus, the debate over the normative perspective of neoclassical thinking significantly retains its validity. An evolutionary perspective does not necessarily mean that one arrives at different (normative) conclusions from different methodologies. The view that a person's actual and normative knowledge may change leads to the conclusion that this process is likely to affect both the potential of normative decisions and judgements and their content. The actual experience of some norms and the pre-existing knowledge may influence preferences and final decisions, and this usually leads to a strong norm-relativism.

This approach is directly associated to the sources of economic vision in moral philosophy. What new insights can an evolutionary perspective contribute at this level, that is, to the normative foundations of economic policy-making? An exhaustive discussion is hardly possible here. However, the range of problems likely to be encountered in future research can perhaps be highlighted by elaborating on two points (Witt, 2003):

- The first relates to the normative judgements to which evolutionary economics implicitly subscribes when it is applied to policy advice—which, up to now, has happened mostly in connection with questions of R&D, technological progress, innovations and growth.
- The second point relates to a more general problem. In the evolutionary perspective, the basis for normative judgements may change: the ends and results of policy-making are assessed in a way which is itself evolving.

References

Acemoglu, D., Robinson, C., & Verdier, T. (2012). *Can't We All Be More Like Scandinavians? Asymmetric Growth and Institutions in An Interdependent World*. NBER Working Paper No. 18441.

Amenta, E., & Ramsey, K. L. (2010). Institutional Theory. In K. T. Leicht & J. C. Jenkins (Eds.), *Handbook of Politics: State and Society in Global Perspective* (pp. 15–39). Berlin: Springer, Science+Business Media.

Arrow, K. J. (1963). Uncertainty and the Welfare Economics of Medical Care. *The American Economic Review, 53*(5), 941–973.

Bartlett, C. A., & Ghoshal, S. (2002). Building Competitive Advantage Through People. *Sloan Management Review, 43*(2), 34–41.

Baumol, W. J. (1965). Informed Judgment, Rigorous Theory and Public Policy. *Southern Economic Journal, 23*(2), 137–145.

Bertola, G., Boeri, T., & Nicoletti, G. (2001). *Welfare and Employment in a United Europe*. Cambridge, MA: MIT Press.

Black, D. (1948). The Decisions of a Committee Using a Special Majority. *Econometrica: Journal of the Econometric Society, 16*(3), 245–261.

Boeri, T. (2002). *Let Social Policy Models Compete and Europe Will Win*. Presented at the Conference Hosted by the John F. Kennedy School of Government, Harvard University. Retrieved from https://pdfs.semanticscholar.org/750a/3ef492809a1dc6ab7eb2ec7b42233300a76f.pdf?_ga=2.242053122.1272309523.1584027716-832695318.1584027716

Boeri, T., Brugiavini, A., & Calmfors, L. (2001). *The Role of the Unions in the Twenty-first century*. London, Oxford: Oxford University Press.

Bruno, M. (1989). *Economic Analysis and the Political Economy of Policy Formation*. NBER Working Paper No. w3183. https://doi.org/10.3386/w3183

Buchanan, J. M. (1965). An Economic Theory of Clubs. *Economica, 32*(125), 1–14.

Buchanan, J. M. (1988). Market Failure and Political Failure. *Cato Journal, 8*(1), 1–13.

Buchanan, J. M., & Tullock, G. (1962). *The Calculus of Consent* (3rd ed.). Ann Arbor, MI: University of Michigan Press.

Chapman, G. B., & Johnson, E. J. (1999). Anchoring, Activation, and the Construction of Values. *Organizational Behavior and Human Decision Processes, 79*(2), 115–153.

Coase, R. H. (1937). The Nature of the Firm. *Economica, 4*(16), 386–405.

David, P. A. (2001). Path Dependence, Its Critics and the Quest for "Historical Economics". In P. Garrouste & S. Ioannides (Eds.), *Evolution and Path Dependence in Economic Ideas: Past and Present*. Cheltenham, UK: Edward Elgar.

Dosi, G., & Nelson, R. R. (2010). Technical Change and Industrial Dynamics as Evolutionary Processes. In B. H. Hall & N. Rosenberg (Eds.), *Handbook of the Economics of Innovation* (pp. 51–128). Amsterdam & Boston: Elsevier.

Ferrera, M. (1998). The Four 'Social Europes': Between Universalism and Selectivity. In M. Rhodes & Y. Mény (Eds.), *The Future of European Welfare*. London: Palgrave Macmillan.

Firestone, W. A. (1989). Educational Policy as an Ecology of Games. *Educational Researcher, 18*(7), 18–24.

Freeman, R. B. (2005). *Can the Social Dialogue EU Compare with the Market-Driven US?* Presented at the Conference on Social Impacts, Employment and Growth: A Reappraisal of Ezio Tarantelli's Thought, Faculty of Economics, University of Rome "La Sapienza", Rome.

Giddens, A. (1990). *The Consequences of Modernity*. Cambridge: Polity Press.

Giddens, A. (1991). *Modernity and Self-identity*. Cambridge: Polity Press.

Grunwald, A. (2013). Modes of Orientation Provided by Futures Studies: Making Sense of Diversity and Divergence. *European Journal of Futures Research*. https://doi.org/10.1007/s40309-013-0030-5

Hall, P. A. (1993). Policy Paradigms, Social Learning, and the State: The Case of Economic Policymaking. *Comparative Politics, 25*(3), 275–296.

Hall, P. A., & Gingerich, D. W. (2004). *Varieties of Capitalism and Institutional Complementarities in the Macroeconomy: An Empirical Analysis*. MPIfG (Max-Plank Institute for the Study of Societies) Discussion Paper 04/5. https://doi.org/10.1007/978-1-4757-4062-2_3

Hall, P. A., & Soskice, D. (2001). *Vaerieties of Capitalism. The Institutional Foundations of Comparative Advantage*. Oxford: Oxford University Press.

Hall, P. A., & Taylor, R. C. R. (1996). Political Science and the Three Institutionalisms. *Political Studies, 44*(5), 936–957.

Hayek, F. A. (1945). The Use of Knowledge in Society. *American Economic Review, 35*(4), 519–530.

Heclo, H. (1972). Policy Analysis. *British Journal of Political Science, 2*(1), 83–108. Retrieved from http://www.jstor.org/stable/193311

Henning, M., Stam, E., & Wenting, R. (2013). Path Dependence Research in Regional Economic Development: Cacophony or Knowledge Accumulation? *Regional Studies, Taylor & Francis Journals, 47*(8), 1348–1362.

Hoeffler, S., Ariely, D., & West, P. (2006). Path Dependent Preferences: The Role of Early Experience and Biased Search in Preference Development. *Organizational Behavior and Human Decision Processes, 101*(2), 215–229.

Hotelling, H. (1929). Stability in Competition. *Economic Journal, 39*(153), 41–57.

Jenkins-Smith, H., & Sabatier, P. (1993). Methodological Appendix. In P. Sabatier & H. Jenkins-Smith (Eds.), *Policy Change and Learning: An Advocacy Coalition Approach* (pp. 237–256). Boulder, CO: Westview Press.

Jerzmanowski, M. (2006). Empirics of Hills, Plateaus, Mountains, and Plains: A Markov-Switching Approach to Growth. *Journal of Development Economics, 81*(2), 357–385.

John, P. (2003). Is There Life After Policy Streams, Advocacy Coalitions, and Punctuations: Using Evolutionary Theory to Explain Policy Change? *Policy Studies Journal, 31*(4), 481–498.

Keynes, J. M. (1919). *The Economic Consequences of the Peace*. New York: Harcourt, Brace and Howe.

Kiser, E. (1999). Comparing Varieties of Agency Theory in Economics, Political Science and Sociology: An Illustration from State Policy Implementation. *Sociological Theory, 17*(2), 146–170.

Maliranta, M., Määttänen, N., & Vihriälä V. (2012). Are the Nordic Countries Really Less Innovative Than the US? *Vox, CEPR Policy Portal*. Retrieved from https://voxeu.org/article/nordic-innovation-cuddly-capitalism-really-less-innovative

March, C. J., & Olsen, J. (1984). The New Institutionalism: Organizational Factors in Political Life. *American Political Science Review, 78*(3), 734–749.

Millett, M. S. (2011). *Managing the Future: A Guide to Forecasting and Strategic Planning in the 21st Century*. Triarchy Press.

Mintzberg, H. (1994). The Fall and Rise of Strategic Planning. *Harvard Business Review, 72*(1), 107–114.

Molina, O., & Rhodes, M. (2007). The Political Economy of Adjustment in Mixed Market Economy: A Study of Spain and Italy. In B. Hancke, M. Rhodes, & M. Thatcher (Eds.), *Beyond Varieties of Capitalism: Conflict, Contradictions and Complementarities in European Economy* (pp. 223–251). Oxford: Oxford University Press.

Mueller, D. C. (1976). Public Choice: A Survey. *Journal of Economic Literature, 14*(2), 395–433.

North, D. C. (1990). *Institutions, Institutional Change and Economic Performance*. New York: Cambridge University Press.

O'Toole Jr., L. J. (1995). Rational Choice and Policy Implementation: Implications for Interorganizational Network Management. *The American Review of Public Administration, 25*(1), 43–57.

Olsen, E. (2012). *Strategic Planning Kit for Dummies* (2nd ed.). Hoboken, NJ: John Wiley & Sons, Inc.

Ostrom, E. (1990). *Governing the Commons: The Evolution of Institutions for Collective Action*. Cambridge: Cambridge University Press.

Petrakis, P. E., Valsamis, D. G., & Kafka, K. I. (2016). From an Optimal to a Stagnated Growth Prototype: The Role of Institutions and Culture. *Journal of Innovation & Knowledge, 2*(3), 97–105.

Pierson, C. P. (1994). *Dismantling the Welfare State?* Cambridge: Cambridge University Press.

Popper, K. R. (1957). *The Poverty of Historicism*. London: Routledge & Kegan Paul.

Rae, D. W. (1969). Decision-Rules and Individual Values in Constitutional Choice. *American Political Science Review, 63*(1), 40–56.

Rasmus, D. W. (2011). *Welcome to the Serendipity Economy, The Serendipity Economy Quantification Study Pilot Project Report.* Serious Insights. Retrieved from https://www.seriousinsights.net/welcome-to-the-serendipity-economy

Rawls, J. (1971). *A Theory of Justice.* Cambridge, MA: Harvard University.

Sapir, A. (2006). Globalization and the Reform of European Social Models. *Journal of Common Market Studies, Wiley Blackwell, 44*(2), 369–390.

Schmidt, V. (2002). *The Futures of European Capitalism.* Oxford: Oxford University Press.

Sen, A. K. (1966). A Possibility Theorem on Majority Decisions. *Econometrica: Journal of the Econometric Society, 34*(2), 491–499.

Sen, A. K. (1970). The Impossibility of a Paretian Liberal. *Journal of Political Economy, 78*(1), 152–157.

Strack, F., & Mussweiler, T. (1997). Explaining the Enigmatic Anchoring Effect: Mechanisms of Selective Accessibility. *Journal of Personality and Social Psychology, 73*(3), 437–446.

Stratmann, T. (2004). Logrolling 1. In C. K. Rowley & F. Schneider (Eds.), *The Encyclopedia of Public Choice.* Boston, MA: Springer.

Sutton, C. (1937). The Relation Between Economic Theory and Economic Policy. *The Economic Journal, 47*(185), 44–52.

Taleb, N. N. (2007). *The Black Swan: The Impact of the Highly Improbable.* New York: Random House.

Tullock, G. (1970). A Simple Algebraic Logrolling Model. *The American Economic Review, 60*(3), 419–426.

Weir, M., & Skocpol, T. (1985). State Structures and the Possibilities for 'Keynesian' Responses to the Great Depression in Sweden, Britain, and the United States. In P. B. Evans, D. Rueschemeyer, & T. Skocpol (Eds.), *Bringing the State Back* (pp. 107–164). Cambridge: Cambridge University Press.

Wernerfelt, B., & Karnani, A. (1987). Competitive Strategy Under Uncertainty. *Strategic Management Journal, 8*(2), 187–194.

Wicksell, K. (1896 [1958]). Finanztheoretische Untersuchungen. (Jena: Gustav Fischer. Engl. A New Principle of Just Taxation). In A. Musgrave & A. T. Peacock (Eds.), *Classics in the Theory of Public Finance* (pp. 72–118). London: Macmillan.

Williamson, O. E. (1973). Markets and Hierarchies: Some Elementary Considerations. *American Economic Review, American Economic Association, 63*(2), 316–325.

Williamson, O. E. (1981). The Modern Corporation: Origins, Evolution, Attributes. *Journal of Economic Literature, 19*(4), 1537–1568.

Williamson, O. E. (1985). *The Economic Institutions of Capitalism*. New York: The Free Press.
Winter, S. C. (2003). Implementation Perspectives: Status and Reconsideration. In B. G. Peters & J. Pierre (Eds.), *Handbook of Public Administration* (pp. 212–222). London: SAGE Publications.
Witt, U. (2003). Economic Policy Making in Evolutionary Perspective. *Journal of Evolutionary Economics, 13*(2), 77–94.

CHAPTER 5

The Determinants of Economic Policy Formation

5.1 Introduction

Economic science may formulate the determinants of economic growth, but it is the political system and the policy-makers who influence the outcome of the development process through their decisions. Shaping economic policy is a complex process that hinges on several determining factors.

The area where economic policy-making occurs and where most decisions are made is politics (Sect. 5.2). So, we need to analyse the importance of the political function in economic policy formulation (Sect. 5.2.1), the role of pressure groups and elites (Sect. 5.2.2), the importance of multi-level governance (Sect. 5.2.3), networks, partnerships and agency theory (Sect. 5.2.4). Learning theories, diffusion and punctuated equilibrium (Sect. 5.3) are concepts that underlie economic policy theories, while disruptive innovations also play an essential role (Sect. 5.4).

Institutions and cultural background (Sect. 5.5) have their share of responsibility and are therefore discussed in more detail later in the book (Chap. 7). Finally, we consider the behavioural approach to policy-making (Sect. 5.6).

P. E. Petrakis et al., *Economic Growth and Development Policy*,
https://doi.org/10.1007/978-3-030-43181-5_5

5.2 Political Systems and the Formation of Economic Policy

Political institutions are a way of allowing for the expression of individual preferences while balancing the collective conflicts that exist in society. They include the processes by which decisions are made and the control of administrators (governments, administrations, etc.) through the systems of electing representatives. They influence to a very large degree the way in which the social decision-making system is organized. Also, they create the right conditions for reducing the pressure from various interest groups that cause problems both in the smooth functioning of the economy and in the distribution of income and thus in economic growth. Of course, the way in which public administration is exercised and its effectiveness are also important. The interconnection of politics, and political institutions in general, with governance is a crucial issue in every society, in terms of conceptions of development and of growth. This is because politics takes precedence over the economy, in terms of ordering the importance of social priorities and making final decisions. In view of all this, the role of the economist is expanding as the problems of economies become increasingly complex.

In addition, political institutions are a way of aggregating or even concentrating individual preferences and conflicts that develop within society. Different political institutions shape different winners and losers and, therefore, represent a different balance of forces. This leads to an endless presence of social tension around the formation of political institutions.

It is now widely accepted that economic institutions are always important in terms of their effects on growth and are mainly shaped by political institutions. The system of government, the organization of the state, electoral law, the party system and the distribution of political influence are determinants of economic growth. So, for example, societies in which political institutions operate for the benefit of powerful elites possessing de facto political power—whether or not it is legitimized in the form of de jure power—are unable to create incentives for dynamic economic growth as the distribution of the social product is to their advantage and reproduces their dominant position.

There is thus a strong link between the way governance is run, or, in other words, the way politics is exercised, and the way an economy operates. Particularly in the last century, the relationship between economics and politics, and especially between economists and politicians, has completely changed (Rodrik, 2013). While this relationship was extremely distant, with economists avoiding politics, economists have now begun to examine political behaviour using the same conceptual framework they use for the market decisions of consumers and producers (Rodrik, 2013).

It is therefore established that (a) politicians may depend on the influential elites of societies, (b) those who benefit from commercial protectionism are usually clustered and exert political influence, while consumers are scattered and disorganized and unable to advance their interests, (c) the political elite (cf. Sect. 5.2.2) obstructs reforms that would promote growth and development because growth and development would undermine its political leverage and (d) banks intervene in the political processes, taking excessive risks. As a result, political decisions play an important role in economic developments (Rodrik, 2013).

Finally, economic activity influences political decisions and political decisions affect the state of the economy (Frey & Steiner, 2012). In particular, (a) the government systematically influences economic activity, through a large number of policy tools, from taxation and public expenditure to many different kinds of regulations, and (b) economic activity, as reflected in the size of and change in GDP, the unemployment rate and inflation, affects how popular a government is with the people and, hence, whether it will be re-elected.

5.2.1 Policy Change and Reforms

The modern world and economy are constantly changing under the influence of economic policies. The latter may cause smaller or greater gradual changes or may even take on the aspect of major reform programmes. Policy change should be differentiated from the concept of policy reform, which has far more ambitious goals than a gradual policy change (Cerna, 2013).

So, then, the distinction between the concepts of policy change and reform plays a very important role in the whole process. Moreover, a reform is characterized as a policy for the following reasons: (a) it represents a choice of values that expresses a particular view of society, (b) it has distinct distributional effects on the distribution of benefits and costs, (c) it promotes competition between groups seeking to influence the above consequences, (d) its institutionalization or non-institutionalization is closely linked to political events or political crises and (e) it can have very significant implications on the political stability of a regime (Reich, 1995).

At all events, what is needed for a reform to be successful? In answering the question, Reich (1995) argues that policy-makers need effective methods of analysing the relevant political conditions and formulating appropriate policy correlations which will favour political reform. In this context, he investigates three cases of political conditions under which policy reforms can occur. These are:

1. The model of political will, which is characterized by rational decision-making, while, however, ignoring the political constraints on political reform. It is more likely to emerge under political conditions, such as "a strong imperative, a strong state, a close coalition and a strong leadership".
2. The model of the political group, according to which politicians seek to satisfy the desires of different groups—interest groups, political parties. The reform, then, takes place when it distributes increased benefits to specific groups who are voters of government leaders.
3. The political survival model, in which government actors seek to protect their interests and to maintain or extend their position in power. So, politicians can operate opportunistically, to manipulate decisions in order to achieve desirable results for themselves. That is to say, there is reform made for personal reasons—that is, for political survival or the interests of political leaders (Reich, 1995).

A crucial factor in the success of reforms is the timing of their implementation. Thus, a change is more likely to take place at the beginning of a regime's coming to power, when major events can create political opportunities and room for reform. Therefore, drastic changes require not only careful design and execution but also the choice of the right time for implementing them. By contrast, smaller and gradual changes are less time-dependent (Reich, 1995).

Finally, Reich (1995) proposes a policy mapping model in which he examines dimensions that policy-makers must take into account for successful policy change. These are (a) the consequences of reform efforts, (b) the behaviour of the strategic players who interact during the whole process (i.e. whether they are in favour of or against the reform), (c) the analysis of the parties' intentions, (d) the relations of players within the political network, (e) ongoing transitions that create opportunities and (f) building strategies for change.

5.2.2 *Pressure Groups and Elite*

The term "elite" means the maintenance of much of the power by a small portion of society, a force that is independent of the democratic electoral process of a state. These are usually members of society who are directly involved in economic policy-making and have a significant influence on government policy decisions, as they usually hold strong positions in businesses and organizations and are directly involved with decision and policy centres—think tanks or policy discussion groups. In addition, elites also include large industrial and financial clusters.

Correspondingly, the term "pressure groups" generally refers to any social group, small or large, whose members share at least one common trait. This feature is most often about achieving a common goal. In economic science, the term "interest groups", in its broad meaning, refers to any non-governmental social group that seeks to pressure policy-makers exercising power in a particular direction, in order to safeguard or promote its goals, interests and objectives in general. The concept of a "pressure group" consists of three main features: (a) it is an organized group, (b) it defends specific interests and (c) it exerts pressure on power. Pressure groups include associations, industrial unions and professional associations.

Both elites and pressure groups exert pressure on the state in order to achieve their own goals. These two groups could be described by the common term "interest groups", the difference being (a) that the elite members are usually closer to the rulers than the members of a pressure group, which is also one reason their interests are more readily attainable and (b) that elites usually consist of a smaller number of members than pressure groups.

Olson (1965) further elaborated the basic principles of interest group theory which had been introduced by the mid-1960s. Olson's main conclusion was that without coercion or selective motivation, rational persons who are members of large groups would not take collective action, nor would they act to promote their collective interests. He also argues that special interest groups are active and are a crucial factor in how capital accumulates and technological progress evolves. Olson (1965) concluded that interest groups reduce investments as well as innovation through their activity and thus have a negative impact on economic progress. His theory was the kick-off for intense study and research on the subject, as well as grounds for intense debate. In particular, it is argued that interest groups provide collective goods to their members, often resulting in free-riding phenomena (Coates, Heckelman, & Wilson, 2007). Olson (1982) argues that society cannot expect to achieve a certain allocation of resources through a process of negotiating with these groups. Furthermore, established groups, as opposed to groups whose interests are not represented, are characterized by the fact that they dominate the market.

5.2.3 *Multi-Level Governance*

Multi-level governance (MLG) describes the diffusion of formal decision-making at multiple spatial levels (Hooghe & Marks, 2001). It was initially used in studies of the European Union as it was argued that European integration challenged the role of the state (Hooghe & Marks, 2003).

MLG offers a useful transition from policy change to policy implementation. For this reason, approaches such as "top-down" and "bottom-up" have been used. The first concerns the transition from a national to a lower level, while the second concerns the involvement of the local level in decision-making and its subsequent impact on higher levels.

Marks (1993) initially characterized MLG as the result of a "centrifugal process in which decision-making is diverted from the Member States in two directions", that is, to the subnational and supranational levels. Thus, it is a "system of continuous negotiations between governments at different levels—supranational, national and local" (Marks, 1993).

The MLG is divided into two types and is classified as either Type I or Type II, based on the following four questions: (a) Should responsibilities be designed around the particular character of the communities or should they be designed around particular policy problems? (b) Should responsibilities be combined or should they work in a specific context? (c) Should responsibilities be limited in number or not? (d) Should responsibilities be designed to be maintained or should they be subject to change? (Hooghe & Marks, 2003).

The first type of MLG consists of general-purpose jurisdiction at different levels. It mainly concerns the interaction and sharing of responsibilities. It also includes non-intersecting memberships, jurisdictions at a limited number of levels and a system-wide durable architecture (Hooghe & Marks, 2003). It is therefore related to a state-centred concept of policy (Conzelmann, 2008).

The second type of MLG is characterized by task-specific jurisdictions, intersecting memberships, many jurisdictional levels and the existence of flexible design, which means that responsibilities can change (Hooghe & Marks, 2003).

According to the first type of MLG, responsibilities take the form of a "trias politica" structure, which includes a legislative, executive and judicial body (Conzelmann, 2008). An example of the first type is the US federal government, while the second type is widespread locally in Swiss communities or even in specific areas of the USA (Hooghe & Marks, 2003).

5.2.4 *Networks, Partnerships and Representation*

A critical theory of policy change is the one described in the "Advocacy Coalition Framework (ACF)" (Sabatier, 1988). The ACF background includes the notion that there are ideological alliances which link causality and value outcomes for specific policies. Policy change is deemed acceptable because of the ability of these ideological alliances to answer specific questions about the operational consequences of the proposed policies.

The policy change model is based on a system of relatively stable parameters, which include the essential characteristics of the problem to be solved, the basic distribution of natural resources, the fundamental sociocultural values and, finally, critical regulatory, structural features.

This basic system influences the way in which external events are perceived, such as changes in socio-economic conditions, public opinion, changes in systemic administrative alliances and, finally, policy decisions, with their consequences on neighbouring decision systems relevant to the issue at stake.

These two conditions of the policy change model, namely the relatively more stable parameter system and the disguised "external" changes, shape the constraints and capabilities of the various subsystems, where the key actors come together in the issue with which policy change is concerned.

This creates alliances of political beliefs and resources that lead to the development of strategy and tools for policy redirection. These alliances may include politicians, lobbyists, researchers and more. In addition, policy brokers work to ensure that the level of political conflict does not exceed certain levels in order to allow for government decisions and programmes that produce concrete results.

The framework discussed above is shown in Fig. 5.1.

The ACF approach uses the concept of political beliefs in comparison to interest systems. Changes to critical aspects of a policy can be driven by changes in the external environment of the main and stable framework of

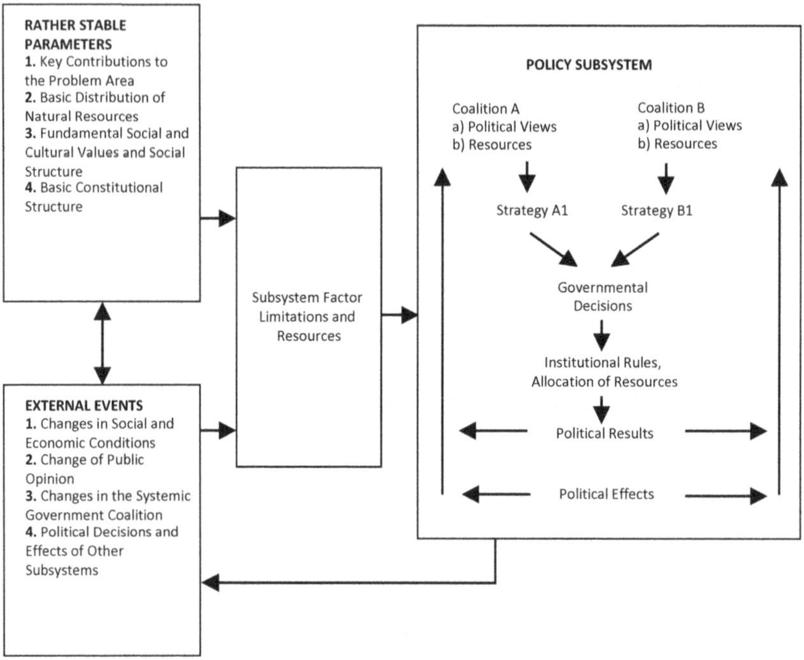

Fig. 5.1 The ACF approach. (Source: Sabatier, 1988, and authors' calculations)

the problem under discussion, such as macroeconomic conditions, the system of government alliance and so on.

At this point, it is useful to refer to the political networks and the theory of representation. The term "policy network" refers to "a group of individuals, where each individual has an interest or goal in a particular policy area and the ability to influence the failure or success of that policy" (Peterson & Bomberg, 1999).

The analysis of policy networks is based on three characteristics. First, modern governance usually operates in a non-hierarchical way, as few political decisions are imposed only by public authorities. Second, in order to analyse and understand the political process, it has to be broken down into its fundamental parts, as relations between groups and the government vary in many areas. Third, governments are fully responsible for governance, but before policies are set by politicians, they have somehow been defined in the negotiation between stakeholders (individuals and pressure groups), including non-governmental actors, all of whom have some vested interest in the policy selected (Peterson, 2003).

But political networks differ among themselves; their different types can be analysed through the Rhodes model of political networks (1990) which answers the following questions:

1. On the relative stability of the network composition: do the same factors tend to dominate decision-making over time, or does this change and adapt to the specific political issue under discussion?
2. On the relative isolation of the political network: is it a closed group that excludes third parties, or does it allow a range of people who may have different goals to access it?
3. On the strength of in-network dependencies: are network members highly dependent on each other, for example, in terms of money or experience, or are most individuals self-sufficient and therefore relatively independent of each other?

As an example of such networks we can consider social movements, which are structures within which organizations negotiate, based on the building of collective identities.

According to König (1998), the political network metaphorically describes the complexities of social and political life but does not explain either why private and public actors depend on each other or how this dependency affects public decision-making; it also does not produce hypotheses that can be checked against the importance of political networks in public decision-making. It is therefore a useful concept but does not constitute a model or theory.

Finally, agency theory—that is, the interaction in the principal-agent relationship and the empowerment of the latter to make decisions for the former—applies to economics, political science and sociology (Kiser, 1999). Political science researchers have emphasized three points: third parties, administrative procedures and where there is more than one principal. But agency theory leaves many questions unanswered, such as who exactly the principal is who is supposed to control the agents' actions and, finally, how the agents are selected.

5.3 Politics, Diffusion and Punctuated Equilibrium

According to the theory of policy diffusion, new policies are "transferred" from one government to another or from one economy to another (Shipan & Volden, 2008). Thus, the political, administrative and institutional dimensions that apply to a particular place at a given time are used for development policies and regulatory reforms in another geographical area at another time.

Shipan and Volden (2008), examining the mechanisms of policy diffusion, examined different types of anti-smoking policies applied to 675 US cities between 1975 and 2000, ultimately identifying four mechanisms by which this process takes place. These mechanisms are learning, economic competition, imitation and coercion.

By observing the implementation of one policy elsewhere, policy-makers can learn from the experiences of other governments. According to Berry and Baybeck (2005), "when faced with a problem, policy makers simplify the need to find a solution by choosing an alternative that has proven successful elsewhere". Thus, Shipan and Volden (2008) define their first hypothesis as follows: The likelihood of a city adopting a policy increases when the same policy has been widely adopted by other cities throughout the state.

The second mechanism is economic competition, which can lead to dispersal of policies from one place to another. This mechanism, together with the preceding one, is the dominant one in the process of policy diffusion. Shipan and Volden (2008) argue that the likelihood of a city adopting a policy decreases when it experiences negative economic impacts by the implementation of policies in nearby cities and increases when such effects are positive.

The third mechanism—imitation—refers to the ability of one government to duplicate the actions of another. The nature of imitation can be perceived by contrast to learning. As part of the learning process, policy-makers focus on the policy implemented elsewhere, in terms of effectiveness and outcomes of its implementation. Instead, imitation focuses on the need to duplicate a policy implemented by another government—what did that government do, and how can we apply it to make it look the same? The crucial distinction is that learning focuses on action (i.e. on the policy adopted by another government), while imitation focuses on the actor (i.e. on the other government that implemented this policy).

Finally, coercion refers to the process of mandatory policy enforcement. This mechanism is different from the other three which are voluntary. For example, countries have the ability to coerce one another directly through trade practices and financial sanctions and indirectly through pressure on international organizations such as the United Nations and the International Monetary Fund.

A rather different perception of policy change formation is that described by the punctuated equilibrium model (Baumgartner & Jones, 1991). This model describes a situation in which one idea of political change competes with others until one of them prevails. This process is triggered by an important external political event that is capable of disrupting existing balances. Then, the dispersal of different policies of change will not cease until one prevails over the others and a new balance is formed, which in turn will be subject to future change. It is a process that involves the interplay of beliefs and values related to a particular policy change, within a specific institutional framework.

5.4 Disruptive Innovation

To the factors that shape policy-making belongs the concept of disruptive innovation. The concept of disruptive innovation comes from management and was coined by C. Christensen in his work *The Innovator's Dilemma* (1997). It is particularly important, especially when referring to drastic changes, and has therefore been used in a wide range of policy areas (Christensen, Aaron, & Clark, 2003). Revolutionary innovation needs to be differentiated from sustainable innovation, with the latter more closely linked to the introduction of improved performance into existing services, systems or products within a defined path (OECD, 2009).

The process of disruptive innovation consists of two stages. In the first, the innovator makes a product simpler and more accessible to use than an existing one, while in the second, additional technological changes in an industry make the process of product upgrading and manufacturing simpler (Christensen, Horn, & Johnson, 2008). In other words, the theory explains the phenomenon in which an innovation transforms an existing market or sector, where there is a complexity and high cost, introducing the following: simplicity, convenience and affordability, thus making the products and services of this sector more accessible to a larger population.

A classic example of revolutionary innovation is Apple in the field of personal computers. Before its entry into the field of computers, the prices and size of Apple's products did not allow them to be acquired by the majority of the population. Gradually, Apple succeeded in creating a small and economical PC, essentially creating a new market. Similar is the case in the automotive industry with Ford's "T" model, which was essentially the first car to reach a large part of the population. Finally, an example of revolutionary innovation in the field of education is online learning, as it makes learning more economical and feasible for people who otherwise would not have access to knowledge (Christensen et al., 2003).

5.5 The Role of Institutions and Cultural Background

Streeck and Thelen (2005) have developed a useful typology for the concept of institutional change. Institutions are "standardized precepts that can be enforced through third parties". While institutional change is not necessarily identical to policy change, these two concepts can interact. Theories of institutional change can also be theories of policy change, with policies being institutions, in the sense that they are in some ways rules for individuals (Streeck & Thelen, 2005).

Initially, Streeck and Thelen (2005) presented a typology of outcomes and processes of change, processes that indicate whether the change is incremental or abrupt. Moreover, they divide the effect of change into continuous and discontinuous. For example, with incremental and continuous change, we would expect reproduction through adaptability. But when change is abrupt and discontinuous, we would expect breakdown and replacement of institutions. The above are presented in Table 5.1.

Table 5.1 Typology of results and processes

		Result of change	
		Continuous	*Discontinuous*
Process of change	Incremental	Reproduction through adaptability	Gradual transformation
	Abrupt	Survival and return	Breakdown and replacement

Source: Streeck and Thelen (2005), and authors' creation

Streeck and Thelen (2005) then introduce five different types of change: displacement, layering, drift, conversion and exhaustion. These types of changes are discussed below:

- In the first case, institutional formations are susceptible to change, as traditional structures resist new institutions and are unable to incorporate changes into fixed behaviours. Such changes often occur through the discovery or activation of institutional forms.
- The second type—layering change—involves modifications, additions or revisions to existing institutions. Changes occur when the introduction of new elements displaces or replaces the old system over time.
- In drift, institutions are subject to corrosion or atrophy if they do not adapt to the changing political and economic environment. The drift can be created by gaps in rules.
- In conversion, institutions are redirected to new goals, functions or goals. This can occur as a result of environmental changes, through changes in the allocation of forces or through political disputes over existing institutions and the functions/purposes they serve.
- Finally, exhaustion can occur when there is a gradual collapse of an institution over time.

5.6 The Behavioural Approach

Behavioural economics assumes that humans do not behave in a perfectly rational way. Thus, behavioural economics incorporate into their analysis elements from other social sciences, such as psychology and sociology. According to the World Bank report (2015): *Mind, Society, and Behavior*, individuals make decisions in a variety of ways.

First, a great many individual decisions are made automatically, based on what comes to mind without further thought. In other words, individuals use patterns of ideas that derive mainly from past decisions, while operating through mental shortcuts. They are, therefore, based on a narrow framework, which can lead to unrealistic approaches to reality. The above contradicts the view that individuals consider all possible choices or consequences of their actions.

Second, individuals think within the broader rules imposed by their social environment. They have innate characteristics such as altruism, cooperation and reciprocity and are influenced by the networks of their communities. Therefore, their preferences and decisions are influenced by what other people think, expect and do. Besides, social recognition and the power of social incentives—social status, reward—are significantly involved in decision-making and behaviour.

Third, individuals do not respond to an objective experience but to mental representations that come from their experiences and the cultural/spiritual model in which they live. People have access to multiple and often conflicting spiritual models that provide them with an interpretation of the world and include concepts, stereotypes and worldviews. Therefore, what people perceive and how they explain it depends on the context in which they see the world around them. Most spiritual models in a society are shared experiences that can be passed on to future generations and have the characteristics of perseverance and non-functionality (World Bank, 2015).

From the foregoing, it becomes apparent that even seemingly irrelevant details, such as how a situation is presented, can influence individuals' perceptions as they tend to make decisions in the light of limited information while thinking non-rationally. Thus, small changes in circumstances can have a major impact on behaviour and on achieving policy goals.

In this context, according to Dawnay and Shah (2005), policy-makers must consider the seven principles that characterize human behaviour. These are (a) the behaviour of other people affects an individual's way of thinking (the person copies, observes, does something they think is acceptable), (b) habits are essential and difficult to change, (c) people are motivated to do something which they consider "right, (d) expectations influence people's behaviours (i.e. their actions depend on their values and commitments), (e) individuals have a loss-averse attitude, (f) individuals have difficulty in making calculations when making decisions (they cannot calculate probabilities and do not worry about unexpected events) and (g) in order to make a change, people want to feel that they are involved and effective in this process.

In this context, the role of the "Choice Architect" (CA) is particularly important. A CA is anyone who can organize the context in which people's decision-making takes place, presenting a set of options and making a choice more attractive or easier to choose than its alternatives (Thaler & Sunstein, 2008).

Governments are just one player among many trying to influence the choices people make. For example, banks frame the complexity of their loan packages by making them more attractive. Elites of all kinds use informal rules to shape public opinion for the benefit of the groups they represent. Consequently, several stakeholders try to exploit people's tendency to think automatically for their own benefit. At this point it is reasonable to pose the following question: Should governments intervene and act as CAs?

According to conventional economics, the main justification for a government to intervene involves cases where the market fails to function effectively, such as when there are monopoly conditions on the market, externalities, public goods, asymmetric information and cases of disruption in the wider macroeconomic stability. Yet, the government has still another reason to intervene, and that is when social practices and the broader social context lead individuals to a state of perpetual poverty and underdevelopment. As decision-making is often based on the most accessible information—influenced by social/spiritual models—individuals' preferences and immediate goals do not always promote their own interests. In addition, social practices may not support prosperity but lead individuals to low expectations/ambitions—due to pessimism, social discrimination, inequality and so on (World Bank, 2015).

Political interventions should, therefore, be aimed at improving confidence, encouraging collective action and, finally, exposing individuals to new ways of thinking (alternative experiences) that extend their spiritual boundaries (such as women's leadership). In addition, policy-makers should keep in mind that the role of incentives is more complex than generally thought, as social incentives may be more powerful than economics. Recognition of the above can lead to an understanding of the causes of specific policy failures and to the development of policies and interventions that promote prosperity and reduce poverty.

But how can governments act as CAs? First, the main component of shaping choices is through simplifying them. Simplifying the choice environment can help individuals make choices to their advantage, as the variety/complexity of options can lead them to avoid/postpone a decision or make the wrong choice. The foregoing has important implications for policy-making.

For example, the political intervention in 1998 that simplified the voting process in Brazil had significant social consequences. Elections in Brazil were held through paper ballots, in which voters filled in the name of the candidate of their choice. But as only about 60% of voters had partially completed primary education, less than 70% of voters filled in the ballots correctly and the rest were declared invalid. In early 1998, Brazil changed its voting system. The new system required voters to fill in the candidate's number using a simple keypad, and when the voter filled in the number, the candidate's face appeared on the screen. The voter confirmed his choice by pressing a green button or cancelling it by pressing orange. When Brazil simplified the electoral process, more people—who were illiterate, fully or partially—were able to cast valid ballots in the ballot box, and the reduction in invalid votes fell immediately to 11%. Thus, with the increased influence of poorer sections of the population on the electoral process, more candidates from parties friendly to them were elected; this led to a 34% increase in public spending on public health within eight years, an increase in the rate of illiterate women who visited the doctor before pregnancy by 20%, the increased health of new-borns and a 6% decrease in low birth weight infants (World Bank, 2015).

Second, governments can act as CAs through nudge policies. These policies are aimed at changing people's behaviour without really changing the set of options. They do not prohibit or reward any choice. Rather, they turn people towards a particular choice (Thaler & Sunstein, 2008). For example, if the government's goal is to increase the consumption of healthy foods, banning unhealthy foods is not the solution. On the contrary, a policy that requires stores to place healthy products on shelves at eye level or near the cash register is a nudge for the buyer to choose them (Kroese, Marchiori, & de Ridder, 2016; Thaler & Sunstein, 2008).

An attempt to increase savings through psychological interventions could also be considered a "nudge" policy (Choi, Haisley, Kurkoski, & Massey, 2012). For example, psychological interventions, in the case of a corporate retirement savings plan—employees accept to have an amount deducted from their monthly pay—are savings goals and savings limits—the maximum contribution or the minimum contribution paid by the employee. Choi et al. (2012) have shown that if saving cues are used in the messages received by employees to participate more actively in the savings plan, then savings contributions will increase.

Nudge policies have received strong criticism regarding their "moral" dimension (Schubert, 2016; Smith, Goldstein, & Johnson, 2013). According to Schubert (2016), in the evaluation of these policies the following questions arise: (a) Do they really increase people's well-being? This question stems from the inability of behavioural economists to give a widely accepted definition of well-being. (b) Do they affect individuals' autonomy? Does simplifying the set of choices ultimately lead to the manipulation of freedom of choice? (c) Do they affect the integrity of individuals? The policy of promoting post-mortem organ donation has proven fairly effective, yet it is a policy that may contradict the argument on integrity (Smith et al., 2013).

As we saw above, governments can act as CAs by simplifying procedures and through nudge policies. There are some areas—education, early childhood development, financial management, productivity—in which governments could intervene, especially in the case of poor households (World Bank, 2015).

Many factors need to be taken into account before designing a policy programme aimed at helping people in poverty. For example, if the government wants to increase children's participation in secondary education, it can do so through funding, an information campaign, or through scholarships. In this decision, the government should take into account the cognitive-psychological factors and the social barriers that may be involved. If the intervention coincides with a period of low income, a policy-maker may shift the decision to a more financially sound period, while if the reluctance of the family to enrol their child in secondary education stems from the lack of ambition in society, then programmes aimed at tackling wider pessimism may prove more useful.

Also, children who grow up in low-income families face a considerable lack of prospects. Thus, anti-poverty measures can have an indirect effect on the development of children by reducing the psychological burden of interacting with parents. Many of the most successful early childhood development programmes educate local community members and provide parents with psychological and social support in order to improve the parents' interaction with their children.

Also, the consequences of biased economic decision-making can be profound for people in poverty, as they tend to base their decisions on limited data rather than looking at their overall economic situation. For example, they cannot understand the real costs of a loan as, according to experiments, the probability of these individuals borrowing through payday loans (payable within four months) is reduced by 11% once they are aware of the accumulated liabilities in case the loan remains pending for three months (World Bank, 2015).

Finally, in the field of productivity, too, more factors need to be taken into account when selecting policies aimed at increasing it. First, there are many non-numerical aspects of labour that affect employee performance, and the effectiveness of interventions varies due to the heterogeneity of individuals. Time lag between effort and pay, for example, can cause employees to procrastinate and can reduce their efficiency. Moreover, merely acknowledging good performance—a no-cost policy—can lead to improvement. Second, it's not only policy intervention that is important, but also the process of its implementation. For example, a policy implemented in Kenya aimed at increasing agricultural productivity, through a discount to farmers on fertilizers, was most effective when the discounts were applied directly after the harvest—when farmers had cash in their hands—compared to when they were applied several months later (World Bank, 2015).

References

Baumgartner, F., & Jones, B. (1991). Agenda Dynamics and Policy Subsystems. *The Journal of Politics, 53*(4), 1044–1074.

Berry, W. D., & Baybeck, B. (2005). Using Geographic Information Systems to Study Interstate Competition. *American Political Science Review, 99*(4), 505–519.

Cerna, L. (2013). The Nature of Policy Change and Implementation: A Review of Different Theoretical Approaches. *Organisation for Economic Cooperation and Development (OECD) Report.* Retrieved from http://www.etudes-fiscales-internationales.com/media/01/00/2853304334.pdf

Choi, J., Haisley, E., Kurkoski, J., & Massey, C. (2012). Nudges to Nudge up the Savings Rate. *Vox, CEPR Policy Portal.* Retrieved from https://voxeu.org/article/nudges-nudge-savings-rate

Christensen, C. M. (1997). *The Innovator's Dilemma: When New Technologies Cause Great Firms to Fail.* Boston: Harvard Business School Press.

Christensen, C. M., Aaron, S., & Clark, W. (2003). Disruption in Education. *Educause Review, 38*(1), 44–54.

Christensen, C. M., Horn, M., & Johnson, C. (2008). *Disrupting Class: How Disruptive Innovation Will Change the Way the World Learns.* New York: McGraw Hill.

Coates, D., Heckelman, J. C., & Wilson, B. (2007). Determinants of Interest Group Formation. *Public Choice, 133*(3), 377–391.

Conzelmann, T. (2008). A New Mode of Governing? Multi-Level Governance Between Cooperation and Conflict. In T. Conzelmann & R. Smith (Eds.), *Multi-Level Governance in the European Union: Taking Stock and Looking Ahead.*

Dawnay, E., & Shah, H. (2005). *Behavioural Economics: Seven Principles for Policy Makers.* London: New Economics Foundation. Retrieved from http://www.neweconomics.org/gen/z_sys_PublicationDetail.aspx?PID=213

Frey, B. S., & Steiner, L. (2012). Political Economy: Success or Failure? *Contemporary Economics, 6*(3), 10–21. Retrieved from https://ssrn.com/abstract=2179859

Hooghe, L., & Marks, G. (2001). *Multi-Level Governance and European Integration*. Lanham, MD: Rowman & Littlefield.

Hooghe, L., & Marks, G. (2003). Unravelling the Central State, but How? Types of Multi-Level Governance. *American Political Science Review, 97*(2), 233–243.

Kiser, E. (1999). Comparing Varieties of Agency Theory in Economics, Political Science and Sociology: An Illustration from State Policy Implementation. *Sociological Theory, 17*(2), 146–170.

König, T. (1998). Introduction: Modelling Policy Networks. *Journal of Theoretical Politics, 10*(4), 382–407.

Kroese, F. M., Marchiori, D. R., & de Ridder, D. T. D. (2016). Nudging Healthy Food Choices: A Field Experiment at the Train Station. *Journal of Public Health, 38*(2), 133–137.

Marks, G. (1993). Structural Policy and Multilevel Governance in the EC. In A. W. Cafruny & G. G. Rosenthal (Eds.), *The State of the European Community, The Maastricht Debates and Beyond* (pp. 391–410). Boulder, CO: Harlow Longman.

OECD. (2009). *OECD Reviews of Regional Innovation: 15 Mexican States*. Paris: OECD Publishing.

Olson, M. (1965). *The Logic of Collective Action*. Harvard Economic Studies. Cambridge: Harvard University Press.

Olson, M. (1982). *The Rise and Decline of Nations: Economic Growth, Stagflation and Social Rigidities*. New Haven: Yale University.

Peterson, J. (2003). Policy Networks. *IHS Political Science Series Working Paper* No. 90. Retrieved from http://aei.pitt.edu/764/1/pw_90.pdf

Peterson, J., & Bomberg, E. (1999). *Decision-Making in the European Union*. Basingstoke and New York: Palgrave.

Reich, M. (1995). The Politics of Health Sector Reform in Developing Countries – 3 Cases of Pharmaceutical Policy. *Health Policy, 32*(1–3), 45–77.

Rhodes, R. A. W. (1990). Policy Networks: A British Perspective. *Journal of Theoretical Politics, 2*(2), 293–317.

Rodrik, D. (2013). The Tyranny of Political Economy. *Project Syndicate*. Retrieved from https://www.project-syndicate.org/commentary/how-economists-killed-policy-analysis-by-dani-rodrik?barrier=accesspaylog

Sabatier, P. A. (1988). An Advocacy Coalition Framework of Policy Change and the Role of Policy-Oriented Learning Therein. *Policy Sciences, 21*(2–3), 129–168.

Schubert, C. (2016). A Note on the Ethics of Nudges. *Vox, CEPR Policy Portal*. Retrieved from https://voxeu.org/article/note-ethics-nudges

Shipan, C. R., & Volden, C. (2008). The Mechanisms of Policy Diffusion. *American Journal of Political Science, 52*(4), 840–857.

Smith, C. N., Goldstein, D. G., & Johnson, E. J. (2013). Choice Without Awareness: Ethical and Policy Implications of Defaults. *Journal of Public Policy & Marketing, 32*(2), 159–172.

Streeck, W., & Thelen, K. (2005). Institutional Change in Advanced Political Economies. In W. Streeck & K. Thelen (Eds.), *Beyond Continuity: Institutional Change in Advanced Political Economies*. Oxford: Oxford University Press.

Thaler, R. H., & Sunstein, C. R. (2008). *Nudge: Improving Decisions About Health, Wealth and Happiness*. New York: Penguin Books.

World Bank. (2015). *Mind, Society, and Behavior*. World Development Report. Retrieved from https://www.worldbank.org/content/dam/Worldbank/Publications/WDR/WDR%202015/WDR-2015-Full-Report.pdf

CHAPTER 6

Targets, Instruments and Policy Implementation

6.1 Introduction

This chapter focuses on the targets of economic policy and the instruments for shaping it. Specifically, the conditions for implementing economic policy are presented, along with the relationship between targets and policy instruments in the course of implementing economic policy.

The discussion about the relationship between targets and instruments is based on the contribution of Tinbergen and Theil (Sect. 6.2.1) on the number of means available as regards the targets, and on the contribution of Lucas (Sect. 6.2.2), about the impact of the changing process of structural relationships themselves, during the implementation of economic policy. The role of game theory in economic policy development is then analysed (Sect. 6.2.3).

Finally, as regards economic policy implementation (Sect. 6.3), the factors are described that influence the methodology of economic policy, followed by the distinction between "top-down" and "bottom-up" approaches or combinations thereof.

6.2 Targets and Instruments

The instruments and targets for achieving economic policy are critical to understanding the process of policy-making and change. Policy change may occur at three hierarchical levels or orders (Greener, 2002). The first order occurs when only the parameters of existing policy instruments

P. E. Petrakis et al., *Economic Growth and Development Policy*,
https://doi.org/10.1007/978-3-030-43181-5_6

change, while the second order occurs when the policy instruments themselves change. Finally, the third order applies when policy-makers reject the existing framework of ideas for understanding the world—and the broader significance of the policy targets they set—and replace it with another model (policy paradigm shift).

More specifically, in the context of pursuing economic policy targets, policy-makers act on the basis of a specific policy model. Often, however, the results of their actions conflict with the targets they set. This raises the question of the relationship between policy targets and instruments.

Three areas of concern are developed in this context. The first area is presented through the relationship between policy targets and instruments, as formulated by Tinbergen and Theil's contribution (Theil, 1964a; Tinbergen, 1952, 1956). The second area arises from the observation that during the performance of economy policy actions, the condition to which all the parameters of the system change and not only the effects are of particular importance. Lucas' Critique made the most significant contribution. Finally, the third area concerns the role of games.

6.2.1 *Targets of Tinbergen and Theil and the Policy Means (Instruments) Approach*

The theory of economic policy was founded by Dutch economist Jan Tinbergen (1939), who developed econometric models of economic policy implementation before and after World War II, as director of the Netherlands Central Planning Bureau.

Tinbergen's view assumed that an economy—and the economic system in general—can be satisfactorily represented in a system of linear equations. In particular, he argued that the question of controlling the relationship between targets and means of achieving them can be resolved if there are a set of independent policy targets to be achieved and a set of specific means (instruments) for doing so (Tinbergen, 1952, 1956). The above-mentioned issue can be managed if the "golden rule" is followed, according to which the number of independent instruments is equal to the number of independent targets that have been set. At the same time, the instruments should be linearly independent, since it is necessary to produce independent results, which in turn influence the target set. This is a first-best policy action, which constitutes a necessary and sufficient condition for controlling the economic policy system.

During the same period, Theil (1964b) identified four obstacles in the formulation of first-best policy solutions. These relate to uncertainty about (a) the data used, (b) the variables, targets and instruments—insofar as these are controlled by decision centres, for example, lobby groups, (c) the model used and (d) the choice of variable targets.

It is clear, then, that Theil's analysis was based on the incorporation of uncertainty deriving from Tinbergen's need to set specific policy targets and instruments. Theil argues that it is preferable to assume that the decision-maker maximizes a preference function or minimizes a loss function, setting as limitations to the problem the ability of the economy to function. So, he successfully avoids the a priori selection of variable targets and, after a manner, solves the problem that arises when the available instruments are less than the targets. He can, thus, solve policy problems in a non-Tinbergen world.

Theil basically enters the field of public choice theory (see Chap. 4, Sect. 4.7) as it could conceivably provide solutions in the area of economic policy-making. He also fosters the presence of an objective function and substantially develops the theory of economic policy along a dynamic axis, by introducing the concepts of optimal control theory (Bellman, 1961). Issues of the dynamic approach to economic policy-making have also been treated by others, including Preston (1974) and Leontief (1976).

The above-mentioned two approaches may help formulate a unique sequence of actions that help to control the decisions and policies of the system wherein economy, policy targets and policy instruments function. Alternatively, second best solutions may emerge.

In any case, the main objective of economic policy theory is to develop general rules for its control. Also based on the general rules is the debate on the available instruments and targets of economic policy in other economics fields (Hansen, 1958), which continue to this day. A typical example is the debate that has emerged on the changes identified in macroeconomics—mainly after the great crisis of 2008—to do with understanding short-term, non-macroeconomic developments (Blanchard, 2017).

Macroeconomic attention over the past 30 years has focused almost exclusively on solving a problem—for example, nominal rigidities of key economic variables such as wages—using only one tool at a time. Because of this logic, analysts and decision-makers have come up with an oversimplified analysis and a poor arsenal for dealing with the great crisis of 2008. Obviously, however, the variables targeted by economic policy are many more and much more complex. This is the oversight whereby economists were unable to foresee the onset of the 2008 crisis and understand the means at their disposal for dealing with it (Blanchard, 2017).

6.2.2 *Lucas' Structural Change*

Lack of understanding of policy problems, the choice of targets and the instruments to achieve them, is one side of the problem of effective economic policy implementation. The other side of the problem occurs when the whole system is changing, with the structural parameters, which actually link policy targets and instruments, changing as well.

In his paper, "Econometric Policy Evaluation: A Critique" (1976), Lucas argues that economic policy is ineffective due to the fact that it changes the structure of the economic system. The quantitative change in policy targets affects the coefficients of the estimated behavioural equations, as the expectations of firms and households depend on the policy means under consideration. Lucas' Critique has helped change economists' view of large-scale macroeconomic models (mainly Keynesian) in the 1960s and early 1970s. According to Lucas' Critique, econometric estimates and analyses, based on past experience, cannot be used to predict in advance the impact of economic policy.

Lucas Jr. (1976) essentially criticizes macroeconomic models that do not take into account changes in the estimated coefficients of the model's behavioural equations. The problem, according to Lucas, comes from the fact that the behaviour of households and firms often depends on the very rules of government policy. The solution given by Lucas is that private actors form rational expectations, based on all available information, in order to respond to changes in policy rules.

In actual fact, by introducing rational expectations into the economic system, Lucas adds the concept of losing control over economic policy as well. Thus, economic policy decision-makers are weakened regarding the strength of the policy they support. So, potentially, this policy maybe is not useful. The real question, however, is whether, in the context of rational expectations, the reactions of individuals and firms are strong enough to neutralize economic policy. Also, the way now opens for the introduction of conflicts into the analysis.

6.2.3 Policy and Games

Over time, the recognition of conflicts and the introduction of games, as a key platform for balancing economic policy, have replaced the traditional approach of Tinbergen and Theil (Acocella, Di Bartolomeo, & Hallett, 2012). This gave us the opportunity to analyse a situation, which accepts the possibility that the decision-making system may react to the formulation of a policy as a result of the development of opposing targets by the leading stakeholders.

For example, in the case of monetary policy, a game is formed between the central bank—which has the changing nominal interest rates as policy instrument—and the private sector—which has nominal wages at its disposal. Here, we can see that, under conditions of rational expectations, there is a complete elimination of the effects of monetary policy on the real product—monetary policy neutrality.

But the rules of the game that lead to policy neutrality may be affected when (a) there is uncertainty in the system (Rogoff, 1985), (b) non-competitive markets are introduced into the analysis or (c) the mix of policy targets and instruments is differentiated.

Thus, in order to avoid or promote the neutrality of economic policy, the potential conflicts between the targets of the different centres that shape it have to be considered, along with the extent to which and number of policy means-instruments available to each policy-maker. In addition, in order to formulate a sustainable economic policy programme, the mutual compatibility between the targets and the strategies followed must be assessed.

These observations lead to a general golden policy rule, between targets and means to achieve them, in the presence of many economic policy-makers/players, according to which the total number of instruments available to all players must not exceed the total number of targets of all players. This is a prerequisite for achieving a Nash equilibrium (Acocella, Di Bartolomeo, & Hallett, 2011). Finally, this rule—to the extent that it is applicable—reveals both its design conditions and the conditions for an ideal institutional framework.

6.3 Policy Implementation

In the context of the implementation of economic policy, two dimensions are analysed. The first concerns the factors affecting the implementation of economic policy, and the second concerns the distinction between "top-down" or "bottom-up" approaches, or a combination of the two. Then, their advantages and disadvantages are analysed.

6.3.1 *Factors Affecting Economic Policy Implementation*

Policy implementation is in line with policy change, as the former may take the form of a political decision that may be incorporated by a government bill or take the form of important implementing/judicial decisions (Mazmanian & Sabatier, 1983). Also, another policy decision recognizes the problem that needs to be addressed and defines the targets and structures of the implementation process (Sabatier & Mazmanian, 1979). However, in order to be considered successful, new policies require their proper implementation by policy-makers.

But what are the factors that affect the process of implementing a policy? In general, we could consider the following as factors that enhance the likelihood of successful policy implementation: (a) the ability and will of policy-makers, (b) the positive political climate, (c) the existence of the necessary resources to support policy implementation, (d) setting clear targets, (e) the compliance of those responsible with the framework directives and (f) defining which authorities are to be accountable for achieving specific targets (Fullan, 2009; McLaughlin, 1987).

However, it considered quite challenging to identify and delineate specific factors, as successful implementation depends on a broader correlation of uncertain political, social and economic factors. Thus, the search for general solutions can lead to policies that are not suitable for all situations ("one-size-fits-all"). It is, therefore, necessary to identify the broader context and the particular circumstances in force in each case.

Even if policy implementation seems to be successful, there is no guarantee that success will last. Therefore, a number of factors must be satisfied in order to increase the likelihood of a successful and sustainable implementation, making the task more difficult (Fullan, 2000).

6.3.2 "Top-Down" and "Bottom-Up" Approaches

The literature on policy-making and implementation gives particular emphasis to two approaches, namely "top-down" and "bottom-up". These two present a range of factors, such as the role of actors, their relationships and the types of policies being implemented.

"Top-down" theorists perceive policy-makers as central actors, focus on factors that can be centrally manipulated and prioritize clear policies (Cerna, 2013; Matland, 1995). The most detailed version of this approach was presented by Sabatier and Mazmanian (1979), who initially identified a range of variables (legal, political, etc.) that affect the policy implementation process at different stages. Then, they grouped these variables into a list of six, generally necessary and sufficient conditions for effective policy implementation. These variables are as follows:

1. Clear and consistent targets, as these provide a template that can be used by those responsible for implementation as a measure for ongoing project evaluation.
2. Adequate causal theory, in the sense that the implementation of a policy must contain a theory—through useful guidelines—aiming at causing social change.
3. Legal infrastructure for the implementation process, as there must be a range of legal mechanisms (sanctions, incentives, vetoes, etc.) to ensure the compliance of those responsible for implementation and wider social groups with the new policy.
4. Loyal and skilful officials.
5. Continuing political-social support to the new policy over time—for example, by interest groups/lobbies and state authorities.
6. Changes in socio-economic conditions that will not undermine political support and causal theory. For example, a war, military or commercial, may have a dramatic impact on the implementation of a policy (Sabatier, 2005).

By contrast, "bottom-up" theorists argue that policy is implemented locally (Cerna, 2013). They further emphasize on the networks of individuals—their targets, strategies, activities and contacts—that are involved in policy implementation at one or more local levels. Then, they use these elements to develop a networking technique for identifying local, regional and national dimensions involved in the planning, financing and implementation of relevant governmental and non-governmental programmes (Hanf, Hjern, & Porter, 1978). This process offers a mechanism for moving from local actors to policy-makers (Sabatier, 2005).

Both approaches have advantages and disadvantages. The "top-down" approach seeks and develops general policy recommendations that can be used as templates in various areas of policy implementation. On the other hand, the "bottom-up" approach, focusing on the local level, does not provide regulatory advice, but describes the factors that impede the achievement of the targets pursued. Therefore, it provides—through the identification of targets, strategies and activities of the people involved at the local level—the information necessary to adapt policy implementation strategies at the local level (Cerna, 2013; Matland, 1995). Nevertheless, the first approach, by not taking into account the local level, offers a management process that relies solely on policy-maker level. Correspondingly, the second approach places too much emphasis on the level of local autonomy, not taking into account that power derives from a central level that remains accountable to its voters.

A growing literature focuses on a combinatorial approach (i.e. micro-level variables from the "bottom-up" approach and macro-level variables from the "top-down" approach) to implementation research, so as to take advantage of both approaches and allow different levels (local-central) to interact regularly (Cerna, 2013; Fullan, 2007; Matland, 1995). The combination of the two approaches allows for differentiation even between policy areas (e.g. implementation strategies are not the same in tertiary and secondary education). As a result, implementation varies depending on the different content and types of policies (Cerna, 2013).

Finally, Suggett (2011) develops an area between the level of political controversy—about the targets or intentions of a policy—and the level of uncertainty—about the means or actions of achieving a target. This framework shows that the two approaches may differ depending on policy areas. For example, strategies using the "bottom-up" approach appear more often in areas of low conflict, high uncertainty and lack of consensus about the means of achieving a target, such as education. On the contrary, "top-down" strategies are more common in high-conflict areas with respect to the target and relatively high uncertainty as to how they must be implemented, for example, in the taxation of a particular industrial sector (Cerna, 2013; Suggett, 2011).

References

Acocella, N., Di Bartolomeo, G., & Hallett, H. A. (2011). Tinbergen Controllability and N-Player LQ-Games. *Economics Letters, 113*(1), *32–34.*

Acocella, N., Di Bartolomeo, G., & Hallett, H. A. (2012). *The Theory of Economic Policy in A Strategic Context.* Cambridge: Cambridge University Press.

Bellman, R. (1961). *Adaptive Control Processes, A Guided Tour.* Princeton: Princeton University Press.

Blanchard, O. (2017). *Macroeconomics* (7th ed.). London, UK: Pearson.

Cerna, L. (2013). *The Nature of Policy Change and Implementation: A Review of Different Theoretical Approaches.* Organization for Economic Cooperation and Development (OECD) Report. Retrieved from https://www.oecd.org/education/ceri/The%20Nature%20of%20Policy%20Change%20and%20Implementation.pdf

Fullan, M. (2000). The Three Stories of Education Reform. *Phi Delta Kappan, 81*(8), 581–584.

Fullan, M. (2007). *The New Meaning of Educational Change.* New York: Teacher's College Press.

Fullan, M. (2009). Large-Scale Reform Comes of Age. *Journal of Educational Change, 10*(2), 101–113.

Greener, I. (2002). Understanding NHS Reform: The Policy-Transfer, Social Learning, and Path Dependency. *Governance, 15*(2), 161–183.

Hanf, K., Hjern, B., & Porter, D. (1978). Local Networks of Manpower Training in the Federal Republic of Germany and Sweden. In K. Hanf & F. Scharpf (Eds.), *Interorganisational Policy Making: Limits to Coordination and Central Control* (pp. 303–344). London: Sage.

Hansen, B. (1958). *The Economic Theory of Fiscal Policy.* London: Allen & Unwin.

Leontief, W. (1976). National Economic Planning: Methods and Problems. *Challenge, 19*(3), 6–11.

Lucas Jr., R. E. (1976). Econometric Policy Evaluation: A Critique. *Carnegie-Rochester Conference Series on Public Policy, 1*(1), 19–46.

Matland, R. (1995). Synthesizing the Implementation Literature: The Ambiguity-Conflict Model of Policy Implementation. *Journal of Public Administration Research and Theory, 5*(2), 145–174.

Mazmanian, D., & Sabatier, P. (1983). *Implementation and Public Policy.* Glenview: Scott, Foresman.

McLaughlin, M. W. (1987). Learning from Experience: Lessons from Policy Implementation. *Education Evaluation and Policy Analysis, 9*(2), 171–178.

Preston, A. J. (1974). A Dynamic Generalization of Tinbergen's Theory of Policy. *The Review of Economic Studies, 41*(1), 65–74.

Rogoff, K. (1985). The Optimal Degree of Commitment to an Intermediate Monetary Target. *Quarterly Journal of Economics, 100*(4), 1169–1189.

Sabatier, P. (2005). From Policy Implementation to Policy Change: A Personal Odyssey. In A. Gornitzka, M. Kogan, & A. Amaral (Eds.), *Reform and Change in Higher Education: Analyzing Policy Implementation* (pp. 17–34). Dordrecht: Springer.

Sabatier, P., & Mazmanian, D. (1979). The Conditions of Effective Implementation: A Guide to Accomplishing Policy Objectives. *Policy Analysis, 5*(4), 481–504.

Suggett, D. (2011). The Implementation Challenge: Strategy Is Only as Good as Its Execution. *State Services Authority Occasional Paper* No. 15.

Theil, H. (1964a). Some Developments of Economic Thought in the Netherlands. *The American Economic Review, 54*(2), 34–55.

Theil, H. (1964b). *Optimal Decision Rules for Government and Industry*. Amsterdam: North Holland.

Tinbergen, J. (1939). *Statistical Testing of Business Cycle Theories: Part II: Business Cycles in the United States of America, 1919–1932*. New York: Agaton Press.

Tinbergen, J. (1952). *On the Theory of Economic Policy*. Amsterdam: North Holland.

Tinbergen, J. (1956). *Economic Policy, Principles and Design*. Amsterdam: North Holland.

CHAPTER 7

Institutional Change and Cultural Change

7.1 Introduction

Institutions frame human activity as the rules of the game (North, 1990), and, hence, the way in which they change is of particular significance. The reason is straightforward: since, on the basis of specific measures and criteria—maximizing growth, maximizing benefit, optimal allocation of resources and so on—institutions do not have proper organization, the question is how they might change so as to acquire it.

The very same concern applies to the cultural background of a society. The change in cultural values over time is an issue of concern to economic science, as this change is responsible for shaping economic, political and social life.

At the same time, the functioning of economies depends heavily on the interconnection of prevailing institutions and preferences. When institutions and cultural background are compatible with an optimal growth pattern, innovation and entrepreneurship are facilitated. On the contrary, when there are distortions in the development and co-evolution of institutions and cultural background, conditions of stagnated growth may occur, causing intense and permanent distortions in entrepreneurship and innovation.

The contents of this chapter are as follows: Sect. 7.2 raises the issue of institutional change and, more specifically, the types and origins of institutional change. Emphasis is also placed on the evolutionary process of institutional change and on the spatio-temporal evolution of institutions.

P. E. Petrakis et al., *Economic Growth and Development Policy*,
https://doi.org/10.1007/978-3-030-43181-5_7

Section 7.3 analyses the concept of cultural background change and discusses individual issues related to this process, such as factors affecting change and the speed of change, cultural background evolution, its key transmission strategies and cultural pace of adjustment. Section 7.4 analyses the hypothesis of the co-evolution of institutions and cultural background, as well as the issue of their asynchronous evolution, leading to uncertainty and a stagnated growth prototype. Finally, in Sect. 7.5, the importance of ideas for changing institutions and cultural background and the conflicting approaches to the role of ideas in institutional change is presented.

7.2 Institutional Change: Endogenous Versus Exogenous

The contribution of institutions to economic growth (Acemoglu & Robinson, 2012; Ostrom, 1990) is clearly defined, but much less is known about institutional change (Aoki, 2007; Greif & Laitin, 2004; Hodgson, 2004; Kingston & Caballero, 2009).

The sources of institutional changes come from causes which are perceived by the actors and may be related to the external environment, the knowledge and the skills of society and of individuals. Usually, change in institutions is a mixture of external influence and endogenous attainment of new requirements and knowledge. For example, entrepreneurs continuously calculate the benefits of maintaining the existing conditions of their business (products, technologies) and the effects on their business of changes within the institutional framework (e.g. changes in the tax system).

The process of change is always gradual and slow. The reason is that, in a given situation dominated by specific institutions, there are winners and losers. Obviously, any change in this situation creates new winners and losers and is accompanied by the creation of rivals and of opposing forces. In addition, the interactions, created by the networks developed in the transition process, always work in favour of the present situation and against the expected situation.

The debate about institutional change can be considered through two theoretical approaches (Kingston & Caballero, 2009):

1. The first approach introduces theories that see institutional change as a result of deliberate design and
2. the second approach refers to the case where the change may be spontaneous and follow an evolutionary process (see Sect. 7.2.1).

Both of them are crucial for understanding institutional change. However, the distinction between the two approaches is not easily visible. This may be because both the design and evolution of new institutions are associated with gradual changes in a multitude of parameters related to beliefs and knowledge. The main reason for the changing of institutions is simply that policy-makers try to update existing institutions to meet new realities.

Human accumulation, new knowledge, learning and new technology might change both formal and informal institutions. Exogenous technological change is the main source of institutional change (Ayres, 1944). "Technological development forces change upon the institutional structure by changing the material setting in which it operates" (Ayres, 1944).

Whether an exogenous shock will lead to a change in an institution depends on the distribution of benefits among agents, both in the current and in the emerging situation. That is to say, if a change is expected to negatively affect a group of the population, then, depending on its strength, it will attempt to impede an impending change. Once these obstacles are overcome, the process of change can take place gradually and over time, through formal and informal rules.

The exogenous determinants of institutional change may be due to the following causes (Libecap, 1989):

1. shifts in preferences and other political preferences,
2. changes in the technology of enforcing and defining property rights and
3. shifts in relative prices.

Political power and political actors in general, in turn, influence the allocation of resources of the economy, through the formation of the institutional background. One characteristic approach is that institutional change is the result of supply and demand forces in the society (Alston, 1996). That is, change in institutions is merely the result of the "negotiation" between suppliers (e.g. government) and demanders (e.g. pressure groups/lobbies).

By contrast, other theories support the neutrality of political actors in determining the institutional framework. Although politicians are being pressured by population groups to change the formal rules (Kantor, 1998), they nonetheless have their own incentives to guide their actions and face constitutional constraints, which, in turn, can also change at much slower rates.

7.2.1 *Evolutionary Process of Institutional Change*

Theories of endogenous institutional change are based on the Darwinian approach, offering significant insights into this process. In their attempt to demonstrate the importance of endogenous institutional change, Greif and Laitin (2004) introduce "quasi-parameters". This term refers to the parameters which are exogenous in the short run but gradually change over time and become endogenous. Changes in quasi-parameters may extend the range of the potential equilibrium points of the institutions. But they can also undermine the current situation by moving the economy away from an optimal condition. Thus, institutional changes may cause a "punctuated equilibrium" process, as gradual changes in quasi-parameters may lead to a shock, since the patterns of behaviour no longer constitute an equilibrium (Kingston & Caballero, 2009). In addition, institutional change may be combined with frequent and short periods of deliberate institutional change and experimentation, interspersed with longer periods during which these experiments are weeded out through competition (Aoki, 2001).

In this context, institutional change may follow a "path-dependent" process, where the institutional framework, at a given time, is a function of both current conditions and precedent institutions and conditions (Kingston & Caballero, 2009). At the same time, seeing change in institutions as a process where participants (agents, policy-makers) have limited cognitive capacity and knowledge makes it understandable that they may be led to erroneous conclusions about the changes they are promoting. Therefore, despite the fact that institutional change is influenced by exogenous factors, the overall process may follow an evolutionary pattern.

Veblen (1899) considers institutions as "prevalent habits of thought with respect to particular relations and particular functions of the individual and of the community". In this manner, the evolutionary theory of institutional change focuses on the habits based on the natural selection hypothesis. Change in social structures is a result of natural selection as the new institutions incorporate habits and preferences of individuals and the community.

In the evolutionary theory, there is no common model or central design that can cause a coordinated change in formal rules, as they are perceived by all players (economic agents and policy-makers). On the contrary, some institutions tend to dominate others, resulting in new formal rules that are not the result of collective choice or political process.

At the heart of the Darwinian Theory stands the principle of "selection", where in the process of evolution, the strongest characteristics of every species survive via the process of inheritance, whereby the successful traits are replicated. The evolutionary process of institutional change is the result of deliberate human action with bounded rationality, with humans acquiring knowledge through experience, interactions with others, imitation and experimentation. Thus, evolutionary theorists provide a theoretical framework, which integrates the study of cognition, ideas and decision-making with institutional change and human evolution (Lewis & Steinmo, 2012).

In the early twentieth century, a debate arose where many scientists assumed that natural selection could operate, not only at the level of individuals but also at the level of populations and ecosystems. It has therefore been called into question whether genes alone ought to be considered the fundamental unit of selection (Dawkins, 1976). And so, the debate has re-emerged as to whether individuals should be considered the key factors that lead to group selection or whether attention should be focused on the behaviour of organized groups of the wider population.

On the one hand, according to the basic principles of natural selection—which supports individual selection—those genes that are more capable of replication will increase their prevalence in the total population of genes and are thus more likely to pass on to the next gene generation. So, these are "selfish genes", each trying to perpetuate itself (Dawkins, 1976). That means that individuals would not altruistically sacrifice anything for the sake of a group.

On the other hand, group selection is an evolutionary mechanism where natural selection is imagined to act at a group level and not at the individual level. That means that in group selection, individuals can indeed act altruistically and are able to sacrifice much for the sake of a group. Groups that work well together are able to survive and reproduce, and this is called multi-level selection (MLS) theory (Sober & Wilson, 1998).

van den Bergh and Gowdy (2009) argue that human nature is such that—unlike other mammals—humans have a much higher ability to adapt their behaviour, achieve sophisticated communication, cultural transmission, social organization and the tendency to behave in a partisan manner. Humans also show a much higher capacity for cooperation and altruism when they are in groups, so group selection is more appropriate for understanding human behaviour.

Thus, evolutionary theory now includes group selection as an integral part, and, in literature, there is a distinction between genetic group selection—replacement of genes where vertical cultural transmission prevails—and cultural group selection—imitation of others and replacement of the cultural values of individuals where horizontal cultural transmission prevails (van den Bergh & Gowdy, 2009). Another distinction of group selection is between kin selection—relating to family-sized groups—reciprocal selection—medium-sized groups where every group member knows the characteristics of every other member—and cultural group selection—very large groups (van den Bergh & Gowdy, 2009). Nevertheless, the two kinds of selection, genetic and cultural, may interact—as has been said—leading to a co-evolution between genes and culture.

Hayek (1973) focuses on the selection at the level of the social group. Rules of conduct evolve in line with social groups, which have managed to evolve and dominate. As a result, "thinking and acting are governed by rules which have evolved by a process of selection in the society in which one lives, and which are thus the product of the experience of generations" (Hayek, 1973). However, in Hayek's analysis, there is also the notion of expectations, which vary in different situations, that is, by exogenous parameters. These exogenous parameters are integrated by institutions and lead to their evolution.

In conclusion, the evolution of institutions is the product of a complex endogenous or exogenous process, activated by the political factor. The question that arises is why do societies not easily agree on the formation of better financial institutions, so that through the process of growth and development, they can ensure the greatest possible share—consumption and growth—for their members? There are two possible answers to this question (Acemoglu, 2009):

- The first is that there is indeed a better situation than the current one in which the society finds itself, and everyone would be better-off from the transition to it, but society cannot find its way to it. In the long run, however, this is not acceptable. In other words, it is not possible for a desired balance to exist but society not being able to find it over time.

- The second answer seems to be gaining ground and plausibility: there are contradictions and opposing interests within society. Therefore, there are no changes that would make everyone better off. In other words, the transition to a new situation makes some winners and others losers, raising the issue of distributing the extra resources created by this transition. Thus, it is likely that changes in institutions were promoted by elites who, in turn, safeguard their interests.

So, to understand the sources of different institutional changes, we must understand the winners and losers in every different situation, even when the institutional change generates new wealth, but, despite this, losers are not compensated, and winners manage to bend the resistance of losers.

Apart from these considerations, a particular characteristic of institutional organizations is their dynamic character that determines the evolution of institutional equilibrium. The evolutionary process of institutional change interprets "institutions-as-equilibria" (Greif & Kingston, 2011) by contrast to the institutions-as-rules approach (North, 1990). The institutions-as-rules approach is based on the rational choice of agents, denying the dynamic character of an evolutionary process, while it fails to explain how institutions are shaped, as it does not address issues of human behaviour and motivation. If, however, human interaction is included in the analysis, then, we can understand institutional change as a continuous process of seeking equilibrium, based on the interests of different social groups. The evolutionary process of institutional change does not always lead to an optimal and stable equilibrium of institutions. Optimal institutions may evolve into a sub-optimal condition (Kingston & Caballero, 2009).

Even if the institutional framework of a society was initially described as "efficient" at a given time, in an evolutionary process, these rules can prove to be "inefficient". In other words, the equilibrium point may change over time, reflecting the particular circumstances at a given moment. Adapting institutions to new conditions is not an easy process and, as a result, institutions are often "outdated" and unable to fulfil the purpose for which they were originally created.

7.2.2 Evolution of Institutions in Time and Space

The change and the evolution of institutions are a matter of time and space. Over time, change in formal rules leads to a gradual assimilation of informal rules which "had gradually evolved as extensions of previous formal rules" (North, 1990). At the end of the process, a new institutional nexus has been created, offering a new equilibrium to the economy. Therefore, institutions are not a static construct initially emerging from a central, deliberate design by policy-makers, but they have a dynamic character which, over time, incorporates elements of the external environment and, in particular, aspects of society cultural background.

Observing how fast institutions change, that is, the flexibility of institutions in the social context is a critical issue, in order to understand their impact on the evolution of economies. The flexibility of institutions passes through the channel of the cultural background. In turn, changing the cultural background (Sect. 7.3) affects the shaping of institutions. An endless feedback loop of the evolution process of both constructs is therefore created. If both constructs can change at the same rate, that is, if there is co-evolution, then the economy is approaching a new equilibrium point, enhancing the efficiency of the economic system.

The literature has very much concerned itself with the process of institutional change (Davis & North, 1970; North, 1971; North & Thomas, 1973). Davis and North (1970), as well as North and Thomas (1973), see changes in relative prices as the major force that causes changes in institutions. In addition, Hayek (1973), trying to illustrate an evolutionary approach of institutional change, states that expectations change under different situations, that is, by exogenous parameters incorporated by institutions, which lead to their evolution.

Table 7.1 describes the flexibility of institutions under normal conditions. The term "normal conditions" means that the course of the economy is not interrupted by an external shock (e.g. war, economic crisis, natural phenomena) that can affect the path of institutional change. That is to say, we are trying to "isolate" the economy from possible external influences.

Institutions are classified in three major categories: (a) economic institutions, (b) political institutions and (c) social institutions. Their temporal evolution is distinguished in short-medium term (1–5 years) and long-very long term (over six years).

Table 7.1 The flexibility of institutions in the social context under normal conditions

			Short-medium term 1–5 years	*Long-very long term 6+ years*
Market institutions	Economic institutions	Property rights		*
		Rule of law		*
		Accountability		*
		Government effectiveness		*
		Labour market	*	
		Product market	*	
		Taxation system	*	
		Social security system	*	
		Public infrastructure		*
		Financial system	*	*
		Economic openness		*
		Shadow economy	*	*
Non-market institutions	Political institutions	Parliament		*
		Quality of democracy		*
		National government (political cycle)	*	
		Politicians/political parties	*	
		Municipalities	*	
	Social institutions	Family		*
		Army		*
		Education system		*
		Healthcare system		*
		Non-governmental organizations	*	
		Public companies and organizations	*	
		Police and law enforcement agencies		*
		Judicial system		*
		Legal system		*
		Mass media	*	
		Firms	*	*
		Religion		*
		Labour unions	*	
		Internet	*	

Source: Authors' own creation

Based on the dimension of time, we can classify institutions as slow moving and fast moving (Roland, 2004). Changing slow-moving institutions needs a long period through a gradual and continuous evolution process. On the contrary, fast-moving institutions are more receptive to change. The first category includes, for example, political institutions, and the second category includes social norms. Political institutions may change overnight either through the legislative process or due to revolutionary moments (Roland, 2004). Of course, a political change may be the result of political developments over time. Labour market, legislative framework and justice are examples of rapidly changing institutions. Also, not all economic institutions change at the same speed.

Much of the institutional framework seems to be changing in the long run. This refers to institutional constructs concerning social benefits and the regulatory context, for example, the insurance system, which have a long-term action.

Correspondingly, social networks, and in particular the institution of family, remain unchanged over time, forming the core of society. The institution of religion is of particular interest. Societies tend to be committed to values and stereotypes that are influenced by religion.

Specifically, the underdevelopment observed in some Muslim countries can be explained by the inheritance system as dictated by the Quran (Kuran, 2007). According to this, two-thirds of each property is bequeathed to a large portion of relatives, and the remaining one-third concerns the allocation of individual responsibilities of the will. Through this inheritance system, everyone had a reasonable share of ownership, and wealth accumulation was limited. However, this system has hindered the retention of successful enterprises or other assets from generation to generation.

Freedom is often seen as a source of wealth. A totalitarian regime tends to neglect the opportunities offered. In China, in the post-revolutionary period, this regime had led to the rejection of everything "foreign" and to the obstruction of adopting new ideas. One of the factors that led to this attitude was the aversion of Confucianism to scientific research. However, this trend changed at the end of the twentieth century and early twenty-first century, offering valuable interpretations to scholars of institutional change. By contrast, Protestant societies generally support and promote development.

The levels of corruption and the retention of the shadow economy reflect the quality of institutions. Economic growth is affected by corruption, which is considered harmful when it is unpredictable and continuous. Paldam (2001) refers to two groups of religions, which reduce citizens' perceptions of corruption, Reformed Christianity (Protestants and Anglicans) and tribal religion.[1] No significant statistical results were found for Catholic and Orthodox Christians and Muslims.

Particularly enlightening for the geographical diversification of institutions (the dimension of space) are the findings from the Corruption Perception Index 2019 of Transparency International (Table 7.2). While European countries appear to have the lowest levels of corruption, African countries face serious corruption problems.

The evolution of the quality of institutions reflects the change in the institutional background over time. Figure 7.1 illustrates the evolution of the quality of institutions in the past decades across major economies and European countries under austerity programmes. From 2008 onward, the quality of Greece's institutions showed significant deterioration, and Greece fell behind other countries in indices measuring institutional quality. The case of Greece is a typical example of the deterioration of institutional quality in the last decade, while, after 2012, there has been an improvement with the implementation of a number of reforms, although 2016 seems to be approaching the same low levels again.

Table 7.2 Institutions and geography diversification: Corruption Perception Index 2019

	Average score	*Top scorer*	*Lowest scorer*
EU and Western Europe	66/100	Denmark (87)	Bulgaria (43)
Asia Pacific	45/100	New Zealand (87)	Afghanistan (16)
Americas	43/100	Canada (77)	Venezuela (16)
Middle East and North Africa	39/100	United Arab Emirates (71)	Syria (13)
Eastern Europe and Central Asia	35/100	Georgia (56)	Turkmenistan (19)
Sub-Saharan Africa	32/100	Seychelles (66)	Somalia (9)

Source: Transparency International and authors' calculations

Note: Low values indicate highly corrupt. Less than 50 = serious corruption problem

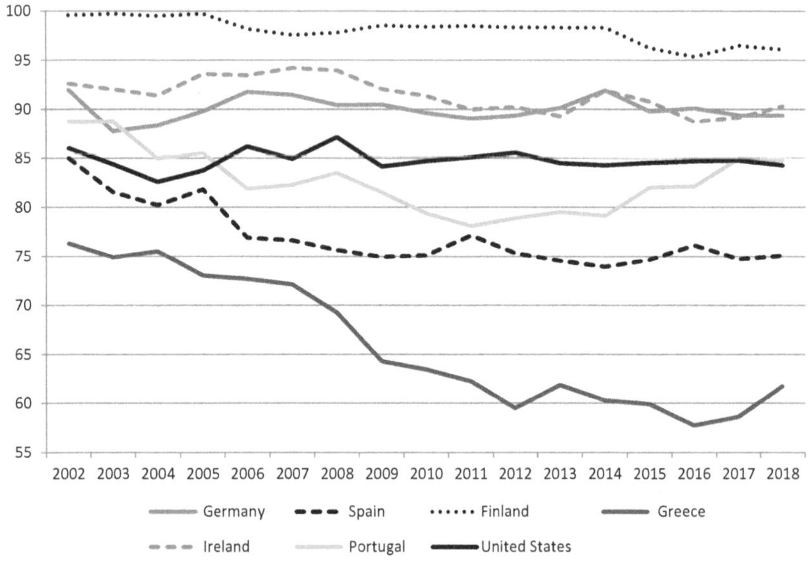

Fig. 7.1 Quality of institutions on time. (Source: Worldwide Governance Indicators-The World Bank and authors' calculations. Note: The data present an average of six variables: voice and accountability, political stability/absence of violence, government effectiveness, regulatory quality, rule of law, and control of corruption. The highest value is 100, that is, the best quality institutions)

7.3 Change in Cultural Background

Although the evolution of societies may be intertwined with economic growth, our question is whether the map of values of each society is a dynamic dimension affected by economic factors. Trying to find the diachronic changes over time in cultural values is a challenging field for research, as it is quite difficult to perform the same experiment with the same population sample at different periods. Cultural values are stable in the long term, and the conditions that influence them remain relatively unchanged (De Jong, 2009).

Therefore, the stability of the cultural background or the shifting of society's values over time requires particular observation for policy implications. The extent to which societies focus on particular values tends to favour or prevent[2] economic growth.

Cultural change can be modelled as a Darwinian evolutionary process, in which some cultural values become more common and others diminish (Boyd & Richerson, 2005).

When individuals are faced with conditions and behaviours that differ from those which they consider acceptable, on the basis of their own cultural background, they follow a process that may be called cultural eclecticism, in which they accept and adopt certain behaviours, reject others and partially adopt yet others. The importance of cultural changes is not always the same, as change may occur, for example, because the adoption of a behaviour is considered necessary for human survival or, in other cases, for meeting certain social needs. It should also be emphasized that cultural change is usually cumulative, in the sense that after each change, much is added and little is lost. At the same time, changes in the cultural background usually lead to the need for new changes that will complement or supplement the original change.

Through globalization, different cultures interact with each other as a number of processes such as commercial transactions and the migration of populations. The development of technology has also contributed to this. As the process of globalization is unavoidable for both developed and developing economies, it is interesting to note the ways in which societies and individuals adapt to change.

Two conflicting schools of thought have emerged regarding the impact of globalization. The first school of thought, based on modernization theory[3] claims that globalization contributes to the convergence of differences between cultural backgrounds, as political and social forces lead to a change in values. The second school emphasizes the stability and endurance of traditional values against economic and political changes occurring under the influence of globalization. The resistance of traditional values to change comes from the fact that these values are independent of economic change (DiMaggio, 1994). In the process of globalization, a set of values is formed, based on common characteristics between different societies, which interact with local cultures, and ultimately lead to a cultural transformation with high cohesion among cultural backgrounds (Hermans & Kempen, 1998).

7.3.1 *Factors Affecting Cultural Change*

The factors that affect the creation and shaping of the culture of a society are inextricably linked to the specific conditions that prevail in that society.

The fact that external factors affect the shaping of the cultural background was confirmed a few thousand years ago.[4] The most important sources of foreign influence on the formation of cultural background are the available resources, the climate and the geographical characteristics in general (Diamond, 1999; Petrakis, 2014; Triandis, 2009). As these factors form the origins for shaping the cultural background of a society, whatever change occurs in them correspondingly affects the prevailing cultural background.

Factors that can lead to cultural change may come from human psychology—as some ideas are more readily learnt or remembered—or may be social and ecological—some ideas make people richer, live longer or migrate more often, and the resulting selective processes generate culture change (Boyd & Richerson, 2005). According to human psychology and the observation of human tendencies, we find that imitation, the contact of a group exhibiting a "common knowledge" with another group with different kinds of cultural characteristics, is a factor in changing culture. The contact between two societies will change the culture of both through cultural diffusion. In addition, any change in physical characteristics (climate, attitude, place, etc.) will lead to a change in culture, habits and lifestyle.

More specifically, resource availability and mobility (Petrakis, 2014) have a significant impact on culture. The more resources and the more accessible these resources are in a society, the greater the likelihood of people being optimistic rather than uncertain and suspicious. In addition, when the resources available are easy to move, then "honour" psychologies are developed as a means of preventing third parties from assaulting easily movable wealth. A revolutionary technological change that will affect, for example, resource availability and the production process is expected to cause a change in the cultural background of individuals.

Climate affects both social psychology and cultural background (McClelland, 1961; Petrakis, 2014; Tavassoli, 2009). Low temperatures are associated with the adoption of privacy and introversion. Individuals are also more disciplined and obey community rules and regulations (Triandis, 1995). At the same time, climate affects individual behaviour through "homeostasis" (Petrakis, 2014), that is, the process by which the human body, mainly through blood circulation, adapts to the external environment (Tavassoli, 2009).

The geographical terrain of the area is another factor shaping cultural background. If geographical terrain leads to the cultural isolation of society, then homogenized reactions and more highly homogenized cultural backgrounds develop. According to Petrakis (2014) and Triandis (2009), it is likely that cultural regulations will be enforced with greater integrity (tightness).

In addition, if extreme events (earthquakes, floods, etc.) occur frequently, people do not develop programming activities. If this is combined with resource constraints, it magnifies the size of uncertainty. But if resources do exist, then the community may be led to the opposite effect of over-programming for precautionary reasons (Petrakis, 2014).

7.3.2 *Incremental Versus Shock Change*

A key feature of human behaviour is its response to environmental conditions. The greatest differentiation in a person's personality occurs during adolescence (Borghans, Duckworth, Heckman, & ter Weel, 2008). However, changes in traits do arise, if to a lesser extent, later in life. Over time, individuals become increasingly more socially dominant, conscientious and emotionally stable. Overall, social vitality and openness to experience rise in early life and then fall in old age (Roberts, Walton, & Viechtbauer, 2006). The above changes in cultural background are gradual and could, as such, be described as incremental changes.

But there are also significant changes in the cultural background after an external shock. It is a fact of common observation that crisis tends to produce or accelerate cultural changes and, what is more, once the changes are accepted due to the crisis, they tend to persist. Changes of this type may cause high stress to individuals (Eschbach, Hagan, & Rodriguez, 2001), affecting their psychological adjustment to new conditions and may cause—depending on the intensity of the change—a strong shock to the framework of cultural values. The result is a change in the cultural background, which is much faster than the incremental change described earlier. The crises of 1929 and 2008 are such examples. So, in addition to economies, an economic crisis appears to affect societies and, more specifically, the culture and personality traits of the members of a society (Magee et al., 2013). The global financial crisis of 2008 with its resultant financial strain appears likely to have contributed to considerable stress and hardship for individuals (Sargent-Cox, Butterworth, & Anstey, 2011), and just as that of 1929, to have also affected investment and saving behaviours (Petrakis, 2011). A similar example is the time needed for immigrants to be assimilated into the new host environment. The adaptation and integration of immigrants into a new culture is a complex process that requires a considerable period of adjustment. Sociocultural adaptation has been emphasized as a major factor of intercultural adjustment (Searle & Ward, 1990; Ward, Bochner, & Furnham, 2001; Ward & Kennedy, 1992) as it mainly consists of behavioural and cognitive components of cultural learning for performing effectively in a new milieu (Zlobina, Basabe, Paez, & Furnham, 2006).

Similar to the effects of a crisis on all members of a society is the occurrence of a crisis within an organization—a business distress—which may be due either to systemic factors—such as a more general crisis in economic activity—or to internal ones—such as mismanagement (Petrakis, 2015). Whatever the cause of a crisis in the workplace, its effects may have a significant impact on the working conditions and, hence, the working behaviour of employees. Also, business distress may indirectly change the organizational culture of an organization. For example, an organization that had been characterized as employee-oriented but had recently been in economic trouble resulting in collective lay-offs, now tends to be job-oriented, even if it has now balanced its operations and is no longer laying off staff.

The concept of culture shock is also important. Oberg (1960) defined culture shock as the "anxiety that results from losing all of our familiar signs and symbols of social intercourse". Culture shock may occur due to the loss of familiar cues, the breakdown of interpersonal communications or an identity crisis (Weaver, 1994). As culture shock, we could define a change that leads individuals and societies to deal with circumstances that are characterized by conditions different from their previous cultural context (Xia, 2009).

The entry of an individual (through immigration, population movements, etc.) into a society characterized by a culture different from their own is an example of culture change. This change results in this individual not being able to understand the ideology and behaviour of the members of the host society, thus not being able to understand why people act the way they do and how the individual himself should behave (Xia, 2009). Under these circumstances, the individual will suffer—fully or partially—from depression, anxiety and feelings of helplessness (Mio, 1999). The more these symptoms are aggravated, the more difficult the process becomes of learning and adapting to the new cultural background. In general, immigration leads to privacy, as it contains the key element of detachment from a group and living privately (Petrakis, 2014). So, the individual has to adapt to the new cultural environment, which is characterized by different lifestyle, living conditions and business practices. However, this adjustment can only be long term. Studies on the rate of adjustment of immigrants in their new culture use their participation in the workplace as a proxy, where their occupational achievement improves significantly with the duration of residence (Chiswick, Lee, & Miller, 2005; Chiswick & Miller, 2008; Zorlu, 2011). This period can last for even more than a decade with time varying across immigrant groups. For example, an immigrant in the Netherlands coming from a Western country needs up to 15 years to catch up with his Dutch counterpart, with this time increasing for immigrant groups from East European countries (Zorlu, 2011). The individual suffers a culture shock in the new environment as he is exposed to an unfamiliar culture, way of life and attitudes. If the individual fails to appropriately adapt to his cultural background, this can lead to alienation from the new society, psychological confusion and emotional discomfort (Hess, 1994).

7.3.3 The Evolution of Cultural Background

Cultural differences are common amongst humans and amongst other species in nature as well. Behaviour is acquired through social learning. Different behaviours are based on different social learning. Through social learning, a particular behaviour is adopted by subsequent generations, and therefore persistent differences between populations persevere, without recourse to genetic or environmental reasons. Nevertheless, the preservation notwithstanding of particular characteristics that determine behaviour, if we are to focus on human nature, the evolution of culture is important. If the knowledge transfer process follows an adaptive procedure, the question arises as to whether changes in the culture of a society occur over time.

The ability of humans to accumulate socially learnt behaviour over many generations has resulted in the development of technology and the formation of complex institutions (Boyd & Richerson, 1985) that allow them to live in developed societies. However, cumulative cultural change requires some special capacities such as psychological factors (Boyd & Richerson, 1985).

Several studies show that the ability of an individual to acquire new behaviours through observation is essential for the evolution of culture and for cumulative cultural change. Social learners, via observational learning or faithful imitation, understand the function of the elements of the environment, adapting their behaviour by watching (Galef, 1988; Visalberghi & Fragazy, 1990; Whiten & Ham, 1992). Other mechanisms of social transmission include local enhancement, whereby the activity of other species increases the chance that naïve species will learn the behaviour on their own. However, only observational learning allows cumulative culture change (Tomasello, Kruger, & Ratner, 1993). Through observation, individuals use the standard model of behaviour as a starting point, which in turn may lead to behaviours that no individual could perform out of their own initiative.

Cultural change is not the result either of socialization or of the human intelligence. Rather, observational learning requires special psychological mechanisms (Bandura, 1986). Psychological mechanisms enable individuals to observe and understand what is happening in their external environment as a result of the adaptations that have taken place through natural selection.

7.3.4 Social Learning Strategies

The set of rules that govern the processing and assimilation of social information constitute social learning strategies (Laland, 2004). Research on social learning strategies is based on a theoretical background with Rogers' paradox (Rogers, 1988) at the centre of the debate.

Rogers (1988) developed a mathematical model to identify how social learning adapts within a changing environment. His findings suggest that social learning does not increase the population fitness (in other words, the rate of adaptation of individuals to societal traits). Copying is beneficial at low frequency, as social learners obtain information primarily from asocial learners who are part of the environment, but they avoid the cost of asocial learning. However, increasingly copying from other copiers becomes less effective. Rogers' findings can be considered contradictory to some extent, as culture, and thus social learning, is the basis for human population growth, which, in turn, implies an increase in fitness (Richerson & Boyd, 2005).

Social learning strategies reflect two fundamental elements, which make up the learning biases (Boyd & Richerson, 1985): (a) the best way for individuals to acquire information and (b) the proper choice about whom one should learn from. Those biases are detected in a set of characteristics, such as an individual's preferences for social information, the expression of strong emotions, the pay-off associated with a particular behaviour according to time preferences and so on.

During the imitation process, individuals are selective as to the information they accept (Boyd & Richerson, 1985; Rogers, 1988), while natural selection favours the development of adaptive learning strategies. Social learning strategies have been examined through theoretical models based on population genetic models and game theory models (Cavalli-Sforza & Feldman, 1981; Feldman, Aoki, & Kumm, 1996; Kendal, Giraldeau, & Laland, 2009; Schlag, 1999; Wakano & Aoki, 2007).

A well-established category of social learning rules are the frequency-dependent strategies such as conformity and anti-conformity (Boyd & Richerson, 1985; Wakano & Aoki, 2007), which concern individuals who adopt selective characteristics based on how often they appear in society. Boyd and Richerson (1985) define conformist frequency-dependent copying as the disproportionately likely adoption of the most common variant.

Another category of the social learning strategy includes rules based on pay-off, where imitation depends on the performance of individual observations (Schlag, 1998). Analyses based on the game theory approach have shown that the use of social information is proportionate to how effective it can be in individuals (Schlag, 1998, 1999). There are indications that both humans and animals are sensitive to the choice of social learning (Caldwell & Millen, 2008; Mesoudi & O'Brien, 2008).

7.3.5 Culture Pace of Adjustment

In theory, cultural stereotypes that influence human activity present great resistance to change and to their own redefinition (Johnston, 1996). However, the overall complexity, as well as the conditions of human behaviour resulting from it, raise significant questions as to how human action evolves in space and time. According to behavioural economics, individuals and organizations do not always behave rationally. As living organisms—and not as rational models of the economic science—they exhibit consistent irrational biases in decision-making and judgement.

As we have seen, human needs and goals are linked in a logical sequence that forms human action. The starting point of this sequence is the needs of individuals, which form their incentives and organize their purpose, thus forming human activity. A number of cultural values affect the expression of this activity.

Trying to evaluate the degree of flexibility of changing cultural values over time (short-medium term; 0–5 years, long and very long term, over 6 years) in the social context—under normal conditions—a typology is formed as shown in Table 7.3. Table 7.3 shows the speed at which basic behaviours and actions of individuals and organizations change, as well as the cultural values that characterize human society and organizations. The term “under normal conditions” isolates the economy from external influences, as it implies that the course of the economy is not interrupted by an external shock (e.g. war, economic crisis, natural phenomena, etc.) or cultural shock, for example, a situation in which individuals find themselves violently and abruptly in a society with a different cultural background from their own. When external shocks or cultural shocks are observed, the change in some values of the cultural background can be relatively faster—it can happen in the medium or even short term if there is a question of survival.

In general, changes in the basic behaviours and actions of individuals and organizations, as well as in cultural values, are deemed to be slow moving. Factors related to psychology and, therefore, affecting human action change into the long and very long term, since these are deeply rooted behaviours of individuals and are entrenched in their psyche. However, the expectations of individuals appear to change faster, as they are more directly dependent on changes in the macroeconomic conditions of the external environment. Similarly, routines that influence and provide feedback for the behaviour of organizations are also well entrenched in organizations. Thus, the way an organization is managed and the way decisions are made by the few change in the short-to-medium term.

The cultural dimensions of society under normal conditions are considered to change in the long and very long term. Cultural values are stable in the long term as the conditions that influence them remain relatively unchanged (De Jong, 2009). Religion, for example, has a significant influence on the formation of the cultural values of society and is a deeply established viewpoint by means of which individuals perceive the world and the way they behave as members of a society. As such, it is considered to change in the very long term.

Economic action is particularly important in terms of time evolution. The basic economic decisions made by society, as regards consuming, investing and saving, change under normal conditions in the long and very long term, while, if an external or cultural shock occurs, this may affect action in the medium- and perhaps in the short term. By definition,

Table 7.3 Time flexibility of cultural behaviour in the social context (under normal conditions)

			Short-medium-term 1–5 years	*Long-very long term 6+ years*
Psychology and social psychology	Altruism			*
	Cooperation			*
	Maximization of utility			*
	Fulfilment of needs-level of needs			*
	Mimicry			*
	Happiness			*
	Way in which expectations are created		*	
	Investment	Ownership investments	*	*
		Lending investments		*
		Investments in human capital		*
	Property market	Option of owner-occupied housing		*
	Savings/consumption			*
	Entrepreneurship	Entrepreneurship by opportunity—innovation	*	
		Entrepreneurship by necessity	*	
	Taxation/social security system	Attitude towards payment of taxes and social security contributions		*
		Tax avoidance—undeclared labour		*
	Financial system	Credit	*	
		Use of cash		*
		Solvency/debt repayment	*	
	Labour market	Mood for work/rest		*
	Activation in shadow economy		*	*
	Education	Public/private education		*
		Participation in networks of knowledge sharing		*
	Communication	Use of Internet	*	
		Use of magazines/newspapers		*
		Use of television/radio		*
		Face-to-face communication		*

(*continued*)

Table 7.3 (continued)

			Short-medium-term 1–5 years	*Long-very long term 6+ years*
Cultural dimensions of society	Personal traits (Big Five)	Openness to experience		*
		Conscientiousness		*
		Extraversion		*
		Agreeableness		*
		Neuroticism		*
	Schwartz	Egalitarianism		*
		Hierarchy		*
		Harmony		*
		Mastery		*
	Hofstede	Power distance		*
		Masculinity/femininity		*
		Uncertainty avoidance		*
		Long-term/short-term orientation		*
		Indulgence/restraint		*
	House et al.	Human orientation		*
		Performance orientation		*
		In-group collectivism		*
	Religion			*
	Generalized trust			*
	Institutional trust			*
Firms	Firms/routines	Decision-making system—which decisions	*	
		Performance control	*	
		System of returns	*	
		Bankruptcy system	*	
		Organization and structure of property	*	
		Organization and structure of credit	*	
		System of creditors	*	
		Control and company mechanisms	*	
		Work remuneration	*	
	Organizational culture (Hofstede)	Means-oriented vs. goal-oriented	*	
		Internally driven vs. externally driven	*	
		Easy-going work discipline vs. strict work discipline	*	
		Local vs. professional	*	
		Open system vs. closed system	*	
		Employee-oriented vs. work-oriented	*	
		Degree of acceptance of leadership style	*	
		Degree of identification with your organization	*	

Source: Authors' own creation

opportunity entrepreneurship changes in the short term and, correspondingly, necessity entrepreneurship in the medium term. The economic action related to the attitude of society towards the tax, insurance and financial systems, as well as the attitude of individuals towards the shadow economy, changes in the medium term—if, for example, a change is made in law that favours or prevents a specific action. The exception is the use of cash, in any form, a practice that is not easily changed by the incentives created by financial institutions, as it relates to the need for security, liquidity and absence of uncertainty, which a society desires. Concerning the labour market, the attitude towards work/rest changes more slowly, in the medium term, as it relates to both the general choices of the individual and society and to exogenous factors. The productivity and creativity of society change in the short term, influenced by the conditions of the external environment that affect human activity. Also, behaviours relating to the housing market, education and communication change in the long term; the use of the Internet changes in the short term in the modern rapidly expanding world, and real-time (live) communication remains a variable that changes in the very long term.

7.4 The Synchronized Evolution Hypothesis and the Unsynchronized Reality

In recent years, several attempts have been made to illustrate how natural selection operating on both genes and institutions can lead to co-evolution of the two (Bowles, 2006; Bowles, Choi, & Hopfensitz, 2003; Boyd & Richerson, 2002; Choi & Bowles, 2007; Gintis, 2007; for early proponents see for instance Cavalli-Sforza & Feldman, 1981; Durham, 1992; Feldman & Zhivotovsky, 1992; Soltis, Boyd, & Richerson, 1995). Understanding how institutions influence cultural background or individual preferences is a difficult task as institutions are endogenously selected by individuals and because institutions and culture co-evolve (Aghion, Algan, Cahuc, & Shleifer, 2010; Tabellini, 2008).

Samuel Bowles has made great contributions in the field of this co-evolution process (Bowles, 2004, 2006, 2009; Bowles & Gintis, 2000; Bowles et al., 2003; Choi & Bowles, 2007). Much of the impact of economic institutions on behaviour may occur through the ways in which particular institutional settings prompt individuals to draw one or another response from their varied behavioural repertoires (Bowles, 1998).

Furthermore, due to the fact that the structure of social interactions, both within and between groups, affects the pace and direction of cultural evolution, economic institutions and policies which influence residential patterns, ingroup–outgroup relationships and other aspects of these structures, will affect preferences, casting doubt on the economists' canonical premise that preferences are exogenous (Bowles, 2000). In addition, institutions, such as resource sharing or segmentation, reduce the variance of reproductive success within groups and thus weaken the force of selection at the level of individuals (Bowles et al., 2003). The emergence of these institutions depends on the existence of such group-beneficial traits and these, in turn, may only be able to proliferate if these institutions are in place, a conclusion that reinforces the case for a co-evolution process.

Other researchers have also tried to connect cultural with institutional evolution. Veblen's (1898) evolutionary theory of institutional change centres on the notion of "habits of thought", where habits are viewed as durable but (in the long run) adaptable propensities to think and act in particular ways. Because these habits reside within individuals, institutional change involves the simultaneous co-evolution of both shared prevalent habits of thought (institutions) and the habits of individuals (Kingston & Caballero, 2009). Genes and institutions shall be understood as the rules, habits and other culturally transmitted norms that individuals of a species follow when interacting with each other (Antrup, 2013). He shows that evolution may also create institutions that are complementary to the choice of mating partner based on genetically fixed preferences, which can be interpreted as genetically coded information processing. Endogenous interactions among institutions and culture and their co-evolution are important in the course of economic evolution (Tabellini, 2008).

However, we do not have adequate critical information on how economic institutions may impact on preferences, due to the fact that we know very little about the process of cultural transmission, that is, who acquires what trait from whom, under what conditions, why, how and how persistent the traits may be once the initiating environment is withdrawn (Bowles, 1998). Furthermore, there is a shortage of evidence on how culture and institutions evolve over time, and whether they mutually reinforce one another or whether one is a precursor to the other (Murrell & Schmidt, 2011). Thus, the question is open as to whether culture and institutions co-evolve or proceed independently or whether there is unidirectional causality.

The conclusions are of special significance of Bisin and Verdier (2015), who claim that culture and institutions evolve and interact jointly and who focus on the process as determined by the interaction, rather than on the cause of the interaction. To prove joint evolution and interaction, they define the cultural or institutional multiplier, as the ratio of the total effect of the institutional or cultural change on economic prosperity divided by the direct effect, that is, the counterfactual effect which would have occurred had the distribution of cultural traits in the population or the institutions remained constant after the institutional or the cultural change. They thus contribute to the debate of whether culture and institutions co-evolve or whether their evolution is asynchronous.

The big question, then, is whether the cultural background evolves in a way that is compatible with institutions. Institutions need to respond to the cultural background of individuals. Otherwise, they fail to serve the purpose for which they were formed, resulting in conflicts and transaction costs. That means that institutions must respond to the needs of the members of society by enhancing the process of economic growth. In other words, according to the characterization of Acemoglu and Robinson (2012), they should be "inclusive" institutions. Otherwise, they act as "extractive" institutions, creating conditions for low growth capacity. Particularly significant is the evolution of social structure, which drives small "initial" differences to become exceedingly large over time. Thus, the population is constantly in a situation where influences from the past affect the preferences of individuals and the evolution of institutions in general. However, the evolution of preferences and the evolution of institutions are in most cases not the same, as there is a time gap between them. Structures of social interactions appear to be able to increase the rate of the evolution of preferences (Bowles, 2009).

The emergence of new institutions is linked to cultural innovation (Bowles, 2009). Such an evolution is usually the result of complex and numerous processes, which do not take place together but vary in time and space. The adoption of new preferences or behaviours is a process that reflects changes in human behaviour due to influences that individuals have been subject to (Bowles, 1998). Complementarity in the evolution of culture and institutions is essential for the long-term survival of the latter. In the event that the co-evolution is interrupted due to a rapid change of institutions, the efficiency of the economic system is contingent. All of the above-mentioned features compose what we call a "stagnated growth prototype", which is created when the prevailing institutions and cultures are opposed to the growth process and could be described as idiosyncratic. In particular, the co-evolution of culture and institutions, where culture is characterized as idiosyncratic, leads to the formation of idiosyncratic institutions by creating a growth prototype, which is characterized as stagnated (Petrakis, Valsamis, & Kafka, 2016). The implications of the dominance of a stagnated growth prototype, which deviate from the optimal pattern, has crystal clear effects on how economies operate, with perhaps the most important implication being the increase in the level of uncertainty.

So, the asynchronous evolution of institutions and cultural background generates uncertainty. Everyday stimuli shape the reaction and behaviour mechanisms of individuals. Risk perception (Brehmer, 1987) and risk judgements are related to a cognitive process of processing the given information (Kahneman & Tversky, 2000). The events that take place and their consequences are important factors through which we perceive risk (Drottz-Sjöberg, 1991; Sjöberg, 2000). Apart from the obvious source of risk perception, there is a belief that it is a social phenomenon which cannot be considered individually (Boholm, 1996). As the perception of risk is not shaped within the narrow confines of a social vacuum, one cannot account for how individuals perceive risk without considering the social contexts. Risk perception is a social and cultural phenomenon (Douglas, 1978), not defined solely by the particular characteristics of the human personality, needs or preferences.

Asynchronous evolution of institutions and culture causes deviations from the optimal growth pattern, leading to a stagnated growth pattern. This growth pattern is characterized mainly by the existence of idiosyncratic institutions and culture, which are associated with the existence of risk and uncertainty; this entails that the future cannot be reliably anticipated, since there is no sufficient information for attributing the probabilities of the various results being realized (Petrakis, 2014).

Those deviated growth patterns can take several forms and affect economies in various ways. The deviated growth patterns may result either in a pattern characterized as growth episodes generator (the rare case) or a stagnated growth pattern (the most frequent case). A growth pattern characterized by idiosyncratic institutions and idiosyncratic preferences can manifest in different types and combinations (Petrakis et al., 2016). Such idiosyncratic combinations of institutions and culture lead to a stagnated growth prototype without any endogenous energy to break the barriers to growth. Institutions always affect culture and vice versa, through the co-evolution pattern that they follow.

7.5 The Role of Ideas on Institutions and Cultural Change

The role of ideas is important in shaping institutions and cultural changes. The times when economic science strictly distinguished itself from related sciences (e.g. psychology) or basic areas of human activity (politics) are long gone. The role of ideas is central to this new context (Rodrik, 2013).

Ideas play an important role by strengthening, organizing or enabling underlying interests, and they become powerful in the context of a given set of institutions and political conflicts (Acemoglu & Robinson, 2012).

Ideas are the intellectual part of a culture, justifying its set of beliefs, values and norms. Thus, new information, that is, new ideas may change the existing cultural background of societies, as they are the driving force of the human condition (North, 2005). At the same time, understanding institutional change contributes to a better explanation of the role played by ideas and ideology (North, 1990) in political economy.

The continuous and constant change of ideas may create the breeding ground for cultural change. A change in ideology only gives rise to cultural change because the agents' beliefs about the manner in which the game is played are altered by a mass effect (Aoki, 2001). Experimenting with new practices and concepts is a process of changing informal institutions. The shaping of culture is the result of both individual and, ultimately, collective choices. Thus, as culture is passed down from generation to generation, individuals follow an evolutionary process where new ideas influence existing ones and a new situation emerges.

The role of ideas on institutional change has triggered the development of two conflicting theoretical approaches: (a) the constructivist approach and (b) the open functional approach. Their differentiation lies in the importance they attach to ideas as a factor for policy and institutional change.

For the supporters of the constructivist approach, ideas play an important role in the process of policy and institutional change, noting that new ideas can differentiate existing institutional entities (Blyth, 2002; Cox, 2001; Hay, 2002). But how do new ideas affect existing policies and institutions? Ideas are what provides the cognitive roadmap for change, affecting the way in which new policy problems are being "reframed" (Schmidt, 2010). New ideas can have an impact on a particular way of thinking over a given period of time. In this sense, political or institutional changes cannot be the sole outcome of an intentionally acting actor who assembles isolated problems and solutions. In addition, the existence of uncertainty in every aspect of human activity is responsible for the creation of dysfunctional institutions. In this way, new ideas always do matter (Gofas & Hay, 2010).

On the other hand, supporters of the open functional approach emphasize material factors as a source of institutional change, limiting the role of ideas to second place. Vis and Van Kersbergen (2013) defend the open functional approach against the constructivist approaches. They argue that the latter approaches tend to neglect material factors which constrain the possible range of actions. They argue that policy and institutional changes in the modern welfare state are mainly dependent on material factors, such as increasing economic internationalization, an ageing population and changing family structures. As Vis and van Kersbergen (2013) put it, these challenges to welfare states exist "irrespective of whether actors perceive these challenges as such or not, because welfare states' continuation depends on their reform".

Notes

1. Tribal religion is a term used to describe various expressions of religion associated with a particular ethnic group.
2. If societies are committed to a set of values that impede their evolution (e.g. high degree of aversion to uncertainty, low orientation to the future), they are at a disadvantage compared with societies with the opposite characteristics.
3. The basic argument of modernization theory is based on economic growth, which in turn creates new social and economic structures: job specialization, improving living standards, modernizing the education system and so on. At the same time, a number of unpredictable changes are taking place, such as changes in the role of women in society, emphasis on more feminine values, trust in institutions and reduced mortality. Over the years, traditional values have given way to modern values by assisting societies to follow the growth path (Inglehart & Baker, 2000). The convergence of cultural background from different societies is also due to the potential of international trade as people from different parts of the globe use the same goods to meet the

same needs by creating a common set of rules and behaviours. Values that dominate Western, developed societies such as consumerism, privacy and freedom of expression are beginning to be adopted by traditional societies that are in the process of development.

4. Herodotus, 2500 years ago, as well as Thucydides (400 BC) had found that the external environment influences the cultural background through studying the relationship that develops between the degree of soil fertility in ancient Greece and the way in which war conflicts develop. As Triandis (2009) points out, the essence of the observation was not the question of the development of war conflicts, but the shaping of human character and its relation to the degree of soil fertility. So, Athens brought together people who did not like war (since they did not have to defend a fertile land) and thus developed a culture of persuasion and argument, namely democracy. By the term "common knowledge" we avoid reference to cultural identity in specific terms of ethnicity, religion and so on.

References

Acemoglu, D. (2009). *Introduction to Modern Economic Growth*. Princeton: Princeton University Press.

Acemoglu, D., & Robinson, J. (2012). *Why Nations Fail: The Origins of Power, Prosperity and Poverty*. New York: Crown.

Aghion, P., Algan, Y., Cahuc, P., & Shleifer, A. (2010). Regulation and Distrust. *Quarterly Journal of Economics, 125*(3), 1015–1049.

Alston, L. (1996). Empirical Work in Institutional Economics: An Overview. In L. Alston, T. Eggertsson, & D. North (Eds.), *Empirical Studies in Institutional Change* (pp. 25–30). Cambridge: Cambridge University Press.

Antrup, A. H. (2013). Co-Evolution of Institutions and Preferences: The Case of the (Human) Mating Market. *Journal of Theoretical Biology, 332*, 9–19.

Aoki, M. (2001). *Towards a Comparative Institutional Analysis*. Cambridge: MIT Press.

Aoki, M. (2007). Endogenizing Institutions and Institutional Changes. *Journal of Institutional Economics, 3*(1), 1–31.

Ayres, C. E. (1944). *The Theory of Economic Progress*. Chapel Hill, NC: University of North Carolina Press.

Bandura, A. (1986). *Social Foundations of Thought and Action: A Social Cognitive Theory*. Englewood Cliffs, NJ: Prentice Hall.

Bisin, A., & Verdier, T. (2015). On the Joint Evolution of Culture and Institutions. *NBER (National Bureau of Economic Research) Working Paper* No. 23375. Retrieved from http://www.nber.org/papers/w23375

Blyth, M. (2002). *Great Transformations: Economic Ideas and Institutional Change in the Twentieth Century*. Cambridge University Press.

Boholm, A. (1996). Risk Perception and Social Anthropology: Critique of Cultural Theory. *Ethnos, 61*(1–2), 64–84.

Borghans, L., Duckworth, A. L., Heckman, J. J., & ter Weel, B. (2008). The Economics and Psychology of Personal Traits. *Journal of Human Resources, 43*(4), 972–1059.

Bowles, S. (1998). Endogenous Preferences: The Cultural Consequences of Markets and Other Economic Institutions. *Journal of Economic Literature, 36*(1), 75–111.

Bowles, S. (2000). Group Conflicts, Individual Interactions, and the Evolution of Preferences. In S. Durlauf & P. Young (Eds.), *Economic Learning and Social Evolution. Social Dynamics* (pp. 155–190). Cambridge: MIT Press.

Bowles, S. (2004). *Microeconomics: Behavior, Institutions, and Evolution.* Princeton: Princeton University Press.

Bowles, S. (2006). Group Competition, Reproductive Leveling, and the Evolution of Human Altruism. *Science, 314*(5805), 1569–1572.

Bowles, S. (2009). Did Warfare Among Ancestral Hunter-Gatherers Affect the Evolution of Human Social Behaviors? *Science, 324*(5932), 1293–1298.

Bowles, S., Choi, J. K., & Hopfensitz, A. (2003). The Co-Evolution of Individual Behaviors and Social Institutions. *Journal of Theoretical Biology, 223*(2), 135–147.

Bowles, S., & Gintis, H. (2000). Walrasian Economics in Retrospect. *Quarterly Journal of Economics, 115*(4), 1411–1439.

Boyd, R., & Richerson, P. J. (1985). *Culture and the Evolutionary Process.* Chicago University Press.

Boyd, R., & Richerson, P. J. (2002). Group Beneficial Norms Can Spread Rapidly in a Structured Population. *Journal of Theoretical Biology, 215*(3), 287–296.

Boyd, R., & Richerson, P. J. (2005). *The Origin and Evolution of Cultures.* Oxford: Oxford University Press.

Brehmer, B. (1987). The Psychology of Risk. In W. T. Singleton & J. Hovden (Eds.), *Risk and Decisions* (pp. 25–39). New York: John Wiley and Sons.

Caldwell, C. A., & Millen, A. E. (2008). Experimental Models for Testing Hypotheses About Cumulative Cultural Evolution. *Evolution and Human Behavior, 29*(3), 165–171.

Cavalli-Sforza, L. L., & Feldman, M. W. (1981). *Cultural Transmission and Evolution: A Quantitative Approach.* Princeton: Princeton University Press.

Chiswick, B. R., Lee, Y. L., & Miller, P. W. (2005). A Longitudinal Analysis of Immigrant Occupational Mobility: A Test of the Immigrant Assimilation Hypothesis. *International Migration Review, 39*(2), 332–353.

Chiswick, B. R., & Miller, P. W. (2008). Why Is the Payoff to Schooling Smaller for Immigrants? *Labour Economics, 15*(6), 1317–1340.

Choi, J. K., & Bowles, S. (2007). The Co-Evolution of Parochial Altruism and War. *Science, 318*(5850), 636–640.

Cox, R. H. (2001). The Social Construction of an Imperative: Why Welfare Reform Happened in Denmark and the Netherlands but Not in Germany. *World Politics, 53*(3), 463–498.

Davis, L., & North, D. (1970). Institutional Change and American Economic Growth: A First Step Towards a Theory of Institutional Innovation. *The Journal of Economic History, 30*(1), 131–149. https://doi.org/10.1017/S0022050700078633

Dawkins, R. (1976). *The Selfish Gene.* Oxford University Press.

De Jong, E. (2009). *Culture and Economics: On Values, Economics, and International Business.* London: Routledge.

Diamond, J. (1999). *Guns, Germs, and Steel.* New York: Norton.

DiMaggio, P. (1994). Culture and Economy. In N. Smelser & R. Swedberg (Eds.), *The Handbook of Economic Sociology* (pp. 27–57). Princeton, NJ: Princeton University Press and New York: Russell Sage Foundation.

Douglas, M. (1978). Cultural Bias. *Royal Anthropological Institute of Great Britain and Ireland Occasional Paper* No. 35.

Drottz-Sjöberg, B.-M. (1991). Non-Experts Definitions of Risk and Risk Perception. *Rhizikon: Risk Research Report* No. 3. Stockholm: Center for Risk Research.

Durham, W. H. (1992). *Coevolution: Genes, Culture, and Human Diversity.* Stanford: Stanford University Press.

Eschbach, K., Hagan, J. M., & Rodriguez, N. (2001). *Causes and Trends in Migrant Deaths Along the US-Mexico Border, 1985–1998.* Houston: University of Houston, Center for Immigration Research.

Feldman, M. W., Aoki, K., & Kumm, J. (1996). Individual Versus Social Learning: Evolutionary Analysis in a Fluctuating Environment. *Anthropological Science, 104*(3), 209–231.

Feldman, M. W., & Zhivotovsky, L. A. (1992). Gene-Culture Co-Evolution: Toward a General Theory of Vertical Transmission. *Proceedings of the National Academy of Sciences of the United States of America, 89*(24), 11935–11938.

Galef, B. G. (1988). Imitation in Animals: History, Definitions, and Interpretation of Data from the Psychological Laboratory. In T. R. Zentall & B. G. Galef Jr. (Eds.), *Social Learning, Psychological and Biological Perspectives* (pp. 3–28). New Jersey: Lawrence Erlbaum Asssociates.

Gintis, H. (2007). A Framework for the Unification of the Behavioral Sciences. *Behavioral and Brain Sciences, 30*(1), 1–61.

Gofas, A., & Hay, C. (2010). *The Role of Ideas in Political Analysis: A Portrait of Contemporary Debates.* London: Routledge.

Greif, A., & Kingston, C. (2011). Institutions: Rules or Equilibria? In N. Schofield & G. Caballero (Eds.), *Political Economy of Institutions, Democracy and Voting* (pp. 13–45). New York: Springer.

Greif, A., & Laitin, D. (2004). A Theory of Endogenous Institutional Change. *American Political Science Review, 98*(4), 633–652.

Hay, C. (2002). *Political Analysis, A Critical Introduction*. Houndmills: Palgrave.

Hayek, F. A. (1973). *Law, Legislation and Liberty, Vol. 1: Rules and Order*. Chicago: University of Chicago Press.

Hermans, H. J., & Kempen, H. J. (1998). Moving Cultures: The Perilous Problems of Cultural Dichotomies in a Globalizing Society. *American Psychologist, 53*(10), 1111.

Hess, J. D. (1994). *The Whole World Guide to Culture Learning*. Yarmouth: Intercultural Press.

Hodgson, G. M. (2004). *The Evolution of Institutional Economics: Agency, Structure and Darwinism in American Institutionalism*. London: Routledge.

Inglehart, R., & Baker, W. E. (2000). Modernization, Cultural Change, and the Persistence of Traditional Values. *American Sociological Review, 65*(1), 19–51.

Johnston, L. (1996). Resisting Change: Information-Seeking and Stereotype Change. *European Journal of Social Psychology, 26*(5), 799–825.

Kahneman, D., & Tversky, A. (2000). *Choices, Values and Frames, Russell Sage Foundation*. Cambridge: Cambridge University Press.

Kantor, S. E. (1998). *Politics and Property Rights*. Chicago: University of Chicago Press.

Kendal, J., Giraldeau, L. A., & Laland, K. (2009). The Evolution of Social Learning Rules: Payoff-Biased and Frequency-Dependent Biased Transmission. *Journal of Theoretical Biology, 260*(2), 210–219. https://doi.org/10.1016/j.jtbi.2009.05.029

Kingston, C., & Caballero, G. (2009). Comparing Theories of Institutional Change. *Journal of Institutional Economics, 5*(2), 151–180.

Kuran, T. (2007). *Economic Underdevelopment in the Middle East: The Historical Role of Culture, Institutions and Religion* (Unpublished Manuscript). Durham: Duke University.

Laland, K. N. (2004). Social Learning Strategies. *Animal Learning & Behavior, 32*(1), 4–14. https://doi.org/10.3758/BF03196002

Lewis, O. A., & Steinmo, S. (2012). How Institutions Evolve: Evolutionary Theory and Institutional Change. *Polity, 44*, 314–339.

Libecap, G. D. (1989). *Contracting for Property Rights*. Cambridge: Cambridge University Press.

Magee, L., Scerri, A., James, P., Thom, J. A., Padgham, L., Hickmott, S., et al. (2013). Reframing Sustainability Reporting: Towards an Engaged Approach. *Environment, Development and Sustainability, 15*(1), 225–243.

McClelland, D. C. (1961). *The Achieving Society*. Princeton: D. Van Nostrand Company.

Mesoudi, A., & O'Brien, M. J. (2008). The Cultural Transmission of Great Basin Projectile-Point Technology, I. An Experimental Simulation. *American Antiquity, 73*(4), 3–28.
Mio, J. S. (1999). *Key Words in Multicultural Interventions: A Dictionary.* Connecticut: Greenwood Press.
Murrell, P., & Schmidt, M. (2011). *The Coevolution of Culture and Institutions in Seventeenth Century England.* University of Maryland, Mimeo.
North, D. C. (1971). Institutional Change and Economic Growth. *Journal of Economic History, 31*(1), 118–125.
North, D. C. (1990). *Institutions, Institutional Change, and Economic Performance.* Cambridge: Cambridge University Press.
North, D. C. (2005). *Understanding the Process of Institutional Change.* Princeton: Princeton University Press.
North, D. C., & Thomas, R. P. (1973). *The Rise of the Western World: A New Economic History.* Cambridge: Cambridge University Press.
Oberg, K. (1960). Cultural Shock: Adjustment to New Cultural Environments. *Practical Anthropology, 7*(4), 177–182.
Ostrom, E. (1990). *Governing the Commons: Evolution of Institutions for Collective Action.* New York: Cambridge University Press.
Paldam, M. (2001). Corruption and Religion: Adding to the Economic Model. *Kyklos, 54*(2/3), 383–414.
Petrakis, P. E. (2011). *The Greek Economy and the Crisis, Challenges and Responses.* New York & Heidelberg: Springer.
Petrakis, P. E. (2014). *Culture, Growth and Economic Policy.* New York & Heidelberg: Springer.
Petrakis, P. E. (2015). Economic Crisis and Business Distress. In A. S. Antoniou & C. L. Cooper (Eds.), *Coping, Personality and the Workplace: Responding to Psychological Crisis and Critical Events (Psychological and Behavioural Aspects of Risk).* UK: Gower Publishing Ltd.
Petrakis, P. E., Valsamis, D. G., & Kafka, K. I. (2016). From an Optimal to a Stagnated Growth Prototype: The Role of Institutions and Culture. *Journal of Innovation & Knowledge, 2*(3). https://doi.org/10.1016/j.jik.2016.01.011
Richerson, P. J., & Boyd, R. (2005). *Not by Genes Alone.* Chicago: University of Chicago Press.
Roberts, B. W., Walton, K. Y., & Viechtbauer, W. (2006). Patterns of Mean-Level Change in Personality Traits Across the Life Course: A Meta-Analysis of Longitudinal Studies. *Psychological Bulletin, 132*(1), 1–25.
Rodrik, D. (2013). When Ideas Trump Interests: Preferences, Worldviews, and Policy Innovations. *The Journal of Economic Perspectives, 28*(1), 189–208.
Rogers, A. R. (1988). Does Biology Constrain Culture. *American Anthropologist, 90*(4), 819–831. https://doi.org/10.1525/aa.1988.90.4.02a00030

Roland, G. (2004). Understanding Institutional Change: Fast-Moving and Slow-Moving Institutions. *Studies in Comparative International Development, 38*(4), 109–131.

Sargent-Cox, K., Butterworth, P., & Anstey, K. J. (2011). The Global Financial Crisis and Psychological Health in a Sample of Australian Older Adults: A Longitudinal Study. *Social Science & Medicine, 73*(7), 1105–1112.

Schlag, K. H. (1998). Why Imitate, and If So, How? A Boundedly Rational Approach to Multi-Armed Bandits. *Journal of Economic Theory, 78*(1), 130–156.

Schlag, K. H. (1999). Which One Should I Imitate? *Journal of Mathematical Economics, 31*(1), 493–522.

Schmidt, V. A. (2010). Taking Ideas and Discourse Seriously: Explaining Change Through Discursive Institutionalism as the Fourth 'New Institutionalism'. *European Political Science Review, 2*(1), 1–25.

Searle, W., & Ward, C. (1990). The Prediction of Psychological and Sociocultural Adjustment During Cross-Cultural Transitions. *International Journal of Intercultural Relations, 14*(4), 449–464.

Sjöberg, L. (2000). Factors in Risk Perception. *Risk Analysis, 20*(1), 1–11.

Sober, E., & Wilson, D. S. (1998). *Unto Others: The Evolution and Psychology of Unselfish Behavior*. Cambridge, MA: Harvard University Press.

Soltis, J., Boyd, R., & Richerson, P. J. (1995). Can Group-Functional Behaviors Evolve by Cultural Group Selection?: An Empirical Test. *Current Anthropology, 36*(3), 473–494.

Tabellini, G. (2008). The Scope of Cooperation: Values and Incentives. *Quarterly Journal of Economics, 123*(3), 905–950.

Tavassoli, N. T. (2009). Climate, Psychological Homeostasis, and Individual Behaviors Across Cultures. In R. S. Wyer, C. Chiu, & Y. Hong (Eds.), *Understanding Culture: Theory, Research, and Application* (pp. 211–222). New York: Psychology Press.

Tomasello, M., Kruger, A. C., & Ratner, H. H. (1993). Cultural Learning. *Behavior and Brain Sciences, 16*(3), 495–552.

Transparency International. (2019). Retrieved from https://www.transparency.org/country

Triandis, H. C. (1995). *Individualism & Collectivism*. Colorado: Westview Press.

Triandis, H. C. (2009). Ecological Determinants of Cultural Variation. In R. S. Wyer, C. Chiu, & Y. Hong (Eds.), *Understanding Culture: Theory, Research and Application* (pp. 189–210). East Sussex, UK: Psychology Press.

van den Bergh, J. C. J. M., & Gowdy, G. M. (2009). A Group Selection Perspective on Economic Behavior, Institutions and Organizations. *Journal of Economic Behavior and Organization, Elsevier, 72*(1), 1–20.

Veblen, T. (1898). Why Is Economics not an Evolutionary Science? *Quarterly Journal of Economics, 12*(4), 373–397.

Veblen, T. (1899). *The Theory of the Leisure Class: An Economic Study of Institutions*. New York: Macmillan.

Vis, B., & Van Kersbergen, K. (2013). Towards an Open Functional Approach to Welfare State Change: Pressures, Ideas, and Blame Avoidance. *Public Administration, 91*(4), 840–854.

Visalberghi, E., & Fragazy, D. M. (1990). Do Monkeys Ape? In S. T. Parker & K. R. Gibson (Eds.), *Language and Intelligence in Monkeys and Apes* (pp. 247–273). Cambridge: Cambridge University Press.

Wakano, J. Y., & Aoki, K. (2007). Do Social Learning and Conformist Bias Coevolve? Henrich and Boyd Revisited. *Theoretical Population Biology, 72*(4), 504–512. https://doi.org/10.1016/j.tpb.2007.04.003

Ward, C., Bochner, S., & Furnham, A. (2001). *The Psychology of Culture Shock* (2nd ed.). London: Routledge.

Ward, C., & Kennedy, A. (1992). Locus of Control, Mood Disturbance, and Social Difficulty During Cross-Cultural Transitions. *International Journal of Intercultural Relations, 16*(2), 175–194.

Weaver, G. R. (1994). Understanding and Coping with Cross-Cultural Adjustment Stress. In G. R. Weaver (Ed.), *Culture, Communication and Conflict: Readings in Intercultural Relations* (pp. 169–189). Needham Heights, MA: Ginn Press.

Whiten, A., & Ham, R. (1992). On the Nature and Evolution of Imitation in the Animal Kingdom: A Reappraisal of a Century of Research. In P. J. B. Slater, C. Beer, M. Milkinski, & J. S. Rosenblatt (Eds.), *Advances in the Study of Behavior, 21* (pp. 239–283). New York: Academic Press.

Worldwide Governance Indicators-The World Bank. Retrieved from http://info.worldbank.org/governance/wgi/#home

Xia, J. (2009). Analysis of Impact of Culture Shock on Individual Psychology. *International Journal of Psychological Studies, 1*(2), 97–101.

Zlobina, A., Basabe, N., Paez, D., & Furnham, A. (2006). Sociocultural Adjustment of Immigrants: Universal and Group-Specific Predictors. *International Journal of Intercultural Relations, 30*(2), 195–211.

Zorlu, A. (2011). Occupational Adjustment of Immigrants. *IZA Discussion Paper* No. 6147. Retrieved from https://ssrn.com/abstract=1968098

CHAPTER 8

Structural Changes, Structural Reforms and Economic Growth

8.1 Introduction

In the modern, globalized economic environment, the need for structural reforms is imperative in order for economies to adjust to modern conditions and structural changes.

Admittedly, structural changes have always occurred, and economic policies have always aimed at adjusting economies in changing conditions so as to increase their international competitiveness and, ultimately, their ability to achieve economic growth. For many decades, economic growth (e.g. in the form of closing output gaps) has remained largely the task of monetary and fiscal policy.

Since, however, the end of the twentieth century, the over-indebtedness of the economies, especially developed ones, and the occasionally depleted capacity of the fiscal space, the focus has shifted to structural reforms as a means of enhancing growth.

Section 8.2 discusses the causes that have led to the need for structural reforms, as well as supply-side-targeted policies. These policies were consolidated in the early 1980s, and, after the global crisis of 2008, they came back to the forefront of public debate, notably in the Eurozone, through structural adjustment. Section 8.3 presents changes that are taking place globally and that have a structural impact on how economies operate. Economies trying to gain comparative advantage over their competitors are externally depreciating their currencies, which can lead to currency wars (Sect. 8.3.1), target non-price advantage (Sect. 8.3.2) and offshoring

P. E. Petrakis et al., *Economic Growth and Development Policy*,
https://doi.org/10.1007/978-3-030-43181-5_8

activities that significantly reduce production costs and increase labour productivity (Sect. 8.3.3). Section 8.4 discusses the transition of economies from industry-based to services-based economies, the nature of the Fourth Industrial Revolution and its potential consequences on the structure of economies. Section 8.5 lists the structural changes that are taking place in an economy and may lead to deviations from the optimal growth model. The rationale behind the structural reforms implemented in Europe after the 2008 crisis is also analysed, which was based on internal devaluation policies through fiscal adjustment programmes, in the course of presenting the objectives of fiscal adjustment programmes and their possible effects, especially in economies with low extroversion. Section 8.6 shows the temporal implications resulting from the implementation of structural reforms. Finally, the interaction between the objective of adjusting to reforms and the time required by the economy to adjust to structural reforms is analysed, that is, between the speed at which adjustment is implemented and the flexibility which society presents to these changes.

8.2 The Causes and Nature of Structural Changes

The need for structural reforms arises because of structural changes taking place globally, due to technological change, globalization and so on. Therefore, economies will have to adjust to these changes because of (a) changes in the mode of production globally—as economies have been transformed from industry-based economies to service-based economies, (b) structural changes at domestic level, which deviate from the optimal functioning of economies, and (c) due to the effects of the observed over-indebtedness of economies, which lead to the depletion of budgetary space and restrict the ability to pursue an expansionary fiscal policy so as to cover the emerging output gap.

Differences in the economic performance of countries are often due to structural factors and to the extent to which they undertake structural reforms in the product and service markets and the labour market (de Bandt & Vigna, 2008). As economies evolve and external conditions change, there are new constraints according to which economic policy-makers will have to adjust their reform priorities (Dabla-Norris, Ho, Kochhar, Kyobe, & Tchaidze, 2013).

Structural reforms entail changes in the way policies are carried out and, if effective, they ensure long-term economic growth. This is because they increase GDP, reduce unemployment and "fortify" the economy in the event of negative shocks. To these ends, a structural reform is considered to intervene in the transaction costs of the product and service markets and the labour market, reduce the barriers to entry for new businesses, improve public sector management and strengthen the role of the private sector (Rodrik, 2015). Structural reforms usually include policies that facilitate the market's ability to adjust and respond to a potential shock and liberalize service sectors, increase competition in product and service markets, improve institutions to enhance the efficiency with which markets operate, enhance the business climate and encourage innovative activity (Canton, Grilo, Monteagudo, Pierini, & Turrini, 2014).

In addition, structural reforms are the key to sustainable development (Dabla-Norris et al., 2013), as enhancing productivity promotes the improvement of living standards in emerging and developing economies and leads to the removal of obstacles to the efficient use of resources.

Differences in economic performance between countries raise questions about the impact of structural reforms, leading us to conclude that the same structural reforms cannot be applied in the same way in all countries, nor may the same effects be expected (de Bandt & Vigna, 2008). Therefore, the implementation of structural reforms must take into account the specific economic, political and social characteristics of each country (Rodrik, 2015).

Structural measures are usually implemented through supply-side policies.[1] Supply-side policies require a number of structural reforms related to production, consumption and the sensitivity of consumer choices to price changes. The main objective of supply-side policies is to increase the supply of goods and services and to allow the free market to function more effectively, reducing the role of the state. Such policies may include, inter alia, privatizations—sale of public assets to individuals—and deregulation of (a) the product market—lowering the barrier to entry for new businesses entails increased competition and consequently lower prices, while increased competition increases the quality of goods and services, (b) the money market—reduced regulation of financial markets aims at lower borrowing costs for consumers and businesses and (c) the labour market with the aim of reducing unemployment and increasing competitiveness. They also include a reduction in income tax so as to increase incentives for more work and thus increase product, improvements in the education system and employee skills—as improvement in the education system can improve labour productivity and increase total supply-, reducing the power of labour unions, which can increase the efficiency of businesses and reduce the level of unemployment in a competitive labour market—provision of better information on job opportunities to reduce frictional unemployment, lowering import barriers to facilitate commerce, reduction of bureaucratic structures and improvement of existing transport structures to reduce business costs.

Supply-side policies and structural reforms are considered to have a long-term impact on economic growth. Any policy that intervenes in the productive structure of the economy is a time-consuming process, so the positive effects of policies aimed at improving the productive capacity of the economy—through structural reforms—are proven in the long run. It should be noted that implementing these policies is often very costly, given the investment in education, R&D and infrastructure, and it can be very painful for society—in particular, measures to improve labour market flexibility. In addition, supply-side policies, such as lower tax rates, reduced union power and privatization, can affect the gap between the rich and the poor. Moreover, supply-side structural change policies seem to make sense when there is potential for a future increase in the productivity of the economic system, in order to cope with reduced demand without excessive debt.

In the wake of the 2008 global financial crisis, structural reforms have been at the heart of public debate, as they were considered a necessary condition for getting out of the crisis and re-energizing the economy. For example, the debate on structural reforms in the Eurozone was based on traditional theoretical approaches and basic economic principles. One of the prevailing views, in order to restore equilibrium in the Eurozone, by concentrating economic power in the peripheral countries as well, was to make a satisfactory structural adjustment to the economies. To this end, structural reforms were thought necessary in order to recover sustainability and facilitate macroeconomic adjustment in the Eurozone area (Goldman Sachs, 2012b, 2012c).

Structural adjustment can take place through changes between internationally tradable and non-tradable goods (housing, land). For this reason, structural changes should be made, notwithstanding the structural rigidities in place. In order to achieve this balancing of markets, the price mechanism is crucial, since prices for non-tradable goods should fall in the heavily indebted countries in the Eurozone periphery and rise in the rest of the world. However, structural changes both entail and lead to resource shifts between tradable and non-tradable sectors, while they take time to materialize. Thus, in the economies in which structural adjustment is applied, the following are observed: (a) reduced wages, (b) changes in relative prices and (c) unemployment and underutilization of capital. These lead to a decrease in demand in the economy and to recession. Consequently, the decline in demand is an intended and expected outcome of the process of restructuring economies.

In essence, structural policies coupled with demand reduction are the opposite of a Keynesian demand-type policy. The application of austerity and supply-side policies aims to create a new productive model that will be able to reduce the negative net investment position of economies. By contrast, Keynesian demand growth policy does not include this, but assumes that the older problematic model will continue to operate.

The paradox is, however, that structural reforms face obstacles to their implementation, which are linked to the process of globalization, as social groups are created that may be numerically larger than those of the benefited groups. Thus, a political "trilemma" emerges (Rodrik, 2011), as the global economy is characterized by an effort for globalization, democracy and national sovereignty to coexist simultaneously. In reality, however, the coexistence of these three conditions is not possible. Based on the most optimistic scenarios, we can only have two of the three conditions at a time (Rodrik, 2011), and, as a result, a vicious circle is created. As the market now extends beyond the boundaries of a national economy governed by specific rules, modes of operation and democratic legitimacy, institutions of a universal nature that transcend the barrier of national borders are required for its proper and sustainable functioning. Consequently, globalization creates international governance and international partnerships, where the implementation of structural reforms to tackle distortions in an economy follows the requirements dictated by global economy with the primary objective of increased market efficiency.

8.3 International Structural Changes

Economic conditions and the interconnection between countries cannot remain stable over time. Thus, at the global level, changes are taking place, which have a structural impact on the way economies operate, and structural reforms are needed to cope with these changes.

In order for economies to gain comparative advantages over their competitors, that is, to increase their world trade shares and improve their economic conditions, policies are being adopted that are intended for all time. Thus, the depreciation of their currencies, internal or external, makes their products cheaper and more competitive. Also, due to globalization and technological developments, countries cannot rely only on low prices to achieve a comparative advantage over their trading partners, but they must also improve the quality and reliability of their goods and services. Finally, globalization has dramatically increased the global value chains (GVCs), and, now, production is largely driven by offshoring activities that reduce production costs and increase labour productivity through specialization.

8.3.1 External Devaluations and Currency Wars

Until the beginning of the twentieth century, there was a perception that a depreciated currency was an indication of a weak government. But at a global level, there is a sharp and deliberate devaluation of currencies in order to exert pressure to increase exports and reduce imports so as to recover growth. Specifically, these are currency wars, also known as competitive devaluations, in which economies depreciate their currency aiming to make products shipped to foreign countries relatively cheaper. When the price of a country's currency falls, so does the price of exported goods and services, while at the same time the price of imports to the country increases. The term "currency war" has prevailed because not all currencies can be depreciated globally at the same time, since when one currency is devalued, another becomes stronger (Bénassy-Quéré, Gourinchas, Martin, & Plantin, 2014).

Of course, it should be noted that such a policy may lead to a reduction in the purchasing power of citizens and even to a decline in international trade. In particular, it may reduce the standard of living due to the increased price of imported products and higher prices when traveling abroad, create inflationary pressures and lead to higher costs of servicing public debt, when this debt is denominated in foreign currency. Also, the depreciation of one currency may lead to the depreciation of other currencies in order for them to remain competitive, resulting in unforeseen changes in exchange rates that limit international trade.

Nevertheless, depreciation is favoured as an effective solution when economies have less export revenue than their import costs or when an economy wants to significantly increase its exports or faces high levels of unemployment. Depreciation increases domestic production and employment in order to meet external demand, and it also increases the level of gross domestic product. Thus, depreciation is considered an efficient policy to tackle high levels of unemployment, when public expenditure cannot be further increased, or when a balance-of-payment deficit exists. In addition, maintaining the depreciation for a long time leads to the creation of foreign currency reserves, which can be used to provide liquidity in future financial crises (Benigno & Fornaro, 2012; Steiner, 2014).

During the twentieth century, there were three major currency wars (Rickards, 2012): The first currency war (1907–1945) broke out when countries attempted to recover from the effects of World War I (a monumental devaluation of the German mark in 1921) and, in particular, in the period after the Great Depression in the late 1930s, when countries abandoned the Golden Rule and used monetary depreciation policy to boost their economies. France depreciated the franc in 1925, Britain depreciated in 1931, and in 1933, there was the notorious US dollar depreciation against gold.

The second currency war (1967–1992) began after Great Britain depreciated the pound against the dollar in 1967 and following the collapse of the Bretton Woods exchange rate system in 1971. In 1971, the United States imposed national price controls and disengaged the economy from the Golden Rule. It was an extreme measure aimed at ending the ongoing currency war, which had undermined confidence in the US dollar. The pressure on the dollar by other countries, such as France, was too high so it was significantly depreciated in the 1970s and regained its value in the early 1980s, thanks to the US Federal Reserve policy under the direction of Paul Volcker. Other currencies, such as the Japanese yen and the West German mark, also lost much of their value, while other fluctuations in the dollar followed, such as the Plaza Accord in 1985 and the Louvre Accord in 1987.

Finally, the third currency war is the one that started recently, in 2010, with the United States announcing that they were to double their exports within five years, while a wave of quantitative easing was implemented in the same year. The main participants in the third currency war are the United States, Europe, China and Japan. The central banks of these economies use a combination of policy tools, either directly through government intervention or indirectly through quantitative easing policies, in order to achieve price stability and full employment. Typical examples are the US-China yuan depreciation dispute in 2010–2011; Japan's announcement of a depreciation of its currency in early 2013, which drew the risk of a currency war between Japan and the Eurozone; Japan's ongoing quantitative easing policy in October 2014 (Roubini, 2014), which tripled the purchases of doubtful securities, and the yen fell to a seven-year low against the dollar; the European Central Bank's quantitative easing programme in January 2015; and the depreciation of the Chinese currency in August 2015.

8.3.2 *The Non-price Advantage*

The enormous changes brought about by advances in technology have been catalytic, bringing rapid changes in all areas of human action. Technological changes have had a catalytic effect on changing the landscape of markets in a great many ways. Consumer preferences are not stable, nor are the characteristics of suppliers or of the products they provide. In addition, competitors' actions are likely to vary over time, as they seek to adopt innovative strategies and to constantly discover new opportunities (Hellriegel, Jackson, & Slocum Jr., 2005).

Thus, achieving competitive advantage is a key objective of any economy, especially at a time when consumer needs are changing and competition from other economies is intensifying. Structural reforms are usually required to achieve a competitive advantage in order for economies to meet the new demands of product and service markets. For this reason, globalization is considered one of the main factors causing product switching (Badia, Slootmaekers, & Van Beveren, 2008). Structural reforms should address changes in factors affecting trends in the production and consumption of economies, as well as the sensitivity of consumer choices to price changes. For example, in the case of the Eurozone, Goldman Sachs (2012a) proposed reforms for increasing the share of tradable products in production, improving price elasticity between non-market and market products, and labour market reforms, in order to change the slope of the Phillips curve or to shift it to the right.

However, competitive advantage does not have to be achieved through the lower selling price but also through non-price factors, such as improving the quality of the products or services produced or better labelling of the products exported (Hallak & Schott, 2011; Khandelwal, 2010; Pula & Santabárbara, 2011). For example, the share of emerging countries in world trade has increased significantly in the last 15 years, due to not only price factors but also non-price factors (Benkovskis & Wörz, 2013).

A typical example of an economy whose trade surplus is mainly due to factors other than prices is the German economy. Germany's trade balance was in deficit for very short periods of time—from 1950 onwards—and these deficits were very limited in size. After 2010, there was further widening of the surpluses, while in 2015 the trade surplus was the highest in the European Union and the second highest among developed countries globally, in absolute terms, after China. Germany's competitive advantage is not due to the lower price of German products and services, but to factors other than price levels, which include the quality of goods and services, production technology, product performance, availability, reliability and after-sales services.

8.3.3 Offshore Outsourcing and Production Chains

International trade and the competitiveness of countries are affected by the rapid rise of global value chains (GVCs). GVCs are an important opportunity for countries to integrate into the global economy at a lower cost, producing only some intermediate goods and services rather than integrated final products, while more than half of the developing countries' exports, in value added terms, include GVCs (World Trade Organization, 2014). So, while it was traditionally assumed that all activities in the production of an economy were carried out using only domestic factors, new conditions have now been created, insofar as the production of an economy is now highly fragmented, with much of it taking place overseas and using foreign production factors (Timmer, Los, Stehrer, & de Vries, 2013). Structural changes, observed globally, are changing the way different markets operate and interconnect, as well as the strategic choices of businesses and organizations.

In particular, what is observed in many advanced economies, whose labour-intensive production structure is characterized by unskilled labour, is that they choose to transfer their production to developing economies with abundant low-skilled labour (Park, Nayyar, & Low, 2013). This activity is defined as offshoring, that is, the geographical transfer of the business activities of a company to a lower-cost foreign country (Levy, 2005; Sako, 2006). In contrast to outsourcing, which involves the transfer of supply chain activities outside the boundaries of an industry, offshoring involves the transfer of supply chain activities across geographical boundaries (Park et al., 2013). In the last two decades, due to the great development of information and communication technologies, offshoring is not only about material inputs but also services (Blinder, 2006). The purpose of offshoring is primarily to increase revenues due to reduced production costs, as offshore outsourcing activities can reduce costs by up to 50%

(Park et al., 2013), while revenues may increase by as much as 20% due to profits from the reorganization of the production process and the specialization of employees (Farrell, 2004).

As the transfer of the production process is accompanied by the transfer of job vacancies, there is a fear that there will be a loss of jobs in the country whose companies are offshoring (Groizard, Ranjan, & Rodriguez-Lopez, 2013). Offshoring is expected to increase employment for low-skilled workers in developing countries, while at the same time reducing employment for skilled workers in developed economies.

The benefits of offshoring depend to a large extent on the level of globalization, either between economies or within an industry, which in turn depends on factors such as technical constraints on the ability to share value-added activities, the regulatory environment and the organizational attitude towards change (Farrell, 2004). Thus, only industries and sectors which are characterized as highly globalized can develop the appropriate structures and absorb global resources to make offshoring feasible and profitable (Farrell, 2004).

In particular, there are five stages identified in global transformation and offshoring, based on which, the more we move from the first to the latter, the higher the degree of globalization of the industry or branch being analysed (Farrell, 2004). In the first phase, businesses are seeking to enter new markets in order to increase their global market share and the number of their customers, using product models similar to those they use in the domestic market. The next stage concerns companies that are moving their entire production overseas, with the aim of taking advantage of potentially lower production costs. In the third stage, the production chain is separated into its individual components, which means that different parts of the product are produced in different geographical areas, and each site specializes in producing only specific parts of the product. In the fourth stage, companies reorganize their production process, in order to maximize their efficiency and minimize production costs, taking into account local factors that may affect its production or costs. At the last stage, which concerns a highly global environment, new markets are being created, benefiting from the high globalization that drives down production costs. Thus, new products are created, at significantly lower prices than existing ones, which enter new markets and new geographical areas.

Thus, if an industrial sector presents attractive conditions for offshoring, the next step in the analysis is to consider how to optimize the production chain to generate benefits (Park et al., 2013). To accomplish this, business activities are initially segmented, whereby activities are usually categorized as "core activities" (these activities remain at the original site of production), "critical activities" (these activities can be offshored) and "commodities" (where standard tasks are very attractive for offshoring) (Aron & Singh, 2005). Shadow risks and costs resulting from offshoring, such as exchange rates, transparency and property rights issues, are then taken into account (Park et al., 2013), and it is then decided which activities will be done through offshoring.

8.4 The Transformation of Economies and of the Productive Model

The modern world we live in is the result of a process of industrialization, which involved three waves of the Industrial Revolution—Steam and mechanical production (1760–1840); increased labour division, the arrival of electricity and mass production (1870–1914); and electronics, information technology and automated production (1969 to the present)—which have led to a sustainable increase in productivity (Rodrik, 2015). However, there has been a great deal of change in recent decades, as most economies have shifted from industry-based to service-based economies (Dasgupta & Singh, 2006). This change affects almost all economies, whether developed or developing, and is the result of a long period of increasing relative wages in the workforce and increasing highly skilled labour (Rodrik, 2015). Because of these changes, a new growth model is needed, especially for developing countries. The export- and industry-based orientation of economies may have run its course, while the concurrent reliance of these countries on capital inflows and periods of increased demand in commodity markets make them particularly vulnerable to financial crises (Rodrik, 2014).

There has also been a great debate over whether the growth of the service sector in economies can replace the role of manufacturing and industry. Some argue that services could replace the role of manufacturing and industry as growth drivers (Ghani & O'Connell, 2014), while others argue that as services are constrained by domestic demand and the size of the domestic market, complementarity is required, and at the same time increased productivity in other sectors of the economy, so that the dynamics of services can come into play as a key driver for growth (Rodrik, 2014).

However, the premature onset of de-industrialization is likely to have significant economic and political implications as it slows economic growth, delays economic convergence (Rodrik, 2013) and creates democratic failures (Rodrik, 2015). At the same time, it seems that we are entering a new era that will significantly affect the future conditions of economic activity. This period is driven by the merger of some technological megatrends that are either in physical form (self-propelled vehicles, 3D printing, advanced robotics, new materials), in digital form (anything can be done online) or in biological form (innovations in the sphere of biology, manipulation of genetics, synthetic biology). As a result, while new opportunities are being created, there are also dramatic repercussions on the economy, businesses, society and individuals, both nationally and globally. In other words, there is a process under way of automating and interconnecting processes with rapid changes, while simultaneously using all the positive elements left behind by the third wave of electronics, information technology and automated production. In effect, this change is the Fourth Industrial Revolution (Schwab, 2016).

Indeed, the Fourth Industrial Revolution is likely to be the most painful in world history, as the technological change that is causing it may increase the wealth and profitability of some economies and professional groups, but it will certainly not work for the benefit of the majority of the society. Machinery is already replacing most types of human labour, with the automation of production adversely affecting relatively unskilled workers. As intelligent machines become cheaper and more skilled, they will increasingly replace human labour, all the more so in the more mundane and repetitive tasks.

On the basis of the above-mentioned developments, further depressing labour costs in developing countries may affect the remuneration of workers in developed countries. Developing countries will also have to choose how to respond to these developments—cheap labour ceases to be a comparative advantage for them—as the operation and interconnection of economies change structurally. Indeed, this change may also cause geopolitical imbalances, since cheap labour has so far been the sole factor compensating for the low productivity and low skill levels of developing economies.

8.5 Domestic Structural Changes and Internal Devaluation

As economies can deviate from the optimal growth pattern or from an optimal way of functioning, economic policy-makers need to look for ways to correct what is not working properly. This deviation from the optimal growth pattern is due to certain structural changes that have taken place. Structural change refers to a long-term shift in the fundamental characteristics of an economy, which occurs either because of the dynamic nature of domestic structural changes or because of international structural changes.

The structure of an economy and the conditions of supply and demand change over time. The main reasons for the change in demand are due to fluctuations in income and consumption habits, which, in turn, create changes at the level of production and employment. There may also be a change in the demand and supply side due to changes in the age structure of the population. For example, reducing the proportion of young people in the workforce will force businesses to employ older workers or replace part of the work with capital, resulting in altered employment patterns. At the same time, supply in an economy can change due to technological advances, which can alter the production process, as well as create new products or services, while at the same time rendering some skills obsolete and leading to permanent changes in spending, and hence creating structural unemployment. The reason for a structural change in an economy may be a change in the availability or pricing of resources, which can significantly affect production and employment. The role of competitiveness is also important, which can be reduced due to lower productivity. Finally, there is the role of political and geostrategic changes, which can translate into policies, which have significant economic implications—for example, the fall of communism, the break-up of Korea, the divergent ways in which each country develops and so on. Other examples of structural changes are the shift from an industry-based economy to a service-based economy or the liberalization of markets previously subject to strict rules.

The common problem is that, although many governments are aware of the need for structural reforms in time, they do not possess the required stamina to implement the reforms necessary, since they need to clash with the entrenched interests of pressure groups, and thus endanger their re-election. In other words, institutional modernization under the constraints of growth opportunities is needed in order to tackle structural change.

This is the difference that separates an optimum market model from a peculiar market model in need of change. Institutional modernization and the release from development constraints, therefore, raise the question of the superiority of the optimum market model that incorporates the best features in relation to the peculiar market model which lacks them.

Institutional modernization is an issue that derives from the original Washington Consensus agenda in which the World Bank and the International Monetary Fund played a role. The Washington Consensus contains mainly free-market neoliberal conceptions which favour the free market, reduction of fiscal deficits, liberalization of international trade, international capital movement and strengthening of growth policies that depend on promoting exports (Rodrik, 2006). Subsequently, the concept of "institutional fundamentalism" (Rodrik, 2006) was developed which, in addition to the initial reflection of the Washington Consensus, engaged with issues of corporate governance, a flexible labour market, corruption reduction policies and so on. These changes are summarized in what is called the "Augmented Washington Consensus" (Rodrik, 2006), representing a characteristic mode of thinking which prevailed in the 1990s. It is generally understood that the force of the Washington Consensus, launched in the late 1970s and replacing the Keynesian notions, was maintained until the 2008 crisis. However, it seems to have been abandoned under the pressure of the massive activation of the public sector to fill the demand gaps created by the global financial crisis. Indeed, the G-20 summit in Seoul (November 2010) is considered to have established the "Seoul Development Consensus", which addresses the new needs of economies and aspires to replace the Washington Agreement. The Seoul agreement is moving towards promoting strong, sustainable and balanced growth (Petrakis, 2011).

The structural reforms that have been implemented in Europe since the 2008 crisis have incorporated many features of the original Washington Consensus Agenda—such as reducing deficits, reducing the role of the state, liberalizing markets and so on—relying on the logic of internal devaluation through fiscal adjustment programmes.

Implementing a fiscal adjustment programme requires a series of structural reforms related to production, consumption, the labour market and changes in relative prices. The effectiveness of structural reforms is closely linked to the size and speed of adjustment. The greater and faster the adjustment, the greater the sacrifices and time required to achieve it (Petrakis, Kostis, & Valsamis, 2013). At the same time, it is very difficult to calculate the positive effects of structural reforms in relation to the costs involved. In the short term, the results are uncertain, and it takes time for the expected benefits to become apparent.

However, structural adjustments of changes in demand require a reallocation of resources and time. Thus, the implementation of structural reforms in economies is linked to: (a) wage reductions, (b) price changes and (c) unemployment and underemployment in the productive sector. Supporters of supply-side policies are aware that these policies are causing social upheavals but argue that the negative effects of implementing structural reforms are gradually diminishing.

In addition, different structural interventions require different time horizons to be effective. Concerning the short-term and long-term impact of structural reforms on the Eurozone GDP, interventions in the labour market are producing results that are visible much faster than those in the product market (Barkbu, Rahman, & Valdés, 2012).

As it can be seen from the shift in demand and the contribution of the tradable sector to total production, the implementation of fiscal adjustment programmes has a direct and negative impact on certain sectors of the economy. Therefore, once demand declines significantly, specific sectors of the economy are likely to be hit the hardest, especially in economies based on domestic consumption and low extroversion (such as the Greek economy).

On the other hand, recovering the competitive advantage of the economy—a reduction in unit labour costs—aims to increase exports. Consequently, export-oriented sectors and companies gain in terms of competitive advantage. But the problem in economies that are based on the internal market is that extrovert businesses do not represent a significant part of the economy. Thus, it is easy to understand that the positive effects cannot offset the negative ones, and that the effects of structural adjustment on low-extroversion economies increase structural unemployment.

8.6 The Time Effect of Structural Reforms

The effectiveness of different structural interventions requires different time horizons. A good example is the product market reforms, whose influence is evident in the medium term, in relation to labour market interventions whose impact on GDP is more direct. The impact of labour market reforms on the Eurozone GDP is evident in the short term (the first year since the reform), while the impact of product market reforms is evident in the medium term (five years after the reform) (Barkbu et al., 2012).

Quantification is quite difficult, but some effective estimates have been made on the basis of the QUEST III model (Hobza & Mourre, 2010). The estimates can be evaluated along four key parameters for the European Union economy: debt rates, average GDP, GDP growth (2009–2020) and unemployment rates. These influences can be distinguished in terms of their implementation and depend on the following: (a) the extent of the financial adjustment programme implemented and (b) the extent of the intensity of structural reforms (limited, moderate, or advanced structural reform), which could boost annual growth between 2010 and 2020 from 1.7% in the scenario of limited structural reforms to 2.2% in the scenario of advanced reforms. Benefits could still be significant in terms of working conditions and lower debt rates (Hobza & Mourre, 2010).

In the long run, the effects of structural reform packages could be significantly higher. Due to the inevitable adjustment to the new structural conditions, only some of the benefits of the reform policies seem to have materialized by 2020. The magnitude of the economic benefits and their time scale depend significantly on the speed of implementation of the reforms. If reforms are implemented slowly, they will bring limited benefits by 2020, while a quick implementation will have an entirely different impact on the time profile of GDP, compared to a more "realistic" scenario where potential social costs are taken into account. Table 8.1 presents the structural reform gaps in selected Eurozone economies through a heat map. The darker the colour that corresponds to each sector of each country, the greater the gap in the reforms.

There is, nevertheless, wide agreement on the fact (Aghion & Cage, 2010; de Mello & Padoan, 2010; Mourougane & Vogel, 2008) that many of the structural measures initially deteriorate the economy or create recessionary conditions to recover later, over a period of 10–30 years. Table 8.2 presents an estimate of the time required for some structural measures to be implemented, by means of the relevant "multipliers" for a series of structural measures. In essence, the "multipliers" indicate the extent to which any structural measure affects the future GDP of the country in which it is implemented. What is clear from Table 8.2 is that, over time, the benefits of the impact of structural reforms on GDP are increasing.

The Adjustment Target (AT) (extent, speed), that is, the intensity with which the economy will have to adjust to the fiscal adjustment programme,

Table 8.1 Structural reform gaps in selected Eurozone economies

		Austria	Belgium	France	Germany	Greece	Ireland	Italy	Netherlands	Portugal	Spain
Institutions and contracts	Institutions										
	Range of public property										
	Legal system and property rights										
	Implementation of contracts										
Infrastructures	Infrastructures										
	Sectoral regulation of transportations										
Human capital	Health and primary education										
	Higher education										
	Average PISA score										
Employment protection											
Business regulations	Effectiveness of goods market										
	Business regulations										
	Starting-up businesses										
	Products market regulations										
Opening to trade and foreign investments	Market size										
	Freedom of trade										
	Obstacles to direct foreign investments										
	Cross-border trade										
	Money market growth										
	Credit market regulations										
	Convenience in securing credit										
Innovation	Technological readiness										
	Business complexity										
	Innovation										
	Research and Development financial support										

Source: World Economic Forum (2012), and authors' calculations

given supply-side logic, depends on five key parameters: (a) the share of marketable goods and services in production, (b) the share of non-market goods in consumption, (c) the elasticity of demand for marketable versus non-marketable goods and services, (d) the share of domestic production in all marketable goods and services and (e) demand elasticity domestically against externally produced marketable products.

Essentially, in the transitional period of achieving the adjustment goal, the resulting restructuring generates signals—changes in relative prices, disasters in certain fields and sectors—which re-energize the entrepreneurship that will shape the new production model. It is obvious that this interval will be no less than 3–5 years. The reason is simple: it takes 3–5 years to organize and deliver a new business endeavour. If we include

Table 8.2 Impact of structural reforms on GDP

Policy push	*2 years*	*5 years*	*10 years*	*20 years*	*Steady-state*
(1) Availability of labour factor					
Reduction of replenishment rate of work benefit	0.8	1.3	1.5/1.0	1.7/1.5	
Decrease of salary revaluation	0.4	0.7	0.8	0.9	
Transfer of taxes from work to VAT	0.1	0.2	0.2	0.3	
Transfer of taxes from low to increased specialization work	0.1	0.2	0.2	0.2	
Reduction of tax burden			3.3	5.2	
(2) Human capital					
Secondary education effectiveness (PISA)			0.1		2.0
Average secondary education time			0.6		
(3) Innovation					
R&D tax subsidies	0.0	−0.1	0.0	0.1	
Wage subsidies for R&D	−0.1	−0.1	0.0	0.1	
(4) Product purchases					
Mark-up reduction (final good)	0.3	0.4	0.5	0.6	
Reduction of administrative burden	0.5	0.6	0.6	0.6	
Tangible capital cost reduction	0.1	0.3	0.5	0.9	
Intangible capital cost reduction	−0.1	−0.1	0.0	0.1	

Source: Luiz de Mello and Padoan (2010) and European Commission, European Economic Forecast, Autumn (2010), and authors' calculations

Note: There are other structural policies not listed in the table above. The contribution of all structural measures is not the same in terms of future GDP growth

in this period 1–2 years of implementation of the policy models, we conclude that the interval cannot be less than 6 years, provided there are no external deterrent effects. These usually take various forms related to the acceptance of the reform programmes by the citizens, the pace of changes required in institutions, the cultural background and so on.

The greater the goal of an adjustment, the greater the sacrifices required and the longer the time required to achieve it. Conversely, if the adjustment goal is attempted in a shorter period of time, then the annual size of sacrifices required—adjustment speed—will greatly increase.

Figure 8.1 shows that given a positive relationship between the required time of adjustment, social flexibility and the potential-required adjustment, the greater is the potential-required adjustment that can be achieved.

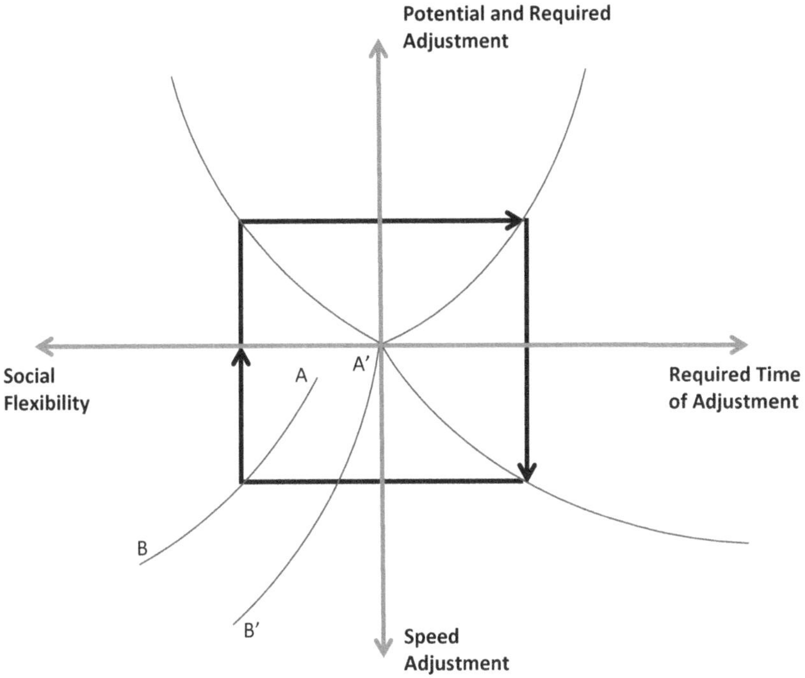

Fig. 8.1 Adjustment goal, time required, speed of adjustment and social flexibility. (Source: Authors' own creation)

Naturally, the greater the potential-required adjustment is, the longer will be the adjustment time required and the greater the speed adjustment necessary.

However, every society that implements an adjustment programme has certain social capabilities to adjust to new circumstances. The conditions that shape a society's flexibility and speed of adjustment are linked to its cultural background, history and social composition. Therefore, adjustment time, extent of adjustment and the speed of adjustment must be ideally combined with reference to social flexibility, in order to achieve the required adjustment.

Note

1. The reasoning of supply-side economic policies is based on the theoretical considerations that shape an organized economic policy platform. These views can be summarized in the following points:
    1. Public or private debt (as a percentage of GDP) needs to be reduced, because, after some level, they pose a threat to medium- and long-term growth.
    2. Implementation of structural measures (including internal devaluation) in order to liberalize production and increase confidence in the economic system. In such a case, future taxes will be reduced, current consumption will increase and the problems caused by fiscal adjustment will be addressed.
    3. If current taxes or debt increase (and, hence, taxes in the future), the level of demand will remain unchanged, reflecting a Ricardian equivalence: increasing savings to pay future taxes to pay off debt and, thus, reducing consumption. Expansionary fiscal policy is therefore not a viable solution.
    4. Monetary policies that encourage excessive investment lead to increased inflation risks and debt costs (i.e. a threat to growth).
    5. Reducing the deficit-ridden Net Foreign Investment Position is a top priority. Budgetary and external deficits should be reduced. This is the reason for imposing an internal devaluation, since there is no option for an external devaluation.

References

Aghion, P., & Cage, J. (2010). Crisis Exit Strategies and Crutch. *Workshop of Structural Reforms, OECD/Bisque de France.*

Aron, R., & Singh, J. V. (2005). Getting Offshoring Right. *Harvard Business Review, 83*(12), 135–143, 154.

Badia, M. M., Slootmaekers, V., & Van Beveren, I. (2008). Globalization Drives Strategic Product Switching. *IMF Working Paper* 08/246.

Barkbu, B., Rahman, J., & Valdés, R. (2012). Fostering Growth in Europe Now. *IMF Staff Discussion Notes* No. 12/07.

Bénassy-Quéré, A., Gourinchas, P. O., Martin, P., & Plantin, G. (2014). The Euro in the 'Currency War'. *CEPR Policy Insight* No. 70.

Benigno, G., & Fornaro, L. (2012). Reserve Accumulation, Growth and Financial Crises. *CEP (Centre for Economic Performance) Discussion Paper* No. 1161.

Benkovskis, K., & Wörz, J. (2013). Non-Price Competitiveness of Exports from Emerging Countries. *ECB Working Paper Series* No. 1612.

Blinder, A. S. (2006). Offshoring: The Next Industrial Revolution? *Foreign Affairs, 85*(2), 113–128.

Canton, E., Grilo, I., Monteagudo, J., Pierini, F., & Turrini, A. (2014). The Role of Structural Reform for Adjustment and Growth. *ECFIN Economic Briefs Working Paper* No. 34. Retrieved from https://doi.org/10.2765/72910

Dabla-Norris, E., Ho, G., Kochhar, K., Kyobe, A., & Tchaidze, R. (2013). Anchoring Growth: The Importance of Productivity-Enhancing Reforms in Emerging Market and Developing Economies. *IMF Staff Discussion Notes* No. 13/8.

Dasgupta, S., & Singh, A. (2006). Manufacturing, Services and Premature Deindustrialization in Developing Countries: A Kaldorian Analysis. *UNU-WIDER, United Nations University Research Paper*, No. 2006/49.

de Bandt, O., & Vigna, O. (2008). The Macroeconomic Impact of Structural Reforms. *Quarterly Selection of Articles – Bulletin de la Banque de France, 11*, 5–23.

de Mello, L., & Padoan, P. (2010). Promoting Potential Growth: The Role of Structural Reform. *OECD Economics Department Working Papers* No. 793. Paris: OECD Publishing. Retrieved from https://doi.org/10.1787/5kmbm6rz4dg6-en

European Commission. (2010). *Commission Staff Working Document*. European Economic Forecast, Autumn.

Farrell, D. (2004). Beyond Offshoring. *Harvard Business Review, 82*(12), 82–90.

Ghani, E., & O'Connell, S. (2014). Can Service Be a Growth Escalator in Low Income Countries? *World Bank, Policy Research Working Paper* No. 6971.

Goldman Sachs. (2012a). Achieving Fiscal and External Balance (Part 1): The Price Adjustment Required for External Sustainability. *European Economics Analyst*, Issue No. 12/01.

Goldman Sachs. (2012b). Can the Euro Area Adjust? *European Economics Analyst*, Issue No. 12/08.

Goldman Sachs. (2012c). Achieving Fiscal and External Balance (Part 4): Escaping the Vicious Circle. *European Economics Analyst*, Issue No. 12/04.

Groizard, J. L., Ranjan, P., & Rodriguez-Lopez, A. (2013). Offshoring, Exporting, and Jobs. *CESifo Working Paper* No. 4550.

Hallak, J. C., & Schott, P. K. (2011). Estimating Cross-Country Differences in Product Quality. *Quarterly Journal of Economics, 126*(1), 417–474.

Hellriegel, D., Jackson, S. E., & Slocum Jr., J. W. (2005). *Management*. London: South-Western College Publishing.

Hobza, A., & Mourre, G. (2010). Quantifying the Potential Macroeconomic Effects of the Europe 2020 Strategy: Stylised Scenarios. *European Economy-Economic Papers* No. 424.

Khandelwal, A. (2010). The Long and Short (of) Quality Ladders. *Review of Economic Studies, 77*(4), 1450–1476.

Levy, D. L. (2005). Offshoring in the New Global Political Economy. *Journal of Management Studies, 42*(3), 685–693.

Mourougane, A., & Vogel, L. (2008). Short-Term Distributional Effects of Structural Reforms: Selected Simulations in a DGSE Framework. *OECD Economics Department Working Papers* No. 648. Paris: OECD Publishing. Retrieved from https://doi.org/10.1787/234214803027

Park, A., Nayyar, G., & Low, P. (2013). *Supply Chain Perspectives and Issues: A Literature Review*. World Trade Organization.

Petrakis, P. E. (2011). *The Greek Economy and the Crisis. Challenges and Responses.* New York and Heidelberg: Springer.

Petrakis, P. E., Kostis, P. C., & Valsamis, D. G. (2013). *European Economics and Politics in the Midst of the Crisis; From the Outbreak of the Crisis to the Fragmented European Federation.* New York and Heidelberg: Springer.

Pula, G., & Santabárbara, D. (2011). Is China Climbing up the Quality Ladder? Estimating Cross Country Differences in Product Quality Using Eurostat's COMEXT Trade Database. *ECB Working Paper* No. 1310.

Rickards, J. (2012). *Currency Wars: The Making of the Next Global Crisis.* US: Portfolio.

Rodrik, D. (2006). Goodbye Washington Consensus, Hello Washington Confusion? A Review of the World Bank's Economic Growth in the 1990s: Learning from a Decade of Reform. *Journal of Economic Literature, 44*(4), 973–987.

Rodrik, D. (2011). *The Globalization Paradox: Democracy and the Future of the World Economy.* New York & London: W.W. Norton.

Rodrik, D. (2013). On Premature Deindustrialization. *Dani Rodrik's Weblog.* Retrieved from http://rodrik.typepad.com/dani_rodriks_weblog/2013/10/on-premature-deindustrialization.html

Rodrik, D. (2014). Are Services the New Manufacturers? *Project Syndicate.* Retrieved from https://www.project-syndicate.org/commentary/are-services-the-new-manufactures-by-dani-rodrik-2014-10?barrier=accessreg

Rodrik, D. (2015). Premature Deindustrialization. *NBER Working Paper* No. 20935.

Roubini, N. (2014). The Return of Currency Wars. *Project Syndicate.* Retrieved from https://www.project-syndicate.org/commentary/world-government-reliance-monetary-policy-by-nouriel-roubini-2014-12?barrier=accesspaylog

Sako, M. (2006). Outsourcing and Offshoring: Implications for Productivity of Business Services. *Oxford Review of Economic Policy, 22*(4), 499–512.

Schwab, K. (2016). The Fourth Industrial Revolution. *World Economic Forum.* Retrieved from https://www.weforum.org/agenda/2016/01/the-fourth-industrial-revolution-what-it-means-and-how-to-respond/

Steiner, A. (2014). Reserve Accumulation and Financial Crises: From Individual Protection to Systemic Risk. *European Economic Review, 70*(3), 126–144.

Timmer, M., Los, B., Stehrer, R., & de Vries, G. (2013). Rethinking Competitiveness: The Global Value Chain Revolution. *Vox, CEPR Policy Portal.* Retrieved from https://voxeu.org/article/rethinking-competitiveness-global-value-chain-revolution

World Economic Forum. (2012). *Global Competitiveness Report 2011–2012.*

World Trade Organization. (2014). *World Trade Report.* Geneva: World Trade Organization.

CHAPTER 9

Entrepreneurship and Economic Growth

9.1 Introduction

Entrepreneurship is the process of generating new opportunities that are incorporated into new businesses. At the same time, it is the process of integrating innovative ideas and business behaviour into existing businesses (Cromie, 2000), which contribute to strategic planning for their growth and the creation of new products (Wennekers & Thurik, 1999). It is a concept directly related to the human factor, as it is the entrepreneur who discovers entrepreneurship opportunities and undertakes to capitalize on them, combining the factors of production so as to generate profit. Driven by their vision and aiming for future prospects, entrepreneurs seek to drive companies to growth (Casson, 1982 [2003]), by increasing their competitiveness in the long run (Leibenstein, 1968).

While it is easy to see the impact of entrepreneurship on growth, no clear conceptual framework has been developed to consider entrepreneurship and correlate it with economic outcome. A possible explanation for this absence, which is discussed in Sect. 9.2, derives from neoclassical theory, which does not consider entrepreneurship as a separate variable in its models.

Section 9.3 presents the micro-foundation of entrepreneurship in growth. Section 9.4 analyses the cognitive process of entrepreneurs seeking growth, and Sect. 9.5 analyses the business development process framework. Section 9.6 analyses a crucial concept of entrepreneurship, the idea of entrepreneurship opportunity and sources of entrepreneurship

P. E. Petrakis et al., *Economic Growth and Development Policy*,
https://doi.org/10.1007/978-3-030-43181-5_9

opportunities. Finally, Sect. 9.7 analyses the process of controlling entrepreneurship opportunities that aim at achieving competitive advantage, and Sect. 9.8 provides policies for promoting entrepreneurship.

9.2 The Absence and Integration of Entrepreneurship

The answer to the question "where can economic growth come from?" has always been a matter of concern for economic science and especially for economic growth researchers. In recent decades, economic literature focuses on the role of entrepreneurship in economic performance. We can reasonably perceive the production process as a mechanism where the factors of production are its input and products are its output.

Although economists have attempted to incorporate entrepreneurship into an economic model (Braunerhjelm, Acs, Audretsch, & Carlsson, 2010; Lucas, 1978; Schmitz, 1989) or to provide a conceptual framework (Kirzner, 1997; Leibenstein, 1968), empirical studies have not been equal to this task. They look at specific cases, limiting the scope of research and the generalizations of results, while in some cases entrepreneurship is considered the residuals of regressions. At the same time, efforts have been made to measure organizational culture[1] (Hofstede, 1980).

The process of converting production factors into products and services is clearly associated to technological progress. According to Adam Smith (1776 [1981]), the division of labour has a limited potential that market economy can exploit. However, entrepreneurs can increase the division of labour and productivity by improving technological progress and innovation. David Ricardo (1817 [1951]), as well as the Malthusian approach to economic growth, believe that declining returns create a constraint on the increase in income of the general population. Investments are what creates new capital, but diminishing productivity returns, population growth and the scarcity of production factors impede economic growth.

The absence of entrepreneurship, both in thought and in the models of economic growth, is associated with neoclassical economics as the dominant school of thought. For the neoclassical economists, there are no profit opportunities, and therefore, there is no concept of entrepreneurship. The neoclassical model is based on the assumption of perfect information and rationality and, thus, leaves no space for the entrepreneur to operate. The price mechanism determines the balance, where supply equals demand for goods and services. As markets work perfectly, there is no incentive for entrepreneurs to take risks or proceed with innovative actions. At the same time, the particular characteristics of the human profile, embodied in the person of the entrepreneur, cannot be integrated into the neoclassical model. *The model is actually a tool for analyzing the optimization of well-defined problems that need no entrepreneur to be solved* (Praag, 1996).

The claim that the differences in the economic progress of countries are due to the absence of entrepreneurship is nothing new (Hoselitz, 1957; Soltow, 1968). However, although many associate entrepreneurship, either directly or indirectly, with economic growth, no specific theory has been formed to explain the process and the way it takes place because reality is quite different. In a non-ergodic world, problems are not always "well defined". The uncertainty that exists in such a world affects decision-making, rejects the basic assumptions of the neoclassical model and necessitates the existence of the entrepreneur and the concept of entrepreneurship, in order to exploit market imperfections and generate profit.

Uncertainty is a crucial feature of the business environment, which creates obstacles to entrepreneurship but also creates opportunities for development. Different businesses face different forms of uncertainty, which by their nature arise from different sources. In order for businesses to understand the form of uncertainty, they need to identify the causes that create uncertainty in each business environment and be able to develop appropriate strategies for dealing with it more effectively (Zichella, 2014).

The nature of entrepreneurship is due to the existence of imperfect knowledge (limited knowledge or subjective uncertainty) or the existence of continuous and volatile processes (system/process variability or objective uncertainty), which may greatly influence the conduct of business activities (van Asselt & Rotmans, 2002; Walker et al., 2003). The existence of uncertainty due to incomplete knowledge can be differentiated through ongoing research, study, experience, continuous evaluation and monitoring of the corporate policies applied.

The uncertainty arising from the volatility of the system (Petrakis & Konstantakopoulou, 2015) is caused by (a) the inherent natural randomness, that is, the existence of an unstable and completely unpredictable function of societies and economies worldwide, which significantly affects business activity, (b) the diversity of values linked to the uncertainty caused by the different approaches and rules under which societies and markets function, (c) human behaviour, where non-rationality and constant variations in the way individuals behave directly affect strategic business planning and hamper the decision-making process, (d) the social variability associated with social, economic and cultural factors and the way they determine the nature of uncertainty, that is, with the different way social processes are carried out in a system of different values, the exercise of social pressure, the way economic institutions operate as well as the diversity of culture, and (e) technological shocks, namely the uncertainty caused by the dynamics of technology and the possibilities of creating new technological achievements and innovations, the infiltration of technology into markets as well as the receptivity to these of the society and economy in which the business operates.

The above-mentioned sources of uncertainty directly influence decision-making and business activity. Parameters such as human behaviour and lack of rationality are in direct contrast to the neoclassical model.

Moreover, market imperfections lead to additional transaction costs. Transaction costs (Coase, 1937; Williamson, 1975, 1985) are inherent in the operating costs of the economy (Arrow, 1969). Since the time of Smith, economists have been convinced that the price mechanism is the driving force behind growth and wealth. In addition, they emphasized the benefits that humanity derives from the specialization of labour. The quantity of goods produced can be increased, without necessarily requiring an increase in production rates, by redistributing production to lower opportunity cost. In the same way, the redistribution of goods and services among consumers with different preferences can increase the social benefit, without necessarily requiring an increase in the production quantity. However, the price mechanism also includes transaction costs, which are a potential barrier to the increase of wealth.

The existence of transaction costs is in conflict with the neoclassical economic theory, according to which they are zero. They therefore constitute a crucial issue, and it is appropriate to approximate their size as optimally as possible in order to understand the type and amount of resources these transactions absorb and their importance to the functioning of the economy. The entrepreneur is called through the hierarchies that he will create, to circumvent the operation of the markets and make a profit. Both Transaction Cost Theory and Institutional Economics see the entrepreneur as the coordinator of the production process, as the price mechanism does not always optimally utilize the allocation of resources within the business.

Finally, Joseph Alois Schumpeter (1911), through his growth model, introduces the role of the entrepreneur whom he identifies with the innovator. He argues that entrepreneurship is a factor of production, which contributes to the composition of the other factors of production. Thus, the role of the entrepreneur is not just limited to his management skills, but it is he who will bring innovation into the production process.

9.3 The Micro-Foundation of Entrepreneurship in Growth

The term "micro-foundation" in economics refers to the microeconomic analysis of the behaviour of households and businesses in macroeconomic models (Barro, 1993). This analysis is closely related to human behaviour and productivity.

As already mentioned, the nature of entrepreneurship is intertwined with the human factor, which is embodied in the person of the entrepreneur, in the form of the cognitive skills and characteristics of the human personality. The behaviour of both the leadership and the workforce, therefore, determines the prospects for business growth at the microeconomic level and, subsequently, throughout the economy, that is, at the macroeconomic level.

Also, the evolution of human personality plays a crucial role in the business environment, as it determines how individuals interact with each other and how they respond to different situations. The connecting link, that is, the parameter that connects the micro-level to the macro-level, is none other than productivity. Productivity is directly linked to the sustainability of a business in a highly competitive environment.

Apart from the cognitive skills that business executives possess, (the) particular characteristics of the human personality may affect productivity levels and growth rates. To this end, and in order for employees, in general, to be more efficient and productive in their employment, it is appropriate to adapt their personality traits to the organizational culture of the business. Thus, the organizational culture of a business or organization is shaped to a large extent by the personality traits of its employees (Hofstede, 1980).

9.4 The Cognitive Process of Entrepreneurs Seeking Growth

The business process of growth requires a set of mental abilities, which are the basic intellectual models that individuals use to organize and process the information they receive (Wright & Stigliani, 2012). These structures attempt through human thinking to create a set of rules that will have general application to a multitude of different situations. Their contribution to the process of seeking entrepreneurship opportunities is especially critical as it helps utilize the information available and to identify opportunities.

The use of these structures may differentiate people who do business from the rest of the population. Numerous studies have focused on this issue examining how entrepreneurs use cognitive structures to make value judgements and identify market imbalances (Bandura, 1977; Gaglio & Katz, 2001; Mitchell et al., 2002). Entrepreneurs tend to develop more precise and complex scenarios that will enable them to perform better in the environment in which they operate (Westhead, Ucbasaran, & Wright, 2009).

In addition, as the entrepreneurial initiative is also linked to the factor of uncertainty, entrepreneurs as personalities tend to make decisions with high risk and uncertainty. On the contrary, some people avoid doing business for fear of the risk and cost of such an initiative (Vecchio, 2003).

Identifying opportunities is about making decisions and evaluating them (Wright & Stigliani, 2012). Decision-making is a process that is undertaken by all entrepreneurs, as they are asked to choose from a multitude of alternatives that have an uncertain outcome. Often, decisions must be made immediately (Markman & Baron, 2003) so that the entrepreneur has to develop the appropriate cognitive mechanisms in order to be able to respond to an emergency. We should note, however, that entrepreneurs, as human beings, do not always make the right decisions, as they are driven by unrealistic expectations (Kahneman, Slovic, & Tversky, 1982).

Regarding the evaluation of entrepreneurship opportunities, this is an integral part of doing business as it differentiates the idea from the opportunity (Hills & Shrader, 1998). Opportunities are mostly evaluated in an environment of high uncertainty and complexity. The acceptability of risk and uncertainty on the part of the entrepreneur depends on his cognitive biases, which in turn affect his decision-making process. Although entrepreneurs differ from the average person in terms of insight and opportunity identification (Kirzner, 1973), the former are not exempt from cognitive biases.

The entrepreneur's intellectual process for seeking the growth of his business is a research field of particular interest and challenges. Research on the importance of cognition and knowledge emphasizes human behaviour and the interaction of the complex environment with human thought (Fiske & Taylor, 1991; Grégoire, Corbett, & McMullen, 2011; Turner, 2001). Empirical studies have shown that successful entrepreneurs use their intuition more often than managers, who tend to prefer a more detailed and linear approach to information processing (Baron, 2007; Groves, Vance, & Choi, 2011).

As a business is a living organism that interacts with its internal and external environment, the intellectual process develops at different levels of analysis (Wright & Stigliani, 2012), starting with the individual himself and ending at the level of society (Hodgkinson & Healey, 2008). However, the dissemination of knowledge within the organization is not an easy task, since it requires the creation of appropriate networks, as does the transfer of knowledge from business to society (Appleyard, 2002; Zander & Kogut, 1995). Knowledge, as an intellectual product and asset of the firm, is therefore diffused into society, working towards economic growth.

9.5 A Framework of Entrepreneurial Growth Process

The growth of a business is achieved by adopting different strategies to make a comparative advantage over its competitors. Initially, in the context of a business process, entrepreneurs, based on their knowledge, experience, education, know-how, cognitive skills, as well as the particular characteristics of their personality, are required to combine the resources necessary to realize their business ideas. Then, they have to find ways of financing their venture on the one hand, and to lead their business to further expansion on the other (Fig. 9.1).

In the process of business growth, it is the entrepreneur who responds to the "who" will help with his experience, knowledge and intellectual skills. The question is also important of whether a novice entrepreneur is able to combine the above so as to cope with a new business venture.

The second big question is "how" the business growth process will be implemented. Access to resources and their effective management are

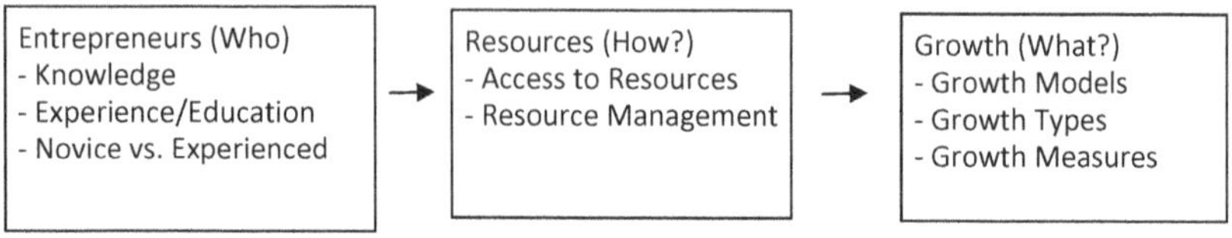

Fig. 9.1 Entrepreneurial growth process. (Source: Wright & Stigliani, 2012, and authors' creation)

issues which the entrepreneur is called to address. However, business growth requires not only material resources but also adequate human capital (Gilbert, McDougall, & Audretsch, 2006). At the same time, technological progress and shared resources also contribute to growth (Wright & Stigliani, 2012), as they help improve human capital and make better use of available resources.

Therefore, the development of strategic planning within the business necessitates the choice of a structure that integrates the human factor and social networks, finds the financial and material resources to exploit opportunities, gains strategic advantage over competitors and eventually expands the business, creating added value (De Clercq, Dimov, & Thongpapanl, 2015; Ireland, Hitt, & Sirmon, 2003; Lechner & Gudmundsson, 2014).

Finally, the third question concerns "what" kind of growth model the business will follow. Will the company, for example, prefer to merge or expand the scope of its operations on its own? Will it internationalize its production or address domestic demand only? These are just some of the many questions about business growth models. But the choice of growth model depends on the mindset and intellectual skills of the entrepreneur. The characteristics of a leader shape the way he thinks and makes decisions about how to invest in business growth (Koryak et al., 2015).

9.6 Sources of Entrepreneurship Opportunities

Entrepreneurship Opportunity (Kirzner, 1973; Schumpeter, 1934) is the result of an activity that involves identifying, evaluating and exploiting entrepreneurship opportunities in order to introduce new products and services, to find a new way of organization, new markets, new processes and raw materials (Shane & Venkataraman, 2000; Venkataraman, 1997). In addition, entrepreneurship opportunities are associated with making better use of existing resources to create a better product than the existing one that will meet the needs of a given market. Hence, market needs are critical to defining entrepreneurship opportunity.

Shane and Venkataraman's approach (2000) focuses on entrepreneurship opportunities by asking three key questions: (a) When, how and why do opportunities for the creation of new goods and services occur? (b) When, how and why do some people—and not others—identify and exploit these opportunities? (c) When, how and why are different modes of action used to exploit entrepreneurship opportunities?

So, then, it is particularly important to understand how individuals (a) use existing knowledge and experience to identify and exploit entrepreneurship opportunities, (b) develop strategies to achieve higher returns from the commitment of resources involved in the activation of an entrepreneurship opportunity and (c) identify and form competitive advantages in an uncertain and competitive environment.

Entrepreneurs have to understand and foresee the future demand for their product, whether it is new or diversified—compared to other similar products in the market—at a given time. It is only through this forecast that entrepreneurs can escape the existing competitive environment, with any deterioration and inefficiencies, and thus guarantee the success of their business initiative.

At this point, it should be made clear that entrepreneurship opportunity should not be confused with innovation. The first is closely related to the process of identifying market needs, while the second relates to ways to improve an existing product or tool to realize an entrepreneurship opportunity. Moreover, entrepreneurship opportunity is associated with people who create innovative forms of entrepreneurship, which significantly improve economic conditions (Schumpeter, 1954 [1982]).

Entrepreneurship opportunities are associated with the activities of individuals, which may be economic or not. The main question associated with the existence of such opportunities is whether they arise as a result of some intentional activity or by accident. A related question is also whether they are endogenously created by individuals involved in the system or are exogenous in nature.

These two questions are particularly critical. The first question relates to the nature of the corresponding business development approach. By contrast, if the existence of an entrepreneurship opportunity is subject to rules, identifying and studying them would be useful, as would be identifying repetition points and the characteristics of the opportunity. It is also important whether the effects of an opportunity are endogenous (e.g. a business activity, generated by the way the financial system is developed) or exogenous (e.g. external factors, such as oil, gold and minerals). In the first case, there is only a "mathematical" search for such opportunities, which exist regardless of the actions of the individuals associated with the financial process. In such a case, the logical sequence of the "finite" opportunities has been created. If entrepreneurship opportunities are endogenously identified, their number is constant or at least fixed.

Important factors that create entrepreneurship opportunities are the level of Research and Development (R&D) spending and technological progress, as resources invested in this area may potentially be used more productively. Research can create new diversified products and boost demand (Casson, 1995), while technological change is the most significant source of opportunities in specific industries (Klevorick, Levin, Nelson, & Winter, 1995). Industries more closely relating to the natural sciences offer more entrepreneurial opportunities, the source of which varies by sector (Klevorick et al., 1995). In some industries, opportunities exist outside manufacturing activities and are found in universities, government agencies and research laboratories. In other industries, opportunities are rarely found within activities and include suppliers or customers. Technological advances can also have adverse effects on some forms of entrepreneurship. For example, high levels of investment and R&D spending can create barriers to market entry.

Management theorists have claimed for decades that the key to business success is understanding customer needs and the supply associated with their needs rather than trying to sell them any product the company owns. Levitt's article "Marketing Myopia" (1960) is perhaps responsible for making entrepreneurs cease to regard their product as a reference point and, instead, focus on consumer needs. However, understanding these needs requires research procedures.

In one of the first studies on the subject, Vesper (1996) presented many methods for identifying new business ideas and proposed the conduct of systemic research. But this method may not always be the most suitable for identifying business activities. For example, it has been found that companies founded due to accidental discoveries managed to achieve higher sales in a shorter period of time than those that used standard research methods.

Studies focusing on practical research methods applied by start-ups show that, although structured consumer research is considered to be of significant value, unstructured and informal ways of collecting consumer information are more commonly used (Fischer & Reuber, 1997).

However, in addition to the appropriate research method, it is well known that market research is significant for identifying entrepreneurship opportunities arising from consumer needs. Market research is also essential at the assessment stage, since entrepreneurs can use the results to predict sales and profits. If entrepreneurs do not conduct market research, they will not be able to properly assess the entrepreneurship opportunity they have identified. Thus, market research can protect entrepreneurs from failure (Twaalfhoven & Muzyka, 1997).

But market research identifies only conscious present needs and not future opportunities. For this reason, entrepreneurs' intuition about entrepreneurship opportunities must not be underestimated.

Entrepreneurship opportunities exist in the entrepreneur's environment. Therefore, sources of new opportunities are identified through market analysis (customers, competitors and suppliers) along with a review of the environment (political, legal, social and technological) in which the company operates. It thus appears that there are many sources where new business activities can be sought, while the entrepreneur's knowledge of changes taking place around him is often the limiting factor.

Prospective entrepreneurs have to be aware of the changes that are taking place around them as they often create entrepreneurship opportunities. According to Timmons (1999), the volume of information in a market is inversely proportional to the quality of the opportunities offered therein. But information is often fragmentary, inaccurate and contradictory, and it depends on the talent of the entrepreneur to improve it and to identify opportunities where others cannot. At this point, the competitive advantage becomes relevant.

9.7 Screening Entrepreneurship Opportunities as a Competitive Advantage

Gaining a competitive advantage is a vital target of any business, and always refers, whether directly or indirectly, to its "vision" or "mission". At a time when consumer needs are changing and competition from other businesses is fierce, an entrepreneur, in order to make a profit, must make his products or/and his business stand out from his competitors. Seeking and identifying entrepreneurship opportunities, as well as innovative activity, are very important steps in gaining a competitive advantage for businesses or organizations.

Competitive advantage is the particular element that distinguishes an entrepreneur's products from those of his competitors. In sum, three sources of competitive advantage can be identified: (a) the business gains "cost advantage" when it can operate at a lower cost than competition; (b) the business gains "diversification advantage" when its products provide greater benefit to customers than those of its competitors; and (c) when the business has a transaction advantage. In this case, the company has lower transaction costs or can create innovative combinations.

Comparative advantage is sought by even businesses that do not face competition, that is, by companies with monopoly power (Dasgupta & Stiglitz, 1980). This happens because their monopoly profits are significant and attract the attention of many others. Thus, businesses search for competitive advantages that will act as barriers to the entry of other companies into the industry. In general, comparative advantage contributes to differentiating a company's products from those of its competitors by helping it gain a greater market share or/and higher profits.

Comparative advantage can also be derived from other factors, such as the rapid response of an entrepreneur to new consumer needs, the ability of the entrepreneur to adopt new technologies and so on. One of the most important factors, as has already been mentioned, is the identification of entrepreneurship opportunities that will allow the business to stand out in the market in which it operates.

One of the main issues raised in the field of entrepreneurship is why entrepreneurs identify opportunities that are overlooked by non-entrepreneurs (Baron, 2007; Kaish & Gilad, 1991; Shane, 2003). The three most convincing and recorded explanations of why entrepreneurs and non-entrepreneurs differ in their ability to identify entrepreneurship opportunities are personality differences, cognitive differences and differences related to their social networking activity.

These characteristics also explain the differences between entrepreneurs in terms of identifying entrepreneurship opportunities. When an entrepreneur has all three of the aforementioned characteristics, he is more likely to identify an entrepreneurship opportunity and, thus, gain a comparative advantage.

Identifying an entrepreneurship opportunity takes place before a company is established. But the entrepreneur, even after identifying an opportunity, must continue to seek opportunities while running his business.

In general, an entrepreneurship opportunity may come from the ability to satisfy a market need with a new product or to creatively combine under-utilized resources, in order to produce a better product to meet that need (Ardichvili, Cardozo, & Sourav, 2003), thereby creating a comparative advantage.

Potential customers may not be able to express their needs, interest or problems. However, even if this expression is not possible, they can recognize the value of a new product or service when it is presented to them and its benefits are explained. When a market need is sufficiently defined—in terms of the benefits which particular customers are looking for—and the potential uses of the resources used to satisfy it are explained, the opportunity will evolve from its original form, and a business idea will emerge.

Business ideas are directly related to the concept of competitive advantage of a business or organization. As an idea evolves, it becomes more complex and, among other things, includes:

- the product or service to be produced,
- the consumers to whom it is addressed and
- how the product/service will reach customers (production chain and marketing planning).

Opportunities are the natural outcome of economic changes and can be identified at any time, with some being recognized and others disregarded. Due to the wide range of opportunities available, the role of the strategy followed by the entrepreneur looking for appropriate opportunities in the appropriate field is important. Long-term success is therefore determined by the strategy used to seek opportunities.

In an economy based on actual business activities or projects (Koopmans, 1951), there are a number of possible actions, some of which are practical, with the level of technology being the main factor for these actions taking place. When an economy is analysed in terms of entrepreneurship, the analysis of the existence of a number of possible actions is rejected, as entrepreneurs themselves use their imagination to create possible implementation actions. Undoubtedly, the choices of economic actors include a number of possible actions, the only difference being that they are exogenous to the choices of entrepreneurs. This is a rigorous approach to entrepreneurship theory.

Entrepreneurs are not able to know in advance whether a business plan is achievable and whether it will provide them with a comparative advantage. Even if the project is considered technologically feasible, the associated costs can be higher than the profit expected. Based on the theory of entrepreneurship, the extent to which a business plan can be implemented is not known.

The cost of a business activity is affected by the cost of information and the cost of searching for it. In addition, collecting and providing specific types of information is more expensive than other types of information. Entrepreneurs have a comparative advantage over most people in terms of business decisions because their personal cost of acquiring information is lower. This is the reason why many non-entrepreneurs lend their resources to entrepreneurs so that the latter can proceed to do business ventures.

9.8 Policies for Promoting Entrepreneurship

The implementation of policies that promote entrepreneurship is inextricably linked to the prevalence of an enabling environment (Acs, Autio, & Szerb, 2014). The question economic policymakers are asked to answer can be summarized as follows: "Does the environment allow the entrepreneur to complete the production function and fill in the missing input markets?" (Acs et al., 2014). Knowledge and its dissemination, human capital and access to finance are parameters that should be given particular emphasis in the implementation of entrepreneurship policies. In combination with the existence of an appropriate institutional background, some countries achieve better entrepreneurial performance than others.

Promoting entrepreneurship-producing innovative products can be achieved through policy intervention (Baumol, Litan, & Schramm, 2007). These kinds of interventions are necessary to create an enabling business environment. In recognition of this need, many countries have developed general and specific policy proposals to promote entrepreneurship. The general policy proposals could include tax and labour market reforms and market regulation. Specific policy proposals include programmes that have been developed in various countries, such as the United States, to increase the survival and growth rates of Small and Medium Enterprises (SMEs) (Gilbert, McDougall, & Audretsch, 2004; Lerner & Kegler, 2000).

Entrepreneurship policies are a set of actions and plans on the part of governments designed to influence and enhance business action and investment decision-making (Audretsch, Grilo, & Thurik, 2007; Klapper, Amit, & Guillén, 2010). The main components of these policies refer to the existence of rules and regulations that enable the launch and enhance the viability of business operations. The purpose of these policies is to improve the competitiveness and profitability of businesses.

Entrepreneurship enhancement policies could be divided into three categories (Table 9.1):

1. access to finance,
2. access to entrepreneurship skills and networks and
3. instruments and rationales in improving the entrepreneurial-enabling environment.

Table 9.1 Policies for promoting entrepreneurship

	Policies	*Instruments*
Limited access to finance	• Facilitating access to financing and expanding financial instruments	• Traditional instruments: grants, loans, loan guarantees • Alternative sources of finance: crowdfunding, peer-to-peer lending, business angel networks, venture capital • Digital finance opportunities: blockchain, fintech
Lack of skills and networks for start-ups and scale-ups	• Providing firms with information, training and coaching	• Information centers • Training courses and e-learning programmes • Mentoring and coaching programmes • Incubators and accelerators
	• Enhancing entrepreneurial networks	• Developing online platforms • Participation in networks and social events
	• Enhancing collaboration among firms and research projects	• Spin-offs • Incubators and accelerators
Entrepreneurial-enabling environment	• Friendly regulatory environment	• Web forums • One-stop shops • E-government services • Consulting about regulations • Bankruptcy code and second chance
	• Entrepreneurial culture	• Entrepreneurial competitions in schools and universities • Laboratories and digital hubs • Entrepreneurship programmes in education
	• Monitoring entrepreneurship policies	• Quantitative assessment • Qualitative monitoring

Source: Authors' own creation

Policies that support access to finance are designed to tackle market failures such as information asymmetries and financing gaps. In addition to traditional funding tools (grants, loans, loan guarantees), alternative sources of finance such as non-bank sources (crowdfunding, business angel networks, venture capital) and digital finance opportunities (blockchain, fintech) have been developed to address the limited funding of the private sector.

Providing alternative sources of finance is especially important for innovative businesses that, due to their high-risk profiles, cannot easily find financing in bank-based traditional instruments. The range of alternative financing options available is large and can cover different financing needs, firm characteristics and risk profiles. Asset-to-firm financing is available to a wide range of firms with low risk of default and low returns. Hybrid instruments that combine debt and equity schemes are more suitable for high-growth firms. Also, new financing opportunities come from a number of technological innovations in financial services such as fintech and blockchain technologies. Finally, governments could facilitate access to financing for start-ups and scale-ups by offering grants (e.g. vouchers), loans or loan guarantees.

The success of an entrepreneurship stimulation programme depends on their funding instruments and several factors related to the ability of public authorities, businesses and entrepreneurs to identify new markets and potential opportunities. To do this, young entrepreneurs need to know how to start or grow a business. Entrepreneurship support programmes can increase prospective entrepreneurs' awareness of the processes needed to start a new business and possible sources of funding. But in addition to the necessary tools, support should be provided such as coaching and mentoring provided by incubators and accelerator programmes.

Concerning the role of networks, public authorities can help link innovation with new business activities both locally and in global networks and value chains. Business networks provide access to new ideas, customers, financing, partners, ideas and sharing knowledge. It is therefore important for policymakers to increase the resources available to potential entrepreneurs by helping them expand their networks, for example, through networking events and forums.

Finally, the prevalence of a positive business environment has a decisive impact on future entrepreneurs. Healthy business requires an external environment that is friendly to investment initiatives and supports the challenges that entrepreneurs face. A friendly regulatory environment contributes to this. In addition to the need for a regulatory framework for business operations, support should be given to a number of actions such as web forums, introduction of e-government services and one-stop shops for information on regulations and support programmes.

Note

1. According to Hofstede, de Hilal, Malvezzi, Tanure, and Vinken (2010), the dimensions that express organizational culture are,
   - Process-oriented versus goal-oriented: it is closely associated with the effectiveness of the organization. In process-oriented cultures, as opposed to goal-oriented cultures, people avoid risk and uncertainty situations and spend only a small portion of their potential at work. A key feature is the way the work has to be done, while individuals are disinclined to face change and they love routine.
   - Employee-oriented versus job-oriented: it reflects the management philosophy of an organization. In employee-oriented cultures, individuals feel that the organization takes their personal problems into account, takes care of the staff—even if this is to the detriment of job objectives—and that important decisions of the organization are made by teams or committees.
   - Local-oriented versus professional-oriented: this dimension shows the contrast between units whose employees largely obtain their identity from the organization (local) with units in which individuals are identified with the type of work (occupation). In local-oriented cultures, by contrast to occupation-oriented ones, individuals feel that the norms of the organization cover their behaviour both at home and at the workplace and that, when it hired them, the company took into account their social and family background along with their professional skills. Furthermore, people in local-oriented cultures are short-term oriented because they believe that the organization will serve its long-term vision over themselves.
   - Open versus closed system: this refers to the accessibility of an organization. In the culture of open systems, individuals consider all members of the organization open to new entrants and to those outside the organization and consider that everyone could join the organization. Therefore, new employees are characterized by adaptability. On the contrary, in the culture of closed systems, the organization is closed and secretive.
   - Loose versus tight control: this refers to the degree of the organization's internal structure. In loose control cultures, no one considers the cost, and meeting times are kept only approximately.

- Normative-oriented versus pragmatic-oriented: this refers to the extent to which the organization is customer-oriented or not. Pragmatic cultures are market-oriented. There is a strong emphasis on meeting customer needs, results are more important than sound procedures and a pragmatic, rather than dogmatic, approach to business ethics prevails. In regulatory cultures, people perceive their work in relation to the outside world as the application of inviolable rules.

References

Acs, Z. J., Autio, E., & Szerb, L. (2014). National Systems of Entrepreneurship: Measurement Issues and Policy Implications. *Research Policy, 43*(3), 476–494. https://doi.org/10.1016/j.respol.2013.08.016

Appleyard, M. M. (2002). How Does Knowledge Flow? Interfirm Patterns in the Semiconductor Industry. In C. W. Choo & N. Bontis (Eds.), *The Strategic Management of Intellectual Capital and Organizational Knowledge* (pp. 537–553). New York: Oxford University Press.

Ardichvili, A., Cardozo, R., & Sourav, R. (2003). A Theory of Entrepreneurial Opportunity Identification and Development. *Journal of Business Venturing, 18*(1), 105–123.

Arrow, K. J. (1969). The Organization of Economic Activity: Issues Pertinent to the Choice of Market Versus Non-market Allocation. In U.S. Joint Economic Committee, 91st Congress, 1st Session (Ed.), *The Analysis and Evaluation of Public Expenditures: The PBB-System* (pp. 47–64). Washington, DC: U.S. Government Printing Office.

Audretsch, D. B., Grilo, I., & Thurik, A. R. (2007). *Handbook of Research on Entrepreneurship Policy*. Cheltenham: Edward Elgar.

Bandura, A. (1977). Self-efficacy: Toward a Unifying Theory of Behavioral Change. *Psychological Review, 84*(2), 191–215.

Baron, R. A. (2007). Behavioral and Cognitive Factors in Entrepreneurship: Entrepreneurs as the Active Element in New Venture Creation. *Strategic Entrepreneurship Journal, 1*(2), 167–182.

Barro, R. J. (1993). *Macroeconomics* (4th ed.). New Jersey: John Wiley & Sons.

Baumol, W. J., Litan, R. E., & Schramm, C. J. (2007). *Good Capitalism, Bad Capitalism, and the Economics of Growth and Prosperity*. New Haven, CT: Yale University Press.

Braunerhjelm, P., Acs, Z. J., Audretsch, D. A., & Carlsson, B. (2010). The Missing Link: Knowledge Diffusion and Entrepreneurship in Endogenous Growth. *Small Business Economics, 34*(2), 105–125.

Casson, M. C. (1982 [2003]). *The Entrepreneur, An Economic Theory*. Aldershot: Edward Elgar.

Casson, M. C. (1995). *Studies in the Economics of Trust*. Cheltenham: Edward Elgar.

Coase, R. H. (1937). The Nature of the Firm. *Economica, 16*(4), 386–405. https://doi.org/10.1111/j.1468-0335.1937.tb00002.x

Cromie, S. (2000). Assessing Entrepreneurial Inclinations: Some Approaches and Empirical Evidence. *European Journal of Work and Organizational Psychology, 9*(1), 7–30.

Dasgupta, P., & Stiglitz, J. (1980). Uncertainty, Industrial Structure, and the Speed of R&D. *Economic Journal, 90*(358), 266–293.

De Clercq, D., Dimov, D., & Thongpapanl, N. (2015). Structural and Relational Interdependence and Entrepreneurial Orientation in Small and Medium-Sized Enterprises: The Mediating Role of Internal Knowledge-Sharing. *International Small Business Journal, 33*(5), 514–536.

Fischer, E., & Reuber, A. (1997). The Influene of the Management Team's International Experience on the Internationalization Behaviours of SMEs. *Journal of International Business Studies, 28*(4), 807–825.

Fiske, S. T., & Taylor, S. E. (1991). *Social Cognition* (2nd ed.). New York: McGraw-Hill.

Gaglio, C. M., & Katz, J. A. (2001). The Psychological Basis of Opportunity Identification: Entrepreneurial Alertness. *Small Business Economics, 16*(2), 95–111.

Gilbert, B. A., McDougall, P. P., & Audretsch, D. B. (2004). The Emergence of Entrepreneurship Policy. *Small Business Economics, 22*(3–4), 313–323.

Gilbert, B. A., McDougall, P. P., & Audretsch, D. B. (2006). New Venture Growth: A Review and Extension. *Journal of Management, 32*(6), 926–950.

Grégoire, D. A., Corbett, A. C., & McMullen, J. S. (2011). The Cognitive Perspective in Entrepreneurship: An Agenda for Future Research. *Journal of Management Studies, 48*(6), 1443–1477.

Groves, K., Vance, C., & Choi, D. (2011). Examining Entrepreneurial Cognition: An Occupational Analysis of Balanced Linear and Nonlinear Thinking and Entrepreneurship Success. *Journal of Small Business Management, 49*(3), 438–466.

Hills, G. E., & Shrader, R. C. (1998). *Successful Entrepreneurs' Insights into Opportunity Recognition, Frontiers of Entrepreneurship Research*. Babson Park, MA: Babson College.

Hodgkinson, G. P., & Healey, M. P. (2008). Cognition in Organizations. *Annual Review of Psychology, 59*, 387–417.

Hofstede, G. (1980). *Culture's Consequences: International Differences in Work-Related Values*. Beverly Hills, CA: Sage.

Hofstede, G., de Hilal, A. V. G., Malvezzi, S., Tanure, B., & Vinken, H. (2010). Comparing Regional Cultures Within a Country: Lessons from Brazil. *Journal of Cross-Cultural Psychology, 41*(3), 336–352. https://doi.org/10.1177/0022022109359696

Hoselitz, B. (1957). Non-Economic Factors in Economic Development. *American Economic Review, 47*(2), 28–41.

Ireland, R. D., Hitt, M. A., & Sirmon, D. G. (2003). A Model of Strategic Entrepreneurship: The Construct and its Dimensions. *Journal of Management, 29*(6), 963–989.

Kahneman, D., Slovic, P., & Tversky, A. (1982). *Judgment Under Uncertainty: Heuristics and Biases.* New York: Cambridge University Press.

Kaish, S., & Gilad, B. (1991). Characteristics of Opportunities Search of Entrepreneurs Versus Executives: Sources, Interests, and General Alertness. *Journal of Business Venturing, 6*(1), 45–61.

Kirzner, L. (1973). *Competition and Entrepreneurship.* Chicago: University of Chicago Press.

Kirzner, L. (1997). Entrepreneurial Discovery and the Competitive Market Process: An Austrian Approach. *Journal of Economic Literature, 35*(1), 60–85.

Klapper, L., Amit, R., & Guillén, M. F. (2010). Entrepreneurship and Firm Formation Across Countries. In J. Lerner & A. Schoar (Eds.), *International Differences in Entrepreneurship* (pp. 129–158). Chicago: University of Chicago Press.

Klevorick, A. K., Levin, R. C., Nelson, R., & Winter, S. G. (1995). On the Sources and Significance of Interindustry Differences in Technological Opportunities. *Research Policy, 24*(2), 185–205.

Koopmans, T. C. (1951). *Activity Analysis of Production and Allocation.* New York: Wiley.

Koryak, O., Mole, K. F., Lockett, A., Hayton, J. C., Ucbasaran, D., & Hodgkinson, G. P. (2015). Entrepreneurial Leadership, Capabilities and Firm Growth. *International Small Business Journal, 33*(1), 89–105.

Lechner, C., & Gudmundsson, S. V. (2014). Entrepreneurial Orientation, Firm Strategy and Small Firm Performance. *International Small Business Journal, 32*(1), 36–60.

Leibenstein, H. (1968). Entrepreneurship and Development. *American Economic Review, 58*(2), 72–83.

Lerner, J., & Kegler, C. (2000). Evaluating the Small Business Innovation Research program: A Literature Review. In C. W. Wessner (Ed.), *The Small Business Innovation Research Program: An Assessment of the Department of Defense Fast Track Initiative* (pp. 307–324). Washington, DC: National Academy Press.

Levitt, T. (1960). Marketing Myopia. *Harvard Business Review, 38*(4), 45–56.

Lucas, R. E. (1978). On the Size Distribution of Business Firms. *Bell Journal of Economics, 9*(2), 508–523.

Markman, G. D., & Baron, R. A. (2003). Person-Entrepreneurship Fit: Why Some People Are More Successful as Entrepreneurs than Others. *Human Resource Management Review, 13*(2), 281–302.

Mitchell, R. K., Busenitz, L., Lant, T., Mcdougall, P. P., Morse, E. A., & Smith, J. B. (2002). Toward a Theory of Entrepreneurial Cognition: Rethinking the People Side of Entrepreneurship Research. *Entrepreneurship Theory and Practice, 27*(2), 93–104.

Petrakis, P. E., & Konstantakopoulou, D. (2015). *Uncertainty in the Entrepreneurial Decision Making: The Competitive Advantage of Strategic Creativity.* New York: Palgrave Macmillan.

Praag, C. M. (1996). *Determinants of Successful Entrepreneurship.* Amsterdam: Thesis Publishers.

Ricardo, D. (1817 [1951]). *On the Principles of Political Economy and Taxation.* In P. Sraffa (Ed.), *The Works and Correspondence of David Ricardo, 1.* Cambridge: Cambridge University Press.

Schmitz, J. A. (1989). Imitation, Entrepreneurship, and Long-run Growth. *Journal of Political Economy, 97*(3), 721–739.

Schumpeter, J. (1911). *The Theory of Economic Development.* Cambridge, MA: Harvard University Press.

Schumpeter, J. (1934). *Capitalism, Socialism, and Democracy.* New York: Harper & Row.

Schumpeter, J. (1954 [1982]). *History of Economic Analysis.* London: Allan and Unwin.

Shane, S., & Venkataraman, S. (2000). The Promise of Entrepreneurship as a Field of Research. *Academy of Management Review, 25*(1), 217–226.

Shane, S. A. (2003). *A General Theory of Entrepreneurship: The Individual-Opportunity Nexus.* Massachusetts: Edward Elgar Publishing.

Smith, A. (1776 [1981]). An Inquiry into the Nature and Causes of the Wealth of Nations. In R. H. Campbell & A. S. Skinner (Eds.), *The Glasgow Edition of the Works of Adam Smith, 2.* Indianapolis: Liberty Fund.

Soltow, J. H. (1968). The Entrepreneur in Economic History. *American Economic Review, 58*(2), 84–92.

Timmons, J. A. (1999). *New Venture Creation: Entrepreneurship for the 21st Century.* New York: McGraw Hill.

Turner, M. (2001). *Cognitive Dimensions of Social Science.* Oxford: Oxford University Press.

Twaalfhoven, B., & Muzyka, D. F. (1997). Doing Business in the Wild East. In S. Birley & D. F. Muzyka (Eds.), *Mastering Enterprise* (pp. 199–205). London: FT Pitman.

van Asselt, M. B. A., & Rotmans, J. (2002). Uncertainty in Integrated Assessment Modeling. *Climatic Change, 54*(1–2), 75–105.

Vecchio, R. P. (2003). Entrepreneurship and Leadership: Common Trends and Common Threads. *Human Resource Management Review, 13*(2), 303–327.

Venkataraman, S. (1997). The Distinctive Domain of Entrepreneurship Research: An Editor's Perspective. In J. A. Katz (Ed.), *Advances in Entrepreneurship, Firm Emergence, and Growth* (pp. 119–138). Greenwich, CT: JAI Press.

Vesper, K. H. (1996). *New Venture Experience – Cases Text and Exercises*. Seattle: Vector Books.

Walker, W. E., Harremoës, P., Rotmans, J., Sluijs, J. P., van der Asselt, M. B. A., van Janssen, P., et al. (2003). Defining Uncertainty: A Conceptual Basis for Uncertainty Management in Model-Based Decision Support. *Integrated Assessment, 4*(1), 5–17.

Wennekers, S., & Thurik, R. (1999). Linking Entrepreneurship and Economic Growth. *Small Business Economics, 13*(1), 27–55.

Westhead, P., Ucbasaran, D., & Wright, M. (2009). Information Search and Opportunity Identification: The Importance of Prior Business Ownership Experience. *International Small Business Journal, 27*(5), 659–680.

Williamson, O. (1975). *Markets and Hierarchies: Analysis and Antitrust Implications*. New York: Free Press.

Williamson, O. (1985). *The Economic Institutions of Capitalism: Firms, Markets, Relational Contracting*. New York: Free Press.

Wright, M., & Stigliani, I. (2012). Entrepreneurship and Growth. *International Small Business Journal, 31*(1), 3–22. https://doi.org/10.1177/0266242612467359

Zander, U., & Kogut, B. (1995). Knowledge and the Speed of the Transfer and Imitation of Organizational Capabilities: An Empirical Test. *Organization Science, 6*(1), 76–92.

Zichella, G. (2014). *Entrepreneurial Cognition When Faced with Risk and Uncertainty: Methodological Reflections*. Paper presented at the DRUID Academy Conference. Rebild, Aalborg, Denmark.

CHAPTER 10

Innovation, Creativity and Economic Growth

10.1 Introduction

Globalization exerts considerable pressure on economies and the businesses that operate in them, to develop more aggressive strategies that will allow them to respond to the needs of the global market. Innovative activities are considered one of the most important means for economies to be competitive in the broader environment in which they operate.

The concept of innovation involves a complex set of processes as it relates to a multitude of interdependent factors and processes. For example, the ability of a state to produce innovative activities depends on institutional factors such as the quality of education, knowledge-related infrastructures, research and the healthy functioning of the economy but also on social factors such as individuals' attitudes to risk, future orientation, their performance orientation and so on.

Creativity, a concept intertwined with innovation (Ward, 1994), is considered to be the operative cause of artistic expression, without its effect on the real economy being precisely defined (Polman & Emich, 2011). It refers to the production of new ideas, while innovation refers to the implementation of an idea and, in many cases, is a collaborative venture. Creativity, in a sense, is the process whereby all brilliant ideas are put together and ways of applying them are sought, while innovation is the conversion of these ideas into practice. We could argue that creativity is the ultimate source of innovation, that is, the transformation of creative ideas into products or services. In this sense, it plays a role when

P. E. Petrakis et al., *Economic Growth and Development Policy*,
https://doi.org/10.1007/978-3-030-43181-5_10

innovation leads to economic results. In short, innovation is the application of creativity.

Creativity is linked to psychological factors, insofar as feeling well and being in a positive frame of mind tend to increase individuals' creativity (Isen, 1987). Integrating an individual into a group, the presence of multiple viewpoints and multiculturalism, all lead to undertaking more creative initiatives (Dijksterhuis & Meurs, 2006; Galinsky, Wang, & Ku, 2008; Leung, Maddux, Galinsky, & Chiu, 2008).

Creative intellect is considered a concept intertwined with entrepreneurship (Gilad, 1984; Nystrom, 1993; Schumpeter, 1911; Whiting, 1988). It is called upon to identify scarce business opportunities and to contribute to their successful implementation when the economy is dominated by conditions of high uncertainty and low nominal returns. In addition, the use of scenario planning encourages managers to incorporate the concept of creativity into business culture (Petrakis & Konstantakopoulou, 2015; van Duijne, 2013). At a business level, the businesses that deliver the best performance in the long run are those which are the most creative and innovative. These businesses do not copy others, but they use innovative ideas as a springboard to create something unique. In other words, they are capable of utilizing their creative and innovative potential to achieve long-term success.

Of course, the absence of incentives and rewards (Amabile, 1996; Friedman & Förster, 2000; Markman, Lindberg, Kray, & Galinsky, 2007) hinders the development of creativity. As can be seen, the concept of creativity is multidimensional and contributes to the exploitation of entrepreneurship opportunities, thereby promoting growth.

This chapter is organized as follows: the second section (10.2) analyses the concept of innovation and its relation to competitiveness and growth, while the third section (10.3), the way of incorporating innovation—exogenously or endogenously—into growth models. The fourth section (10.4) presents the connection between business creativity and growth, while the fifth section (10.5) discusses the macro-model of business creativity, in which education and knowledge, scientific and technological creativity, the diffusion of creativity, the cultural background and obstacles or supports to creativity, play an important role. The final section (10.6) provides policies for promoting innovation for entrepreneurship.

10.2 Innovation, Competitiveness and Growth

The stages of economic development and growth, according to the study of Porter, Sachs, and McArthur (2002), are the following: (a) the factor-driven stage, (b) the efficiency-driven stage and (c) the innovation-driven stage.

The first and lowest category is one where society is led by productive resources (factor-driven stage). In this stage, society produces low-value products, using existing knowledge, without creating any new knowledge or innovation. Furthermore, society clearly produces for self-consumption, that is, to meet its own needs, because there is no export sector. This stage is similar to the first stage of the traditional society, developed by Rostow (1960).

The second category is one where society is led by effectiveness (Porter et al., 2002). This category represents the gradual attempts of a society to develop and to become modernized, to make its debut in the international market and to acquire a national identity. Economies increase the efficiency of production and of the training levels of their workforce. In the efficiency-driven stage, economies have efficient production practices to enable them to exploit economies of scale. Self-employment rates decline, with capital, labour and technology appearing to play the most important role in productivity.

Finally, in the third category, society has exhausted every resource (factor-driven) and form of its efficient utilization (efficiency-driven), and the only route for further growth is via knowledge and innovation (innovation-driven). This stage can be considered parallel to the emergence and development of the notion of entrepreneurship, which is still being examined and studied by many modern sciences. The transition to the innovation-driven stage is characterized by business activity based on human capital.

Acs and Szerb (2010) associated these stages with the development of economies. They consider that entrepreneurship does not suddenly emerge when a country enters the third stage, but rather, it has played a role in all stages of development and is an ongoing process.

Particularly important for innovative activity is the role of competition, which is a fundamental challenge for business strategy. For any business to be successful, it is not enough to market a "good" product. In order for a business entity to survive and succeed, it must overcome competition in many different ways, as its products or services have to provide consumers with greater value, either due to their high quality or due to the lower price compared to competition (Besanko, Dravone, & Shanley, 2000). The business has to be more "attractive" to suppliers and distributors of its products, as well as to potential investors. In order to win the competition, companies innovate by seeking competitive advantage. In this way, they will diversify and enhance their performance against competition (Bowman & Faulkner, 1994).

Gaining a competitive advantage is a key objective for any business, and whether directly or indirectly, it always refers to its "vision" or "mission". At a time when consumer needs change and competition from other businesses is fierce, in order for an entrepreneur to make a profit, he must make his products and/or his business stand out from those of his competitors. Seeking out and identifying entrepreneurship opportunities as well as innovative activity are very important steps in this process.

Competitive advantage is the particular element that distinguishes an entrepreneur's products from those of his competitors. In summary, three sources of competitive advantage can be identified: (a) the business gains "cost advantage" when it can operate at a lower cost than competition, (b) the business gains "diversification advantage" when its products provide a more significant benefit to customers than those of its competitors and (c) when the business has a transaction advantage, that is, when the company has lower transaction costs or can create innovative combinations.

Technological changes are the major forces contributing to changing the profile of markets. These can take place in many ways, as, for example, consumer preferences are not constant. Consequently, the characteristics of suppliers and the products they provide vary over time. In addition, competitors' actions are also likely to change over time as they seek to adopt innovative strategies and identify new opportunities (Hellriegel, Jackson, & Slocum Jr., 2005).

The main objective of entrepreneurs is to create a competitive advantage (Hitt, Ireland, & Hoskisson, 2005). To do so, the business must accentuate its differentiation against competition. Many times, businesses—especially when they enter a sector—imitate existing ones and then develop their own strategy. This way, they open up new horizons and new directions. Managers must select the objectives and the strategies of the business so as to match the organizational capabilities of the business with the opportunities presented by the market. This is also the critical point of competitive strategies (Grant, 2005). However, maintaining the competitive advantage over the long term is difficult, especially in conditions of low nominal returns, high levels of uncertainty and high volatility of uncertainty (Petrakis & Konstantakopoulou, 2015).

An effective way to maintain a competitive advantage in the future is by shaping a business culture that is driven by innovative activity. Innovation cannot simply happen but requires a wider favourable environment that promotes the free exchange of ideas among those whose activities centre around a business, from customers to senior executives. Culture must be seen as a strategic tool for gaining comparative advantage through innovation (Petrakis, Kostis, & Valsamis, 2015).

Creating an innovation culture may be an important source of competitive advantage for a business as it encourages creativity. It also motivates the individual or team to adopt a spirit of entrepreneurship, while its diverse characteristics help the team to adopt new ideas, by contrast to groups whose composition is homogeneous. One way to foster an innovation culture is to have the right leaders, who have made clear to all participants in the productive outcome: (a) what the targets are and (b) how the desired outcome will be pursued. By focusing on the outcome, a great deal of valuable energy is released that allows creativity to unfold.

10.3 Innovation: Exogenous or Endogenous

There are divergent views in the literature on how to incorporate innovation into growth models. Thus, a significant part of the literature considers that innovation is incorporated into businesses exogenously, from the external environment, and another part of the literature considers that innovation is incorporated endogenously, that is, produced within the structures of the business.

The role of innovation in economic growth has concerned economists since the earliest steps of economics as a science. Smith (1776 [1981]) argues about the critical role of technological progress in increasing the wealth of societies and economic growth. Ricardo and Malthus, based on A. Smith's theory, added the connection between technological progress and employment. Additionally, J.S. Mill, in agreement with Ricardo and Malthus, views innovation as exogenous to the model of economic growth, so the relationship between technology and growth cannot be analysed within the model. Accordingly, Schumpeter's theory (1921, 1939) relates to a static—from its base—economy, with innovation being incorporated into its models exogenously, as it comes from the entrepreneur. The economy and society—especially the latter—are averse to innovation with the business process being the one that takes on and overcomes this resistance (Piore, 2007).

More specifically, the main idea of Schumpeter (1921, 1939), on the nature of economic growth and entrepreneurship, is based on the assumption that every growth process results in a quantitative change at the micro- and macro-levels. This change could be characterized as a creative destruction whose forces are (a) the introduction of a new good or a significant improvement in the quality of an existing good, (2) the introduction of a new production method, (3) the opening of a new market, (4) the conquest of a new source of supply of raw materials or semi-final goods and (5) the creation of a new kind of industrial organization. This creative destruction cannot be reduced to a path of equilibrium. As a result, the analysis of such a process must include the study of the sources and consequences of disturbances, which are unavoidable in quality change (Gaffard, 2008).

A key feature of capitalist economy is that it never stagnates. Innovation is the element that causes imbalance and, at the same time, moves economy forward. The reason Schumpeter uses the concept of general equilibrium is to highlight the contrast and to explain economic growth when a change occurs through the introduction of innovation into existing corporate routines. For Schumpeter, equilibrium is a theoretical measure, introduced to explain the imbalance caused by innovation. Through innovation, the economic system moves away from the imbalance and, as its effects "disappear", the economic system returns to a new equilibrium (Schumpeter, 1939).

Schumpeter also stresses the importance of innovations in the production process and attributes economic growth to them, which he disassociates from the increase in production rates. He argues that the introduction of innovations allows entrepreneurs to create short-term monopoly situations that make it easy for them to accumulate sufficient money to depreciate the capital they have invested, although the entry of new competitors gradually eliminates big profits. More specifically, he argues that "entrepreneurial innovation" is the process whereby new key technologies driven by new scientific developments emerge, new industries and new product groups are developed and fostered, small businesses play a leading role in innovations, initial technology and markets become mature, average business size and concentration are increased, margins for significant innovations are minimized, customers are better informed, market requirements become more specific, there is little differentiation between competing products and there is competition in price and improved processes to reduce costs (Deakins & Freel, 2010). Moreover, Schumpeter (1911) identifies the motives that drive entrepreneurs to innovate as being: (a) their desire to become independent founders of companies, (b) their desire for victory and (c) their joy at creating and solving problems.

On the contrary, Marx views innovation as an endogenous process. He considers that this is an internal dimension which is inextricably linked to the process of capitalist accumulation, in the sense that it is the cause, the result and the primary source of the increase in the social productive power of labour.

With regard to the endogenous growth model—where innovation is generated through business structures—literature (Lucas Jr, 1988; Rebelo, 1991; Romer, 1986) has discussed the idea that investing in knowledge and learning may affect the growth of economic figures in the long run. This has led to the view that human resource productivity in the future is affected by the dispositions of the present (Lucas Jr, 1988), that is, by decisions to allocate the financial and technological resources needed and encourage business executives to diffuse knowledge and take initiatives. According to Griliches' (1979) Knowledge Production Function Model, the business invests in knowledge inputs in order to achieve innovation outputs. That is, an exogenous factor (the business), with its strategic choices and investments, generates an innovative activity, turning it into an endogenous system variable (Audretsch & Erdem, 2002).

Englmann (1994), in his attempt to develop a model of imbalance of endogenous innovation and growth, has argued that the long-term rate of technological progress should be included endogenously. Actually, this is what Arrow (1962) has also argued about learning by doing, in accumulated investments. However, Arrow did not take into account the fact that much of the technological progress depends on investment in research and development. Thus, Englmann (1994) developed an economic model including investments in research and development, but admitted that a significant part of these investments was stochastic. In addition, he assumes that entrepreneurs invest one part of their operating profits in real capital accumulation and another part in R&D. Because of this stochastic approach, entrepreneurs use routines in the production process, routines that also determine the behaviour of individuals. In addition, he takes into account the process of R&D diffusion. Finally, he argues that in Schumpeter's theory of economic development, the economic impact of technical change is considered an imbalance. Consequently, in a capitalist economy, characterized by a continuous process of diffusion of innovations, the time averages are more important than the steady state, even in the long run.

In this context, the contribution of Acs, Braunerhjelm, Audretsch, and Carlsson (2009) expands the microeconomic foundations of endogenous growth models (Lucas Jr, 1988; Romer, 1990) through the entrepreneurial knowledge diffusion theory. According to it, the creation of knowledge can lead to its diffusion, thus creating technological opportunities (Block, Thurik, & Zhou, 2013).

In conclusion, there are internal and external factors that affect the ability of a business to innovate. Internal factors include the level of education of the entrepreneur or founder, as well as the work experience, qualifications and skills of the workforce, its training, continuous technological efforts, the expenditure of the business in formal or informal research and development and so on. On the other hand, external factors include good networking, geographical proximity and institutional support (Hoffman, Parejo, Bessant, & Perren, 1998; Romijn & Albaladejo, 2002; Wignaraja, 1998). In addition, Yoo, Sawyerr, and Tan (2015) point out that the decision to acquire external knowledge is determined by factors that are both exogenous and endogenous to the company. Exogenous factors, such as the market, technological change and the intensity of competition, are considered to push a company to acquire exogenous knowledge for the sake of innovation, while endogenous factors, such as avoiding ambiguity, organizational inertia and low assimilation capacity, may inhibit the acquisition of external knowledge.

10.4 Entrepreneurial Creativity and Growth

One of the significant challenges for an economy is to determine those factors that drive economic growth. The traditional neoclassical theory claims that economic growth is determined by the supply of capital and labour and the level of technology (Solow, 1956). This, however, ignores any direct impact that entrepreneurship may have on economic growth.

Yet, the contribution of entrepreneurship to economic growth is particularly important as it has the status of both cause and effect (McMullan & Kenworthy, 2015). Entrepreneurship generates economic growth, as the entrepreneur is a potential productive factor for growth. The position of the entrepreneur is crucial as he contributes to change and economic progress, while also being the driving force for the generation of innovation (Schumpeter, 1911). Correspondingly, a country's economic growth promotes entrepreneurship, as it increases demand and creates needs that foster a breeding ground for the development of entrepreneurship.

Audretsch (2009) introduced the concept of "entrepreneurship capital", which refers to the aspects of institutions and the cultural and historical context that favour the creation of new companies, such as the acceptance of entrepreneurship by society, and individuals' intention to share risks and benefits. Thus, "entrepreneurship capital" reflects several different legal, institutional and social forces. Audretsch characterizes some of the "remaining factors" as venture capital. These are the factors that shape the knowledge filter which lies, on the one hand, between investment in knowledge, science and ideas and, on the other, commercialization, which ultimately leads to economic growth (Audretsch, 2007).

Emerging conditions, resulting from the continuously changing environment of globalization, changing economic and political structures, new technologies, the specialized requirements of customers and an emphasis on the quality of products and services, have led economies to assess those factors which shape entrepreneurial development and creativity in the ever-increasing competition of world markets. In addition, the incentives behind entrepreneurship vary considerably and define its objectives. These incentives relate to earning profit to make a living, to identifying and exploiting entrepreneurship opportunities, and to reasons directly linked to creativity and innovation.

Schumpeter spent most of his life working on the interconnection of the concepts of creativity, entrepreneurship and capitalism. Schumpeter's theory (1911) of economic growth (as presented in Chap. 9) was a particularly important step in establishing the relationship between creativity and entrepreneurship. That is why, apart from a theory of economic growth, Schumpeter's theory could be considered as a theory of creativity. Its three different aspects—cyclical flow, new combination and creative disaster—address the role of entrepreneurship as a creative force in the economy as a whole. So, one might argue that Schumpeter's theory is entirely consistent with the field of creativity where the productive change of a system caused by creative people is considered to be a fundamental concept (McMullan & Kenworthy, 2015).

In addition, McCraw (2007) supports Schumpeter's view of business incentives, which are generally regarded as corresponding to incentives for creation. McCraw's perception of the dynamic side of the economy may also be considered compatible with the creative process, which is characterized by uncertainty and ambiguity.

However, Baumol (1993) strongly opposes the utility of the Schumpeterian model as an applied theory of entrepreneurship, arguing that Schumpeter's theory does not attempt to discover what an innovative entrepreneur does or how he can become better (McMullan & Kenworthy, 2015). In order to develop a modern general theory of entrepreneurship, it is necessary to modernize Schumpeter's work by incorporating elements from the field of creativity. The end result would be a general theory that should predict significant business results.

10.5 A Macro-Model of Entrepreneurial Creativity

The factors that influence the creativity of individuals shape entrepreneurship and, by extension, have a major impact on economic growth. In an attempt to capture these factors, McMullan and Kenworthy (2015) present a macroeconomic model that depicts their attempt to modify the concept of Schumpeter's economic growth so as to include factors that influence entrepreneurship growth. This model demonstrates the importance of entrepreneurial and technological creativity in business activity. There are mixed indications that (a) artistic creativity in an area contributes to the size of creative entrepreneurship and (b) community values may drive creativity to or away from entrepreneurship.

According to McMullan and Kenworthy's (2015) model, there are factors that influence entrepreneurial creativity, which in turn leads to economic growth and development. These factors should be taken into account as they make an important contribution to the process of economic growth. They are (a) knowledge and education, which are considered valuable concepts, increasingly prevalent in business practices and, consequently, in innovative activities, (b) scientific and technological creativity, as technological evolution, especially in the last century, is capable of changing the consumer model, creating new needs, producing new goods and services, disrupting the prevailing situation, changing the way people live, think and work and so on, (c) the diffusion of creativity, (d) the role of the cultural background, as it is extremely important to find out whether cultural stereotypes favour—through creativity—the conditions for development or not and (e) the obstacles and supports of creativity, which may be due to the economic, political, cultural and social environment and to the mentality of the individual.

The above-mentioned factors are enriched by the role of incentives, the managing of disruptive technologies and the managing of resources, as well as the institutional background (Petrakis & Kafka, 2016).

The relationships mentioned are shown in Fig. 10.1 and, then, the interconnection of individual factors with entrepreneurial creativity is analysed.

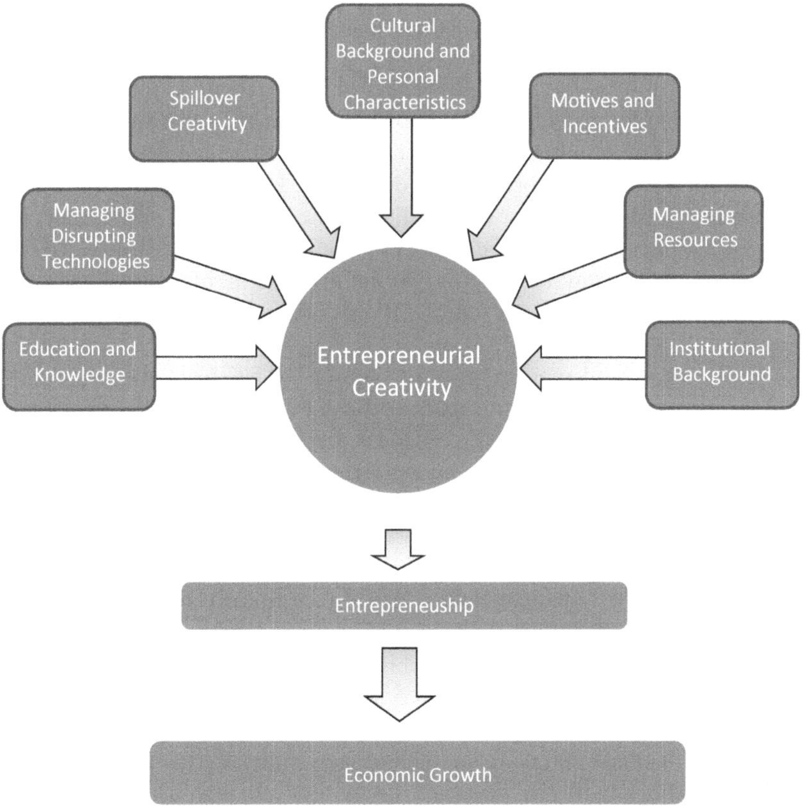

Fig. 10.1 A macro-model of economic growth. (Source: Authors' own creation)

10.5.1 The Role of Education and Knowledge

Knowledge is nowadays considered a valuable commodity, and concepts such as the exchange of knowledge and lifelong learning have become increasingly widespread in business practices and, so, in innovative activities. The expected economic value of knowledge or of a new idea varies widely between actors. Different levels of knowledge, background differences and individual experiences create different conditions related to knowledge, a high degree of uncertainty, information asymmetries and transaction costs, and lead to different levels of decision-making (Audretsch, 2007). The differences mentioned earlier may lead to divergences in the identification, evaluation and decision-making of entrepreneurship opportunities among actors, due to the different approach to the expected value of a new venture.

Creativity is a function of knowledge, curiosity, imagination and evaluation. The higher an individual's knowledge base and curiosity, the more ideas, trends and combinations they can achieve that then lead to the creation of new innovative products and services. However, the existence of a knowledge base alone cannot guarantee the creation of new trends, as there is a process that must be followed, from combining existing ideas to evaluating them and developing them into useful insights. Creativity therefore consists of three stages (a) discovery, (b) invention and (c) creation.

The concept and management of knowledge has been the subject of systematic research into the causes of business growth (Dalmaris, Tsui, Hall, & Smith, 2007; Nonaka, 1994; Randeree, 2006; Smith, 2005; von Krogh, 1998). If businesses use knowledge correctly, they gain a comparative advantage and become more creative, sustainable, competitive and innovative. In addition, investment by companies and organizations in new knowledge creates not only opportunities to achieve comparative advantage for these companies but also the conditions for disseminating that knowledge into other companies (Griliches, 1992).

The role of education also proves to be important. High levels of creativity and innovation are associated with high levels of education and positive attitudes towards science (Lee, 1998). The importance of education is that it trains people from a young age to think in a specific way by providing them with the necessary tools they can use in the future to become creative and develop innovative ideas.

We conclude, then, that the interaction of knowledge with innovation and the impact of this relationship on the competitiveness of enterprises are of particular importance. The challenge for businesses is to be able to retain this knowledge and exploit it through their operation. At the operational level, knowledge enters from the external environment through formal and informal channels (Smith & Temple, 2007). Finally, businesses have an integrated wealth of knowledge that is embedded in their work practices, operating systems and human resources (Petrakis & Kostis, 2012).

10.5.2 Scientific and Technological Creativity

Technology and innovation are a key source of growth in economic activity and standard of living. In the world of supercomputers, genetic engineering and fibre optics, technological creativity is even more the key to economic success (Mokyr, 2011). New business opportunities, new potential customers, new products and new investment options are some of the potential benefits of new technologies. New technologies, which represent a rapid change in capabilities or in the price/performance ratio compared with substitutes and competing products, or related to developments leading to accelerated rates of change or discontinuous capacity improvements, have been characterized as "disruptive technologies" (Manyika et al., 2013).

If new technologies are properly used, they can give a significant boost to the level of creativity of a society. As new technologies nowadays play an important role in people's lives, it is necessary to find constructive ways of exploiting them in a creative direction. As McMullan and Kenworthy (2015) point out, a number of empirical studies have concluded that there is a strong interconnection between the application of creative technological/scientific results and entrepreneurial creativity (Dean, Brown, & Bamford, 1998; Dean & Meyer, 1992; Eckhardt & Shane, 2011).

However, despite the fact that evolution in science and technology have helped in the facilitation of economic production and the daily needs of individuals, concerns have been expressed that the very "smart" and advanced technology negatively affects creativity. The problem is mainly in childhood, as the overuse of smartphones, computers and video games can lead to addiction and adversely affect children's development and creativity.

10.5.3 Creativity Diffusion

The magnitude of the impact of creativity on economic growth depends on the tendency of creative capital to diffuse, that is to say, on a vibrant business environment that favours creativity, exchange of ideas, cultural diversity and entrepreneurship (Audretsch & Belitski, 2015). The availability alone of creative capital does not automatically lead to economic growth, but entrepreneurship facilitates the diffusion and commercialization of these ideas.

As the gains from creativity are uncertain, the degree of creativity diffusion may be an important factor in harmonizing the "Innovation paradox" (Audretsch & Belitski, 2014). The size of the creativity filter and the new innovative businesses (start-ups) have been found to be internal and external factors of creativity diffusion, respectively.

In addition, the level of creativity can vary significantly between countries or regions. Many academic studies have argued that the arts and the cultural background have become one of the main components of local growth (Bille & Schulze, 2006; Chapain & Comunian, 2009; Sanchez-Serra, 2013). Lee, Florida, and Acs (2004) proved that the overall formation rate of new businesses is directly influenced by cultural creativity. Also, recent studies have shown that creative activities are not evenly distributed (Cooke & Lazzaretti, 2008; Florida, 2008; Florida, Mellander, & Qian, 2008; Scott, 2005) and may be more concentrated in metropolitan areas.

10.5.4 The Role of the Cultural Background

Individuals form a cognitive background that reflects the cultural and institutional environment in which they live, as well as their personal temperament and mentality, on the basis of which they understand and specify their needs and desires have been identified, over a period of time, decisions must be made and actions aimed at meeting them must be taken.

This process is based on an individual's collectivist ability, as each person has a different ability to understand in depth the information at their disposal, and then combine and process it in order to make decisions and take actions (Hodgson, 1988, 1997; Lavoie, 1992; Simon, 1955, 1957). At this stage, the cultural and institutional background provide a set of habits and rules that the individual may either use in their entirety or selectively, in order to find the best solution and then act (Hodgson, 1988, 1997; Loasby, 2001).

The dimensions of the cultural background make up the social stereotypes. The composition of social stereotypes forms the prevailing social behaviour. Therefore, it is extremely important to find out whether the prevailing social behaviour portfolio favours growth conditions or not.

Diversity of cultural characteristics also stimulates creativity (Majidi, 2010). The ability of businesses to deal with different cultural aspects in order to achieve better results is a critical issue. In addition, groups with diverse cultural characteristics are better equipped to adopt new views, as opposed to groups with homogeneous characteristics. Cultures reward creativity, encourage their members' individual attainments and tend to achieve better innovation results. In addition, different cultural behaviours have been observed in relation to business formation (Shapero & Sokol, 1982).

A positive relationship between individualism and innovation has been potentially identified, as the greater the freedom of individuals to express their views, the greater the likelihood of finding new ideas (Barnett, 1953). Everyone's creativity, and personal, emotional world, come to differentiate individuals' collectivist behaviour as regards the needs they consider salient and the ways in which they intend to satisfy them (Dequech, 1999, 2001, 2006; Dunn, 2001; Loasby, 2001). Individualistic societies are more likely to encourage their members to express their views and allow the freedom needed for creativity. Finally, specific characteristics of individuals' mentality, such as independence, achievement and encouragement of innovation, are often found in individualistic societies (Shane, 1992).

10.5.5 Obstacles and Props of Creativity

A key factor affecting the level of creativity, either as a barrier or as a support, is the institutional environment (McMullan & Kenworthy, 2015). This environment can be economic, political or cultural (Shane, 2003). The first relates to creativity, mainly through wealth, economic stability, capital availability and taxation (Audretsch & Acs, 1994; Bruce & Mohsin, 2006; Djankov, Ganser, McLiesh, Ramalho, & Shleifer, 2010), while the second relates to creativity through policy freedom and the degree of concentration of power (Roll & Talbott, 2003; Weymouth & Broz, 2013). In addition, the factors of the cultural environment are the general behaviours and beliefs about business activity and the presence of the role of business models (Loasby, 2001; Rutherford, 1994).

The role of the wider social environment is also important. Creative thinking is inherent to all humans, but the way and intensity in which it is fostered vary among individuals, as the wider social environment has a decisive influence on whether and to what extent the creative capacity of individuals is developed. Besides, at the individual level, individual empowerment has dominated in recent decades. Individuals equip themselves with the skills and abilities to respond to the changing conditions of globalization as well as to make decisions and meet their present and future goals. Individuals improve and take control of their decisions, thereby changing their role in society and, then, gaining confidence in decision-making.

Finally, one of the most important factors affecting the level of creativity is the psychology of the individual. The following factors adversely affect individual psychology with regard to creativity (Paraskevopoulos, 2004): (a) The standardization of thought and the absolute dominance of reason. The way our creative intellectual capacities operate is influenced by our past experiences. The human mind possesses critical-converging thinking (logical analysis) and creative-diverging thinking (imagination). In the early years of one's life, from pre-school age, intellectual activity is dominated by imagination. Critical-logical thinking begins to develop later. But as the demands of social adjustment, including the adaptation to the way the school system operates, make one use logical thinking more, simultaneously, creativity is hindered and becomes inactive. It is noteworthy that great scientific discoveries, works of art and business ideas were primarily produced by their creators at a young age. (b) A lack of confidence and self-esteem in one's creative abilities, accompanied by the fear of mistakes and ridicule, results in the creative forces of the individual gradually becoming inactive. (c) The social pressures for compliance with social rules counter the individual's desire for creative output. (d) Psychological insecurity around the new and the unknown. This fear, which is overly pronounced in some people, makes them extremely insecure about exploring new ideas.

10.5.6 *The Role of Motives and Incentives*

An "incentive" is something that motivates, rouses or encourages (when no longer provided, the individual stops being motivated), while a "motive" is a mechanism within the individual; a reason for doing something; anything that prompts a choice of action. Incentives and motives are a key source of stimulation of individual creativity (Friedman & Förster, 2000; Markman et al., 2007). The lack of incentives, motivation and rewards is a basic obstacle in the development of creativity (Friedman & Förster, 2000; Markman et al., 2007). Human needs and objectives are related in the context of a logical sequence that starts from needs and passes through incentives (remunerative, financial, moral, coercive or natural) to organize goals and finally precipitate human activity (Petrakis et al., 2015). Translating creativity into innovation is a function of multiple incentives (Yusuf, 2009). McCraw (2007) argues that business incentives are generally equivalent to the incentives for creation.

Motives can be divided into two types, intrinsic and extrinsic, and both kinds of motivations appear to play roles as determinants of creative behaviour. Intrinsic motives depend on internal sources of the entrepreneur, such as the need for self-actualization or merely the joy of being creative and generating wellness and spontaneity. Conversely, extrinsically imposed motives may be the result of pressure and low self-esteem. This may be a creative behaviour that is a response to external conditions and the external environment of the entrepreneur, for example, an experimental requirement or environmental needs. Entrepreneurial creativity requires a combination of intrinsic and extrinsic motivation, which occurs when there is a combination of personal interest and the promise of a reward, which confirms competence, supports skill development and/or enables future achievement (Amabile, 1996).

Motives arise from the needs of the individual (Maslow, 1948), they guide people's behaviour and help them achieve goals (Lawler III, 1994) which are set and which depend on the external environment. In this way, motives influence the primary start-up of human action—the direction, extent and systematic appearance of free behaviour. Simultaneously, goal-setting activates behaviour and directs choices, and, thus, people get to differ as to the objectives they set and how to reach them. Moreover, the motives behind business activity vary widely and define its objectives. These motives are related to the profit potential for livelihood purposes, the identification and utilization of business opportunities, and to reasons directly related to creativity and innovation.

There is considerable debate in the literature about the extent to which the impact of rewards on creativity can be positive or negative, making it clear that motives significantly determine the creative performance of entrepreneurs. On the one side, Winston and Baker (1985), Eisenberger, Cummings, Armeli, and Lynch (1997), and Eisenberger, Armeli, Rexwinkel, Lynch, and Rhoades (2001) state that rewards are appropriate and desirable for creative performance. Nickerson (1999) claims that since an important factor for creative accomplishment is establishing purpose and intention to be creative, rewards may indeed lead to such a creative orientation. On the other side, Kohn (1993) argues that it is not possible to bribe people to be creative, and Amabile (1996) concludes that working for a reward can be damaging to both intrinsic interest and creativity.

10.5.7 *Managing Resources*

The availability of resources is a particularly critical element in order to form creative capital in a company, an organization or a society. For this reason, apart from the existence of the necessary resources, proper management is particularly significant.

In literature, there are different views as to what is considered a resource, the proper management of which could lead to creative processes, as some claim that a resource comprises fixed entities (Amabile, 1996; Pfeffer & Salancik, 1978), while others consider it anything that arises from malleable objects shaped by individuals (Dutton, Worline, Frost, & Lilius, 2006; Feldman, 2004). However, perhaps more correctly, a resource could be defined as an object that is used in a way that renders it useful (Feldman, 2004; Feldman & Worline, 2011; Sonenshein, 2014).

The connection of resources with the achievement of creative results (Sonenshein, 2014) is also ambiguous in the literature, as there are researchers who argue that the existence of abundant resources is a key component for the development of creativity (Amabile, 1996), while others argue that limited resources also promote creativity, as the difficulty (due to limited resources) in resolving the various processes requires a higher level of creativity (Nohria & Gulati, 1996; Ohly & Fritz, 2010).

10.5.8 *The Institutional Background*

A key factor influencing the level of entrepreneurial creativity is the institutional environment, which may be economic, political, cultural and/or social (McMullan & Kenworthy, 2015; Shane, 2003). The "general national framework conditions"—such as economic, social, political and cultural factors—create the variety of established business conditions, and "entrepreneurial business conditions"—such as the interventionist policies of governments—create the variety of entrepreneurial activity (Reynolds, Chelazzi, & Desimone, 1999).

The different types of institutional backgrounds are interconnected. Originally, the cultural background affects the social/institutional environment, which in turn affects the quality and operation of political institutions. Then, political institutions shape the system of economic institutions, which in turn create structures and incentives for the actions of individuals. The prevailing economic institutions ultimately determine the distribution of wealth and the degree of economic growth.

In particular, the economic environment is associated with creativity, mainly through wealth, economic stability, the existence of capital and taxation (Audretsch & Acs, 1994; Bruce & Mohsin, 2006; Djankov et al., 2010). Accordingly, the political environment is related to creativity through political freedom and the degree of the centralization of power (Roll & Talbott, 2003; Weymouth & Broz, 2013). Furthermore, the protection of property rights seems to be fundamental in economic growth (Acemoglu & Johnson, 2005; North, 1981; Rodrik, Subramanian, & Trebbi, 2004; Rosenberg & Birdzell Jr, 1986) and, so, in creativity and, hence, in entrepreneurship, as entrepreneurship thrives through secured property rights that can be used in voluntary, contractual exchanges. In addition, as pointed out earlier, the cultural environment factors are general attitudes and beliefs about entrepreneurial activity and the presence of entrepreneurial role models (Loasby, 2001; Rutherford, 1994). Finally, regarding the influence of the social institutional environment on creativity, we should note that creative thinking is inherent in all people, but the manner and intensity of its cultivation vary from one to the other, as the broader social environment decisively affects whether and how the creative ability of individuals is deployed.

10.6 Policies for Promoting Innovation for Entrepreneurship

The promotion of innovation by governments encourages economic growth, as higher levels of R&D spending are positive correlated with higher levels of income (Jones, 2015). Developing a framework for innovation requires the creation of a long-term strategic partnership of stakeholders, that is, policy-makers and entrepreneurs. Financing and the legislative and regulatory framework are one side to promoting innovation. Creating an enabling environment, on the other hand, is essential for a robust innovation system to prevail.

Initially, reforms on the regulatory framework are important in order to provide incentives for innovative activity. In this respect, inter alia, it is necessary to take the initiative to reduce bureaucracy in the process of starting and operating businesses, the reduction of the procedures laid down in the bankruptcy code, and speed up the functioning of the judicial system.

Providing tax incentives for R&D is also important for business financing. At the same time, financial support for start-ups is essential. The aim of public policies should be to increase R&D spending as well as to attract venture capital from abroad. To this end, the most powerful tool is the promotion of regulations that will make the country an attractive destination for investors. However, in addition to these regulations, a number of actions need to be taken:

- Introduce R&D tax incentives.
- Create complementarity relationships between public and private investments. The existence of appropriate public infrastructure favours the productivity of private investment.
- Attract venture capitals.
- Provide subsidies to young scientists and innovative entrepreneurs.

In the 1970s, Ireland introduced "patent boxes" as a special case of the tax regime, for applying a lower revenue tax rate derived from the use of patents against other revenues. Subsequently, patent boxes as tax incentives were adopted by other Organisation for Economic Co-operation and Development (OECD) countries (Guenther, Matsunaga, & Williams, 2017). Patent boxes provide a system through which firms can manipulate patent revenues to minimize their global tax burden (Griffith, Miller, & O'Connell, 2014).

However, tax-based policies aiming to support innovation have one major disadvantage: it is quite difficult for tax policies to focus on R&D, which creates the most knowledge spillovers and avoids business-stealing (Bloom et al., 2019). On the contrary, government research grants can be more effective as they are directly addressed to stakeholders such as universities and research centres. A variety of government programmes seek to foster innovation by providing grant funding to universities such as the US National Institutes of Health (NIH). Jacob and Lefgren (2011) argue that these grants produce positive but small effects on research output. However, public R&D grants can create positive spillovers to the private sector, for example, in the form of increased private patents (Azoulay, Fons-Rosen, & Graff Zivin, 2019). Moretti, Steinwender, and Reenen (2019), using data on military R&D spending, document that a 10% increase in publicly funded R&D to private firms results in a 3% increase in private R&D, suggesting an improvement in productivity. Finally, through government research grants, private companies can receive public subsidies.

As ideas are an asset to their owners, a well-designed intellectual property system motivates the creation of new ideas (Bloom et al., 2019). The term intellectual property describes a series of policies relating to patents, copyrights, trademarks and so on. Inadequate protection of intellectual property and lack of confidence limit entrepreneurship, while at the same time hampering the capacity for innovation and growth (Gokhberg & Roud, 2012). Policies focusing on the protection of intellectual property rights are, therefore, an essential undertaking in trying to foster innovation.

Financial constraint is often the main obstacle to small business development. For this reason, innovation policies focus on this aspect. In many countries, R&D tax credit is larger in small firms than in others (OECD, 2018), while small firms appear to respond more positively to innovation and other business support policies than larger firms (Criscuolo, Martin, Overman, & van Reenen, 2019). However, such policies may create disincentives for business development as businesses are, at one point or another, excluded from the beneficial provisions of policy innovation. One policy applied to small firms is their geographical coexistence in a high-density accelerator, incubator and in clusters (Madaleno, Nathan, Overman, & Waights, 2018).

The policies we have mentioned earlier focus on increasing demand for innovation through incentives and an enabling environment for attracting investment funds. However, we also need to focus on the supply side, namely education and human capital, which will train young scientists capable of innovating and doing business. For novices, there should be a solid educational policy that ensures a reliable framework for the operation of universities. Priority should also be given to market needs and to the improvement of digital skills through lifelong learning. Finally, the emphasis should be on increasing the number of individuals with training in science, technology, engineering and mathematics (STEM). For example, Toivanen and Väänänen (2016) argue that individuals growing up around a technical university were more likely to become engineers and inventors.

References

Acemoglu, D., & Johnson, S. (2005). Unbundling Institutions. *Journal of Political Economy, 113*(5), 949–995.

Acs, Z., Braunerhjelm, P., Audretsch, D., & Carlsson, B. (2009). The Knowledge Spill-Over Theory of Entrepreneurship. *Small Business Economics, 32*(1), 15–30.

Acs, Z., & Szerb, L. (2010). The Global Entrepreneurship Index (GEINDEX). *Foundations and Trends in Entrepreneurship, 5*(5), 341–435.

Amabile, T. M. (1996). *Creativity in Context: Update to "The Social Psychology of Creativity"*. Boulder, CO: Westview.

Arrow, K. (1962). Economic Welfare and the Allocation of Resources for Invention. In R. Nelson (Ed.), *The Rate and Direction of Inventive Activity*. Princeton: Princeton University Press.

Audretsch, D. B. (2007). Entrepreneurship Capital and Economic Growth. *Oxford Review of Economic Policy, Oxford University Press, 23*(1), 63–78.

Audretsch, D. B. (2009). The Emergence of the Entrepreneurial Society: The 2008 Geary Lecture. *The Economic and Social Review, 40*(3), 255–268.

Audretsch, D. B., & Acs, Z. J. (1994). New-Firm Startups, Technology, and Macroeconomic Fluctuations. *Small Business Economics, Springer, 6*(6), 439–449.

Audretsch, D. B., & Belitski, M. (2014). The Role of the Creativity Spillover of Entrepreneurship in Reconciling the Innovation Paradox. *Academy of Management Journal, 2014*(1), 17569–17569.

Audretsch, D. B., & Belitski, M. (2015). Creativity Spillover of Entrepreneurship: Evidence from European Cities. In C. Karlsson, U. Grasjo, & S. Wixe (Eds.), *Innovation and Entrepreneurship in the Global Economy, Knowledge Technology and Internationalization, New Horizons in Regional Science Series*. Cheltenham, UK: Edward Elgar Publishing.

Audretsch, D. B., & Erdem, K. D. (2002). *Determinants of Scientific Entrepreneurship: An Integrative Research Agenda, Discussion Papers on Entrepreneurship, Growth & Public Policy*. Germany: Max Plank Institute.

Azoulay, P., Fons-Rosen, C., & Graff Zivin, J. S. (2019). Does Science Advance One Funeral at a Time? *American Economic Review, 109*(8), 2889–2920.

Barnett, H. G. (1953). *Innovation: The Basis of Cultural Change*. New York: McGraw Hill.

Baumol, W. (1993). *Entrepreneurship, Management and the Structure of Payoffs*. London: MIT Press.

Besanko, D., Dravone, D., & Shanley, M. (2000). *Economics of Strategy*. New York: John Wiley & Sons.

Bille, T., & Schulze, G. G. (2006). Culture in Urban and Regional Development. In V. A. Ginsburgh & D. Throsby (Eds.), *Handbook of the Economics of Art and Culture* (pp. 1051–1100). Amsterdam: Elsevier.

Block, J. H., Thurik, R., & Zhou, H. (2013). What Turns Knowledge into Innovative Products? The Role of Entrepreneurship and Knowledge Spillovers. *Journal of Evolutionary Economics, 23*(4), 693–718.

Bloom, N., Bunn, P., Chen, S., Mizen, P., Smietanka, P., & Thwaites, G. (2019). The Impact of Brexit on U.K. Firms. *SIEPR Working Paper* 19-019.

Bowman, C., & Faulkner, D. (1994). Measuring Product Advantage Using Competitive Benchmarking and Customer Perceptions. *Long Range Planning, 27*(1), 119–132.

Bruce, D., & Mohsin, M. (2006). Tax Policy and Entrepreneurship: New Time Series Evidence. *Small Business Economics, 26*(5), 409–425.

Chapain, C., & Comunian, R. (2009). Enabling and Inhibiting the Creative Economy: The Role of the Local and Regional Dimensions in England. *Regional Studies, 44*(6), 717–734.

Cooke, P., & Lazzaretti, L. (2008). *Creative Cities, Cultural Clusters and Local Economic Development.* Cheltenham: Edward Elgar.

Criscuolo, C., Martin, R., Overman, H. G., & Van Reenen, J. (2019). Some Causal Effects of an Industrial Policy. *American Economic Review, 109*(1), 48–85.

Dalmaris, P., Tsui, E., Hall, B., & Smith, B. (2007). A Framework for the Improvement of Knowledge-Intensive Business Processes. *Business Process Management Journal, 13*(2), 279–305.

Deakins, D., & Freel, M. (2010). *Entrepreneurship and Small Firms* (5th ed.). London: McGraw-Hill.

Dean, T. J., Brown, R. L., & Bamford, C. (1998). Differences in Large and Small Firm Responses to Environmental Context: Strategic Implications from a Comparative Analysis of Business Formations. *Strategic Manage Journal, 19*(8), 709–728.

Dean, T. J., & Meyer, G. D. (1992). New Venture Formations in Manufacturing Industries: A Conceptual and Empirical Analysis. In N. Churchill, S. Birley, W. Bygrave, D. Muzyka, C. Wahlbin, & W. Wetzel (Eds.), *Frontiers of Entrepreneurship Research* (pp. 173–187). Babson Park: Babson College.

Dequech, D. (1999). Expectations and Confidence Under Uncertainty. *Journal of Post Keynesian Economics, 21*(3), 415–430.

Dequech, D. (2001). Bounded Rationality, Institutions, and Uncertainty. *Journal of Economic Issues, 35*(4), 911–929.

Dequech, D. (2006). The New Institutional Economics and the Theory of Behaviour Under Uncertainty. *Journal of Economic Behavior and Organization, 59*(1), 109–131.

Dijksterhuis, A., & Meurs, T. (2006). Where Creativity Resides: The Generative Power of Unconscious Thought. *Consciousness and Cognition, 15*(1), 135–146.

Djankov, S., Ganser, T., McLiesh, C., Ramalho, R., & Shleifer, A. (2010). The Effect of Corporate Taxes on Investment and Entrepreneurship. *American Economic Journal: Macroeconomics, 2*(3), 31–64.

Dunn, W. (2001). The Sensations of Everyday Life: Empirical, Theoretical, and Pragmatic Considerations. *American Journal of Occupational Therapy, 55*(6), 608–620.

Dutton, J. E., Worline, M. C., Frost, P. J., & Lilius, J. M. (2006). Explaining Compassion Organizing. *Administrative Science Quarterly, 51*(1), 59–96.

Eckhardt, J. T., & Shane, S. A. (2011). Industry Changes in Technology and Complementary Assets and the Creation of High-Growth Firms. *Journal of Business Venturing, 26*(4), 412–430.

Eisenberger, R., Armeli, S., Rexwinkel, B., Lynch, P. D., & Rhoades, L. (2001). Reciprocation of Perceived Organizational Support. *Journal of Applied Psychology, 86*(1), 42–51.

Eisenberger, R., Cummings, J., Armeli, S., & Lynch, P. (1997). Perceived Organizational Support, Discretionary Treatment, and Job Satisfaction. *Journal of Applied Psychology, 82*(5), 812–820.

Englmann, F. C. (1994). A Schumpeterian Model of Endogenous Innovation and Growth. *Journal of Evolutionary Economics, 4*(3), 227–241.

Feldman, B. (2004). A Skin for the Imaginal. *Journal of Analytical Psychology, 49*(3), 285–311.

Feldman, M. S., & Worline, M. (2011). Resources, Resourcing, and Ampliative Cycles in Organizations. In K. S. Cameron & G. Spreitzer (Eds.), *Oxford Handbook of Positive Organizational Scholarship* (pp. 629–641). New York, NY: Oxford University Press.

Florida, R. (2008). *Who's Your City? How the Creative Economy Is Making Where to Live the Most Important Decision of Your Life*. New York: Basic Books.

Florida, R., Mellander, C., & Qian, H. (2008). Creative China? The University, Tolerance, Talent in Chinese Regional Development. *CESIS Electronic Working Paper Series Paper* No. 145. Retrieved from https://static.sys.kth.se/itm/wp/cesis/cesiswp145.pdf

Friedman, R. S., & Förster, J. (2000). The Effects of Approach and Avoidance Motor Actions on the Elements of Creative Insight. *Journal of Personality and Social Psychology, 79*(4), 477–492.

Gaffard, J. L. (2008). Innovation, Competition, and Growth: Schumpeterian Ideas Within a Hicksian Framework. *Journal of Evolutionary Economics, 18*, 295–311. https://doi.org/10.1007/s00191-008-0102-z

Galinsky, A. D., Wang, C. S., & Ku, G. (2008). Perspective-Takers Behave More Stereotypically. *Journal of Personality and Social Psychology, 95*(2), 404–419.

Gilad, B. (1984). Entrepreneurship: The Issue of Creativity in the Market Place. *The Journal of Creative Behavior, 18*(3), 151–161. https://doi.org/10.1002/j.2162-6057.1984.tb00379.x

Gokhberg, L., & Roud, V. (2012). The Russian Federation: A New Innovation Policy for Sustainable Growth. In S. Dutta (Ed.), *The Global Innovation Index*

2012. Stronger Innovation Linkages for Global Growth (pp. 121–130). Fontainebleau: INSEAD and World Intellectual Property Organization.

Grant, R. M. (2005). *Contemporary Strategy Analysis.* Hoboken, NJ: Wiley-Blackwell.

Griffith, R., Miller, H., & O'Connell, M. (2014). Ownership of Intellectual Property and Corporate Taxation. *Journal of Public Economics, 112*, 12–23.

Griliches, Z. (1979). Issues in Assessing the Contribution of R&D to Productivity Growth, Bell. *Journal of Economics, 10*(1), 92–116.

Griliches, Z. (1992). The Search for R&D Spillovers, Scandinavian. *Journal of Economics, 94*(Suppl), 29–47.

Guenther, D. A., Matsunaga, S. R., & Williams, B. M. (2017). Is Tax Avoidance Related to Firm Risk? *The Accounting Review, 92*(1), 115–136.

Hellriegel, D., Jackson, S. E., & Slocum Jr., J. W. (2005). *Management.* London: South-Western College Publishing.

Hitt, M. A., Ireland, R. D., & Hoskisson, R. E. (2005). *Strategic Management, Competitiveness and Globalization.* Mason, OH: South Western, Thomson.

Hodgson, G. M. (1988). *Economics and Institutions: A Manifesto for a Modern Institutional Economics.* Cambridge: Polity Press.

Hodgson, G. M. (1997). The Ubiquity of Habits and Rules. *Cambridge Journal of Economics, 21*(6), 663–684.

Hoffman, K., Parejo, M., Bessant, J., & Perren, L. (1998). Small Firms, R&D, Technology and Innovation in the UK: A Literature Review. *Technovation, 18*(1), 39–55.

Isen, A. M. (1987). Positive Affect, Cognitive Processes, and Social Behavior. *Advances in Experimental Social Psychology, 20*, 203–253.

Jacob, B., & Lefgren, L. (2011). The Impact of Research Grant Funding on Scientific Productivity. *Journal of Public Economics, 95*(9–10), 1168–1177.

Jones, C. (2015). Pareto and Piketty: The Macroeconomics of Top Income and Wealth Inequality. *Journal of Economic Perspectives, 29*(1), 29–46.

Kohn, A. (1993). *Punished by Rewards: The Trouble with Gold Stars, Incentive Plans, Aís, Praise and Other Bribes.* Boston: Houghton Mifflin Company.

Lavoie, M. (1992). *Foundations of Post-Keynesian Economic Analysis.* Cheltenham, UK: Books, Edward Elgar Publishing.

Lawler III, E. E. (1994). Total Quality Management and Employee Involvement: Are They Compatible? *Academy of Management Executive, 8*(1), 68–76.

Lee, S. Y., Florida, R., & Acs, Z. J. (2004). Creativity and Entrepreneurship: A Regional Analysis of New Firm Formation. *Regional Studies, 38*(8), 879–891.

Lee, T. (1998). Assessment of Safety Culture at a Nuclear Reprocessing Plant. *Work & Stress, 12*(3), 217–237.

Leung, A. K. Y., Maddux, W. W., Galinsky, A. D., & Chiu, C. Y. (2008). Multicultural Experience Enhances Creativity: The When and How. *American Psychologist, 63*(3), 169–181.

Loasby, B. J. (2001). Time, Knowledge and Evolutionary Dynamics: Why Connections Matter. *Journal of Evolutionary Economics, 11*(4), 393–412.
Lucas Jr., R. E. (1988). On the Mechanics of Economic Development. *Journal of Monetary Economics, 22*(1), 3–42.
Madaleno, M., Nathan, M., Overman, H., & Waights, S. (2018). Incubators, Accelerators and Regional Economic Development. *CEP Discussion Paper* No. 1575.
Majidi, M. (2010). *Invest in Diversity as a Competitive Advantage, A Vision on Cultural Diversity.* Rochester, NY: ADP Publication.
Manyika, J., Chui, M., Bughin, J., Dobbs, R., Bisson, P., & Marrs, A. (2013). *Disruptive Technologies: Advances that Will Transform Life, Business, and the Global Economy.* McKinsey Global Institute. Retrieved from https://www.mckinsey.com/business-functions/mckinsey-digital/our-insights/disruptive-technologies
Markman, K. D., Lindberg, M. J., Kray, L. J., & Galinsky, A. D. (2007). Implications of Counterfactual Structure for Creative Generation and Analytical Problem Solving. *Personality and Social Psychology Bulletin, 33*(3), 312–324.
Maslow, A. H. (1948). "Higher" and "Lower" Needs. *The Journal of Psychology, 25*(2), 433–436. https://doi.org/10.1080/00223980.1948.9917386
McCraw, T. K. (2007). *Prophet of Innovation.* Cambridge: The Belkin Press of Harvard University.
McMullan, W. E., & Kenworthy, T. P. (2015). *Creativity and Entrepreneurial Performance: A General Scientific Theory.* Cham, Germany: Springer.
Mokyr, J. (2011). *The Lever of Riches: Technological Creativity and Economic Progress.* Oxford: Oxford University Press.
Moretti, E., Steinwender, C., & Reenen, J. V. (2019). The Intellectual Spoils of War? Defense R&D, Productivity and International Spillovers. *NBER Working Paper* No. 26483.
Nickerson, R. (1999). How We Know—And Sometimes Misjudge—What Others Know: Imputing One's Own Knowledge to Others. *Psychological Bulletin, 125*(6), 737–759.
Nohria, N., & Gulati, R. (1996). Is Slack Good or Bad for Innovation? *Academy of Management Journal, 39*(5), 1245–1264.
Nonaka, I. (1994). A Dynamic Theory of Organizational Knowledge Creation. *Organization Science, 5*(1), *14–37.*
North, D. (1981). *Structure and Change in Economic History.* Cambridge: Cambridge University Press.
Nystrom, H. (1993). Creativity and Entrepreneurship. *Creativity and Innovation Management, 2*(4), 237–242.
OECD. (2018). *Financing SMEs and Entrepreneurs 2018: An OECD Scoreboard.* Paris: OECD Publishing. Retrieved from https://doi.org/10.1787/fin_sme_ent-2018-en

Ohly, S., & Fritz, C. (2010). Work Characteristics, Challenge Appraisal, Creativity, and Proactive Behavior: A Multi-Level Study. *Journal of Organizational Behavior, 31*(4), 543–565.

Paraskevopoulos, I. N. (2004). *Creative Thinking in School and Family*. Athens: Ellinika Grammata.

Petrakis, P. E., & Kafka, K. I. (2016). Entrepreneurial Creativity and Growth. In M. Franco (Ed.), *Entrepreneurship* (pp. 3–20). London: Intech.

Petrakis, P. E., & Konstantakopoulou, D. (2015). *Uncertainty in the Entrepreneurial Decision Making: The Competitive Advantage of Strategic Creativity*. New York, NY: Palgrave Macmillan.

Petrakis, P. E., & Kostis, P. (2012). The Role of Knowledge and Trust in SMEs. *Journal of the Knowledge Economy, 6, 105–124.* https://doi.org/10.1007/s13132-012-0115-6

Petrakis, P. E., Kostis, P. C., & Valsamis, D. G. (2015). Innovation and Competitiveness: Culture as a Longterm Strategic Instrument During the European Great Recession. *Journal of Business Research, 68*(7), 1436–1438.

Pfeffer, J., & Salancik, G. R. (1978). *The External Control of Organizations: A Resource Dependence Perspective*. New York: Harper & Row.

Piore, M. J. (2007). *A Critical View of Schumpeter's 'Theory' of Innovation*. Prepared for Presentation at Conference on Capitalism and Entrepreneurship. New York, NY: Cornell University.

Polman, E., & Emich, K. J. (2011). Decisions for Others Are More Creative Than Decisions for the Self. *Personality and Social Psychology Bulletin, 37*(4), 492–501.

Porter, M., Sachs, J., & McArthur, J. (2002). Executive Summary: Competitiveness and Stages of Economic Development. In M. Porter, J. Sachs, P. Cornelius, J. McArthur, & K. Schwab (Eds.), *The Global Competitiveness Report 2001–2002* (pp. 16–26). New York: Oxford University Press.

Randeree, E. (2006). Knowledge Management: Securing the Future. *Journal of Knowledge Management, 10*(4), 145–156.

Rebelo, S. (1991). Long-Run Policy Analysis and Long-Run Growth. *Journal of Political Economy, 99*(3), 500–521.

Reynolds, J. H., Chelazzi, L., & Desimone, R. (1999). Competitive Mechanisms Subserve Attention in Macaque Areas V2 and V4. *The Journal of Neuroscience, 19*(5), 1736–1753.

Rodrik, D., Subramanian, A., & Trebbi, F. (2004). Institutions Rule: The Primacy of Institutions over Geography and Integration in Economic Development. *Journal of Economic Growth, 9*(2), 131–165.

Roll, R., & Talbott, J. (2003). Political Freedom, Economic Liberty, and Prosperity. *Journal of Democracy, 14*(3), 75–89.

Romer, P. (1986). Increasing Returns and Long Run Growth. *Journal of Political Economy, 94*(5), 1002–1037.

Romer, P. (1990). Endogenous Technological Change. *Journal of Political Economy, 98*(5), 71–10.

Romijn, H., & Albaladejo, M. (2002). Determinants of Innovation Capability in Small Electronics and Software Firms in Southeast England. *Research Policy, 31*(7), 1053–1067.

Rosenberg, N., & Birdzell Jr., L. E. (1986). *How the West Grew Rich: The Economic Transformation of the Industrial World*. New York: Basic Books.

Rostow, W. (1960). *The Stages of Economic Growth*. Cambridge: Cambridge University Press.

Rutherford, M. H. (1994). *Institutions in Economics: The Old and New Institutionalism*. Cambridge: Cambridge University Press.

Sanchez-Serra, D. (2013). Artistic Creative Clusters in France: A Statistical Approach. *Artistes et Territoires Créatifs en Europe, 2*, 6–18.

Schumpeter, J. (1911). *The Theory of Economic Development*. Cambridge, MA: Harvard University Press.

Schumpeter, J. A. (1921). *The Theory of Economic Development*. Cambridge: Harvard University Press.

Schumpeter, J. A. (1939). *Business Cycles, A Theoretical, Historical and Statistical Analysis of capitalist Process*. New York: McGraw-Hill.

Scott, A. J. (2005). *On Hollywood. The Place, the Industry*. Princeton: Princeton University Press.

Shane, S. A. (1992). Why Do Some Societies Invent More than Others? *Journal of Business Venturing, 7*(1), 29–46.

Shane, S. A. (2003). *A General Theory of Entrepreneurship: The Individual-Opportunity Nexus*. Cheltenham: Edward Elgar.

Shapero, A., & Sokol, L. (1982). The Social Dimensions of Entrepreneurship. In C. Kent, D. Sexton, & K. H. Vesper (Eds.), *The Encyclopedia of Entrepreneurship* (pp. 72–90). Englewood Cliffs, NJ: Prentice-Hall.

Simon, H. A. (1955). A Behavioral Model of Rational Choice. *Quarterly Journal of Economics, 69*(1), 99–118.

Simon, H. A. (1957). *Models of Man*. New York: John Wiley & Sons.

Smith, A. (1776 [1981]). An Inquiry into the Nature and Causes of the Wealth of Nations. In R. H. Campbell & A. S. Skinner (Eds.), *The Glasgow Edition of the Works of Adam Smith, 2*. Indianapolis: Liberty Fund.

Smith, A., & Temple, B. K. (2007). *The Impacts of Knowledge Transfer from Educational Programmes on Individuals and SME Business Development*. Management of International Business and Economic Systems (MIBES).

Smith, P. (2005). Knowledge Sharing and Strategic Capital, the Importance and Identification of Opinion Leaders. *The Learning Organization, 12*(6), 563–574.

Solow, R. (1956). A Contribution to the Theory of Economic Growth. *The Quarterly Journal of Economics, 70*(1), 65–94.

Sonenshein, S. (2014). How Organizations Foster the Creative Use of Resources. *Academy of Management Journal, 57*(3), 814–848.

Toivanen, O., & Väänänen, L. (2016). Education and Invention. *The Review of Economics and Statistics, 98*(2), 382–396.

van Duijne, F. (2013). How to Bring More Creativity in Scenario Thinking? *The Futurist.* Retrieved from http://www.wfs.org/blogs/freija-van-duijne/how-bring-more-creativity-scenario-thinking

von Krogh, G. (1998). Knowledge Creation. *California Management Review, 40*(3), 133–153.

Ward, T. B. (1994). Structured Imagination: The Role of Conceptual Structure in Exemplar Generation. *Cognitive Psychology, 27*(1), 1–40.

Weymouth, S., & Broz, J. L. (2013). Government Partisanship and Property Rights: Cross-Country Firm Level Evidence. *Economics and Politics, 25*(2), 229–256.

Whiting, B. G. (1988). Creativity and Entrepreneurship: How Do They Relate? *The Journal of Creative Behavior, 22*(3), 178–183.

Wignaraja, G. (1998). *Trade Policy, Technology and Exports: Sri Lanka's Liberalisation Experience.* London: Macmillan.

Winston, A. S., & Baker, J. E. (1985). Behavior Analytic Studies of Creativity: A Critical Review. *The Behavior Analyst, 8*, 191–205.

Yoo, S. J., Sawyerr, O., & Tan, W. L. (2015). The Impact of Exogenous and Endogenous Factors on External Knowledge Sourcing for Innovation: The Dual Effects of the External Environment. *The Journal of High Technology Management Research, 26*(1), 14–26.

Yusuf, H. O. (2009). Strategies for Improving the Teaching of Reading Comprehension in Primary Schools. *Journal of Educational. Research and Development, 4*(3), 63–68.

Index[1]

A

Absolute advantage, 6, 37, 40, 41
Adjustment Target (AT), 204
Advocacy Coalition Framework (ACF), 129, 130
Agency theory, 109, 110, 123, 131
AK growth models, 3
Arrow-Debreu-McKenzie (ADM model), 71
Augmented Washington Consensus, 202

B

Bad-equilibria, 87
Behavioural economics, 135
Big Push Theory, 38, 39
Black Swan, 97, 98
Bottom-up, 128, 143, 148–150
Bounded rationality, 16, 37, 49, 50, 78, 102, 115, 116, 157

C

Capital productivity, 4
Cass criterion, 10, 30n2
Choice Architect (CA), 136–139
Classical economics, 2, 5, 38, 46
Cobb-Douglas production function, 7
Comparative advantage, 6, 27, 40–43, 189, 193, 194, 200, 219, 224–226, 239, 246
Conventional economic thinking, 100
Coordinated Market Economies (CMEs), 105
Cultural Growth Trap, 81
Cultural innovation, 177
Cultural values, 74, 76, 77, 82, 87n1, 153, 158, 164, 165, 167, 171, 172
Currency war, 189, 194–196
Cycling, 110, 111

[1] Note: Page numbers followed by 'n' refer to notes.

P. E. Petrakis et al., *Economic Growth and Development Policy*,
https://doi.org/10.1007/978-3-030-43181-5

D
Developed economies, 5, 38, 58, 80, 82, 198
Developing economies, 5, 40, 165, 191, 197, 200
Diminishing returns, 1–5, 8, 11, 12
Disruptive innovation, 123, 133–134
Disruptive technologies, 245, 247
Dynamic Stochastic General Equilibrium (DSGE) Models, 15, 37, 55–57

E
Economic development, 12, 18, 22, 24, 28, 80, 85, 95, 125, 237, 241
Economic growth, xv, 5–7, 11, 12, 15, 21–24, 37–40, 56, 64, 74, 75, 79–85, 87, 123, 124, 154, 163, 164, 177, 180n3, 189–207, 213–229, 235–255
Efficiency-driven, 237
Elite, 123–125, 127–128, 136, 159
Endogenous growth models, 3, 7, 11, 21, 241, 242
Entrepreneurial business conditions, 253
Entrepreneurial innovation, 240
Entrepreneurship capital, 243
Evolutionary economics, 59–61, 117
Externalities, 26, 72, 73, 78, 102, 137
Extractive institutions, 22, 77, 177

F
Factor-driven, 237
Ford's "T" model, 134
Fourth Industrial Revolution, 190, 200
Full employment, 7, 44, 195

G
General budgetary revenue, 111
General equilibrium model, 7, 10, 75
General national framework conditions, 252
Global value chains (GVCs), 194, 197
Golden rule, 144, 195
Great depression, 43, 195
Gross Domestic Product (GDP), 4, 20–22, 50, 54, 55, 86, 87, 87n2, 125, 190, 194, 203, 204, 206, 208n1
Growth Paradigm, 12–14

H
Heterogeneous Agent New Keynesian (HANK), 51
Human accumulation, 155
Human capital, 3, 11, 21, 26, 27, 81, 85, 220, 226, 237, 255

I
Idiosyncratic Cultural Values Framework, 77
Imperfect knowledge, 39, 215
Inclusive institutions, 177
Innovation-driven, 237
Innovation paradox, 248
Institutional economics, 64, 216
Institutional fundamentalism, 202
Institutions-as-equilibria, 159
Interest groups, 124, 126, 127, 149
Involuntary unemployment, 46, 47
IS-LM, 16, 43, 44

K
Keynes + Schumpeter (K + S), 60, 62

L

Labour productivity, 4, 40, 41, 51, 190, 191, 194
Liberal Market Economies (LMEs), 105
Loss aversion behaviour, 80
Lucas critique, 45, 48, 144, 146

M

Malthusian Period, 5–7
Marginal cost, 52, 53
Market economy, 91, 103–105, 214
Market efficiency, 48, 78, 101, 102, 193
Market failure, 78, 99, 102, 108, 228
Micro-foundation, 7, 43, 44, 47, 75, 213, 217
Middle-income trap, 80–82, 85
Mixed Market Economies (MMEs), 105
Multi-Factor Productivity (MFP), 4
Multi-level Governance (MLG), 123, 128–129
Multi-level selection (MLS), 157

N

Nash equilibrium, 147
National Institutes of Health (NIH), 254
Neoclassical growth model, 7, 8, 10
Net Foreign Investment, 54, 208n1
New Classicals, 16, 25, 37, 46–49
New Keynesian Phillips Curve (NKPC), 51–53
New Keynesians, 16, 25, 37, 49–56
Non-ergodic world, 215

O

One-size-fits-all, 73, 148
Opportunity entrepreneurship, 175
Optimal Cultural Values Framework, 77
Overlapping Generation Models (OGM), 9, 10, 30n2

P

Pareto optimal, 10, 30n2, 72, 75
Patent boxes, 254
Path-dependent, 78, 156
Phillips Curve, 37, 44, 48, 52–55, 63, 196
Political trilemma, 193
Porter's Advantage, 42
Post-Keynesians, 25
Pressure groups, 115, 123, 127–128, 155, 201
Productivity, 1–8, 12, 22, 24, 31n3, 38, 40, 47, 57, 58, 80–82, 95, 139, 140, 175, 191, 192, 199–201, 214, 217, 237, 241, 254, 255
Product Life Cycle, 42
Product Variety Model, 11, 12
Public choice, 91, 108–115, 145
Punctuated equilibrium, 123, 132–133, 156

R

Rational behavioural assumptions, 110
Rational choice, 109–110, 159
Real Business Cycle (RBC), 10, 47, 51, 55, 56, 63
Research and Development (R&D), 57, 61, 117, 192, 222, 241, 253–255

S

Science, technology, engineering and mathematics (STEM), 255
The second-best theory, 73
Selfish genes, 157
Seoul Development Consensus, 202
Serendipity Economy, 95
Social capital, 39, 63
Social contract, 113, 114
Social welfare function, 109, 114
Solow-Swan, 7
Stagnated growth prototype, 154, 178, 179
State Capitalism, 105
Supply-side policies, 37, 54, 191–193, 203
Sustainable development, 84, 191
Systematic risk, 78–80, 83, 101, 102

T

Taylor's rule, 45
Top-down, 128, 143, 149–150
Total Factor Productivity (TFP), 4, 82
Transaction costs, 16, 26, 72, 75, 78, 79, 101–103, 177, 191, 216, 224, 238, 246
Transaction Cost Theory, 216

U

Uncertainty, xv, 8, 9, 15, 25, 28–30, 42, 59, 61, 62, 74, 78, 79, 81, 83, 85, 93, 97, 102, 103, 109, 113, 145, 147, 150, 154, 167, 175, 178, 180, 180n2, 215, 216, 218, 229n1, 236, 239, 244, 246

V

Varieties of Capitalism (VoC), 104, 105
Vote trading, 111

W

Walras' paradigm, 75

The manufacturer's authorised representative in the EU is Springer Nature Customer Service Centre GmbH, Europaplatz 3, 69115 Heidelberg, Germany. If you have any concerns regarding our products, please contact ProductSafety@springernature.com

Printed and bound by CPI Group (UK) Ltd, Croydon, CR0 4YY

30/09/2026

02225645-0005